Tinkering

Tinkering

Consumers Reinvent the Early Automobile

KATHLEEN FRANZ

PENN

University of Pennsylvania Press

Philadelphia

10 9 8 7 6 5 4 3 2 1

Published by
University of Pennsylvania Press
Philadelphia, Pennsylvania 19104–4011

Library of Congress Cataloging-in-Publication Data

Franz, Kathleen.
    Tinkering : consumers reinvent the early automobile / Kathleen Franz.
    p. cm.
    Includes bibliographical references and index.
    ISBN 0-8122-3881-8 (cloth : alk. paper)
    1. Automobiles—United States—History. 2. Automobile industry and
trade—United States—History. 3. Transportation, Automotive—United
States—History. I. Title.

TL23.F745 2005
629.222′0973—dc22   2004065111

For my grandparents
Alois and Gretchen Franz
and
Frank and Henrietta Schettle

Contents

Introduction

Automobiles in the Machine Age

In 1915, Emily Post wrote one of the first accounts of transcontinental motor travel in the United States, *By Motor to the Golden Gate*.[1] Hired by *Collier's* magazine to travel the newly completed Lincoln Highway from New York City to San Francisco for the Pan American Exposition, Post recorded her impressions of long distance travel by automobile. As a way to sell both the book and motor travel, friend and editor Frank Crownin-shield asked Post to "keep an informal but complete record" of the trip to be published as advice to the legions of middle-class drivers who would follow her. Although the journey proved difficult at times, Post declared driving to be a liberating experience. Having conquered poor roads, breakdowns, and even sleeping outside, Post claimed that traveling by car gave her a new perspective on America, the automobile, and herself.[2]

Typical of many American motorists, Post emphasized the thrill of traveling outside a national system of railroads and urban hotels and the importance of mechanical ingenuity among the new generation of motor travelers. Yet, in an era when many Americans learned to drive and repair their own cars, the advice expert admitted that she knew nothing about auto mechanics and left the driving to her son, Edwin. Post's vehicle, a large, foreign touring car that was both heavy and low to the ground, did not fare well on America's muddy roads. Post used the difficulties of cross-country auto travel to underscore both the inge-nuity and the persistence of American motorists. Both Post and her son advised their readers to purchase an American car with standardized parts and to cultivate their knowledge of automobile mechanics.[3] Most car owners did this without prompting from Emily Post; they were eager to tinker with the new machine.

In the same year, *Fordowner*, a magazine written by and for drivers of the Ford Model T, featured its version of motor travel for the middle classes, "Ford Camp Touring."[4] The journal asked: "By the way, how have you toured? Did you throw a couple of suit cases into the car, and make runs from one hotel to another, paying high prices for poor food, bad service, uncomfortable beds?" *Fordowner* advised its readers to avoid such discomforts and costs by using a little ingenuity to modify the bodies of their cars for touring. The editor of *Fordowner* assured drivers that redesigning their cars would give them a feeling of "absolute independence" from hotels and railroads.[5] The journal encouraged readers to send photographs and stories of how they modified the car for travel. Countless motorists responded by showing off their newly remade vehicles. These stories revealed what both automobility and tinkering meant to middle-class American consumers.

In the first decades of the twentieth century, thousands of enthusiastic motorists, like Post and the contributors to *Fordowner*, reported the benefits of automobility and articulated the links between motor travel, tinkering, and technological authority in America. Indeed motor touring presents an important cultural window onto how Americans used and thought about the new consumer technology of the automobile. In the years surrounding World War I, social and industrial changes put the automobile and the motor vacation within the reach of the broad group of middle-class Americans from white-collar office workers and prosperous farmers to skilled laborers. Coupled with mass production after 1913 and Henry Ford's five-dollar day, the creation of General Motors Acceptance Corporation's (GMAC) installment buying in 1919 lowered the price of cars and made the new machines available to those with not as much ready cash.[6] Buying on credit allowed many wage laborers to purchase cars for the first time. Between 1914 and 1920 automobile ownership in the United States rose significantly and, in 1920, a nationwide census of automobile registrations, produced by the auto industry, claimed the sensational statistic that one out of every fourteen Americans owned an automobile.[7] Motor touring expert J. C. Long argued, "motor cars are more accessible to the laboring man to-day than they ever have been before." Comparing the drop in car prices against rising union wages, he wrote that in 1920 a union carpenter could buy a car with slightly over six months' wages.[8] Translating the figures into national rhetoric, *Literary Digest* declared, "We are the world's motor-country."[9]

Despite *Literary Digest*'s optimism, the automobile census also underscored racial and class inequality among automobile consumers in the years after World War I.[10] The majority of car owners in 1920 were white, middle-class men who lived outside of cities, either in suburbs or on farms.[11] The industry census also reported that few recent immigrants, urban laborers, poor rural whites, or African Americans owned cars.[12] Nevertheless, many members of these communities would join the ranks of auto owners as the resale market made cars even more affordable in the late 1920s and 1930s.

As one of the premier consumer technologies of the twentieth century, the automobile opened a new cultural arena in which different groups of American consumers could demonstrate their technological competency and gain authority in a culture that valued ingenuity. The terrain in which these consumers traveled was as important as the new technology of the car; the imaginary public space of the open road became site of social and cultural struggle in America as the automobile became a viable means of transportation.[13] The automobile and the mechanical know-how required to drive and repair the machine became tools that consumers used to articulate their varying agendas for greater spatial and cultural autonomy. Tinkering, which I equate here with user modification of the automobile body, allowed motor travelers to not only redesign the car but, at the same time, to re-negotiate their cultural identities and their relationships to public space in terms of gender and technical expertise. The popular adoption of the automobile inspired debates about who could drive, tinker, and enjoy the new form of mobility.

Historians of technology have explored how new communications technologies afforded Americans a moment of opportunity to reconfigure public space and gain authority in the public sphere.[14] For example, Carolyn Marvin has asserted that new technologies gave rise to cultural debates over authority in American society based on knowledge of the technology. She has argued that "the history of technology is less the evolution of technical efficiencies . . . than a series of arenas for negotiating issues crucial to the conduct of social life; among them, who is inside and outside, who may speak, who may not, and who has authority."[15] The automobile offered Americans similar opportunities to reconfigure social and technological hierarchies. In these debates the automobile became a tool in power relations among groups of consumers, such as men and women, and between consumers and emerging automotive corporations.

Constructing the Open Road

Automobile advocates in this period wrote extensively on the social and cultural value of the motorcar. The outpouring of advice literature, travel narratives, trade journals and popular magazines contextualized and gave meaning to the material practices of early auto ownership.[16] For many of the white men and women who wrote about auto travel, the social benefits of the new technology were clear: the car provided a means to leave the city and enter what journalist Wilber Hall described as the democratic, regenerative, and unifying space of the open road. Enthusiasts promoted what they called "the free car and the open road." According to Hall, the automobile would help the native, white middle-class or the "elect" to create a new landscape that would act as an antidote to the stress of living in an increasingly diverse and more urban nation. Hall wrote in 1917: "In its finest and most human sense the automobile is an engine of divine origin for carrying the elect to the open road that Whitman sings."[17] Hall defined the open road as a unique, democratic space that anyone could enter as long as they owned a car. The benefits for the auto-touring elect were many: travel by car cured anxiety and physical dissipation caused by urban life and put the middle-class in touch with a national community of "like-minded" Americans. Automobile touring, especially in the form of auto-camping, allowed the traveler to sleep and eat outside an urban system of hotels thus separating leisure from the city and its multitude of social challenges and discomforts, from polluted air to social fragmentation.

By World War I, Americans who could afford a car and a vacation set out for the open road, which could be as close as a country road or as distant as Yellowstone. The open road was as much an ideology as a physical space, and, as such, it embodied many cultural sentiments prevalent in the United States in the early twentieth century including nationalism, anti-urbanism, and technological enthusiasm. Even as inventors worked on the problem of motorized transportation in the 1890s, critics of urbanization and immigration constructed a vision of America that idealized rural and wilderness landscapes as a respite from city life.[18] Living in a period of rapid urbanization, elite advocates of outdoor leisure wrote of the corrupting influences of the city and how the automobile might liberate the individual and the family from the problems of modernity.[19] By the twentieth century the American wilderness had become a redemptive space, a place that city dwellers could go to counter the negative effects of urban life.[20]

Publisher Bruce Calvert described the open road as a metaphoric place where American democracy and individual freedom could be practiced by a select group of Americans. Calvert began publication of *The Open Road*—a "liberal, independent magazinelet of high voltage for people not afraid to think"—in 1908. The pages of the magazine became a forum for the reformer's ideas on urbanization, immigration, and the urgent need for Americans to escape cities and live closer to nature. At the core of Calvert's writings was the argument that the open road, and the way of life it symbolized, was threatened by rapid urbanization. In the inaugural issue he asked: "Why will not tired and restless humanity leave the noisy overcrowded, unwholesome city for the green fields . . . of the country?" The publisher defined "crowdophobia" as the "new disease." Summoning the spirit of Walt Whitman he exhorted his readers: "There's only one cure—take to the woods. Come out with me on the Open Road."[21] Members of the intellectual and economic elite, such as Calvert, were not alone in their construction of an urban-rural dichotomy that set in opposition the libratory promise of the rural highway and the debilitating atmosphere of the city.

Auto touring emerged as a middle-brow and more technological interpretation of Calvert's naturalist manifesto. Motor travelers wrote that they wanted relief from city life.[22] "Mrs. Newton and I were weary of civilization. . . . We wanted to get away from the city," wrote H. C. Newton in a 1911 promotion for the Franklin car company.[23] Camping experts urged motor travelers to avoid urban hotels and restaurants. In "Why We Motor-

Camp," expert Elon Jessup wrote that he preferred to avoid urban institutions because they drew motorists "back [to] the turmoil of the city streets."[24] The stress of urban life contributed to what another autocamping authority, Frank Brimmer, termed "National Vacationitis." In 1923, Brimmer, Chicago radio personality and prolific writer on the benefits of automobile touring, defined the illness as an "annual depression and lack of interest, world blurs drab and irksome, food tastes stale and insipid, there is present a powerful craving to burst collar and conventions and become a boy again."[25] Brimmer placed the automobile at the center of his formula for healthier leisure and predicted that motor travel would become the preferred recreational activity of all Americans.

A search for national unity also permeated the literature on automobility.[26] Nina Wilcox Putnam, a reporter for the *Saturday Evening Post*, described the frustrations of urban life that prompted her to leave New York City on a cross-country automobile tour in 1921. She presented a fictionalized account of her travels in *West Broadway*. For Putnam's heroine, Miss Latour, the streets of New York consisted of a predominantly alien crowd of immigrants and political rabble-rousers. Although Latour had no real contact with strikers, Reds, or anarchists, she noted that the newspapers were full of their activities. Reading the morning news, Latour sunk back in her bed "fairly sick" with the condition of her country. "This was serious," she wrote. "If all that stuff was so much more important than the good news, we as a nation were in a bad way, that was clear to any fool." She reasoned, "if it was true every decent American ought to act and act quick before it was too late. But it couldn't be too late. I wouldn't let it be."[27] Thus she resolved to leave New York and spread true "Americanism" on a cross-country automobile tour.

An increasingly diverse urban population contributed to the image of the city as fragmented. High rates of immigration and migration both from Eastern Europe and the southern United States spurred urbanization at the turn of the nineteenth century. Immigrants were not the only group of outsiders in the city. The migration of southern blacks to northern cities increased sharply after World War I. Racial violence in more than twenty-five cities across the United States in 1919, added to the perception of the urban landscape as divided and dangerous.[28] Members of the growing white middle classes searched for social order in an increasingly diverse society. Cultural historians have observed that the turn of the twentieth century saw a growing sense of fragmentation and multiplicity that seemed to "imperil the very basis of order," not only for native elites but for the white middle classes as well.[29] Indeed, the formation of a middle class was in part due to native white efforts to maintain control of the urban environment and distinguish themselves from the working classes and immigrants by forming exclusive clubs and associations.[30]

While some elites took up social reform efforts to control public space, the middle classes seemed more interested in improving their own lives and maintaining a sense of privacy.[31] The defining characteristics of the middle classes in the 1920s were self-improvement and self-sufficiency rather than social reform.[32] The automobile offered the perfect means of retreat, giving the driver more privacy and greater control over space. Advertisers and manufacturers also told car owners that the new technology would make the open road more accessible.[33]

Henry Ford was perhaps the most vocal authority on the automobile as a cure for the problems of urbanization. In his essay "The Modern City: A Pestiferous Growth," the automobile manufacturer characterized the urban populations as "antagonistic, competitive, mutually exclusive." Ford believed that the fight for "ground space" was misdirected. Instead, he urged Americans to seek out "communities where a man knows his neighbor, where there is a commonalty of interest." In Ford's estimation, technology did not contribute to the disadvantages of urban life, which he defined as "congestion and inequality," rather it provided the solution. "We shall solve the City Problem by leaving the City," he declared. But Ford warned readers to think of cities not as "a sad blunder" but as "a school for the race" that taught Americans how to achieve the benefits of industrialization, namely through new inventions. Ford observed that the consumers could take "the best of the cities with them—those discoveries and inventions which make life safe and pleasant."[34] The industrialist offered a technological solution to a social problem; he believed that the automobile would give Americans more control over public space and a greater sense of community.

Automobile experts reinforced Ford's message that the new machine gave drivers a sense of power over public space. In 1910 Robert Sloss, automobile editor for *Outing*, wrote, "the car has proved that it is capable of . . . bringing its owner into speedy touch with primitive Nature. . . . And the car gets him back again before he has dropped any of the necessary threads of our complex civilization."[35] Twelve years later, Harry Shumway, editor at *Field and Stream*, marveled that cars, "go so fast, perform so creditably, that one finds nowadays that he has but to feel the wish, get out the car and presto—in a few hours he is so far away from the smoke, dust and jazz of the city that, really, its existence is but a dream." The driver, Shumway concluded, was a "near master" of the landscape.[36] Other writers such as Elon Jessup told their middle-class readers, "Time and space are at your beck and call, your freedom is complete."[37]

Some observers, however, worried that the automobile would create class divisions. President Woodrow Wilson warned that automobiles had the dark potential to "spread Socialism" because they were "a picture of arrogance and wealth in all its independence and carelessness."[38] Wilson was in the minority. Respondents to Wilson's speech sought to dispel the notion that the automobile would intensify class divisions and struggles over public space. Leaders of the Automobile Club of America remarked that "Automobiling more than any other sport . . . tends to break down class distinctions and brings the poor man with his small runabout into close sympathy and fellowship with the rich man who owns a high-powered and expensive machine."[39] In November 1910, *American Motorist*, the official publication of the American Automobile Association, observed with a sigh of relief, that "automobiling has not bred anarchy."[40]

Cornelius Vanderbilt, Jr., whose vacation plans did not suffer from financial constraint, endorsed the automobile as an agent of democracy in 1921. Acknowledging Henry Ford's achievements in lowering the cost of the car, he wrote that all "clear-thinking" Americans realized that the "automobile and its manufacturers are helping to solve the . . . social problems of the future." Vanderbilt wrote that there was a "poetic jus-tice of the open spaces, for the ways of the road . . . are those of fair play and democracy for all."[41] During World War I, American motorists flooded national parks, auto camps, and the byways of the open road.[42] Elon Jessup observed, "To my mind the only democratic sport is one in which everybody plays the game. And I hereby elect motor camping the most democratic sport in America."[43]

Despite the democratic rhetoric, the ranks of early auto travelers were limited by class, ethnicity, and race. Many new immigrants and industrial workers could not afford cars or vacations in the early years of automobil-ity and rarely, if ever, appeared in descriptions of auto travel. Further-more, a new class of black professionals who could afford cars was systematically denied access to the open road. Like other public leisure spaces in the early twentieth century, the road was racially segregated.[44] Even though African Americans embraced auto ownership as an alterna-tive to Jim Crow railroad cars, those who wrote about the pleasures of auto travel never equated the automobile with integration or an equal share in democracy.[45] African American drivers between 1910 and 1940 found that the majority of autocamps, resorts, and hotels did not wel-come black motorists.[46] Alfred Edgar Smith described disappointments of African American motorists in *Opportunity* magazine: "With good cars growing cheaper . . . there is still a small cloud that stands between us and complete motor-travel freedom. . . . 'Where,' it asks us, 'will you stay tonight?' An innocent enough question for our Nordic friends. . . . But to you and me, what a peace-destroying world of potentiality." After trav-eling extensively in the United States, Smith remarked that racial discrim-ination against black motorists was not limited to the South; "in spite of unfounded beliefs to the contrary, conditions are practically identical in the Mid-west, the South, the so-called North-east, and the South-west."[47]

Vanderbilt and his fellow motor enthusiasts admired the regional and occupational diversity of motor travelers and, at the same time, enjoyed the racial and ethnic homogeneity of the open road. Nina Wilcox Putnam observed that her fellow travelers hailed from diverse regions of the United States and represented "perfectly good members of the . . . middle-classes" and "American whites."[48] The common racial background of Putnam's motor comrades added to her sense of fraternity and security.[49] Race, class, and national character intertwined in Putnam's evaluation of the importance of the automobile vacation and the open road; if the nation was in crisis in 1919, then the open road offered motorists a place undivided by political factions or different races. Travel writer Frederic Van de Water reiterated the democratic nature of automobility and, at the same time, invoked the rhetoric of 100-percent Americanism.[50] Van de Water declared that auto camping drove out sectionalism and cultivated a community made up of people who were honest, self-sufficient and "like-minded." He wrote: "Sometimes . . . the feeling came over us that we belonged to some great mutual-benefit society of which all those we met were also members. . . . We were Americans and in that part of the nation that is still natively American."[51] To participate in Van de Water's "mutual benefit society" all one had to do was to buy a car.

Tinkering and Technological Authority

In addition to access to the open road, technological authority became one of the chief benefits of auto ownership. Automobile owners quickly became members of a community defined as much by its enthusiasm for technology as by its love of unfettered mobility. Introduced in the first decades of the Machine Age the automobile entered a culture already distinctly and intimately involved with technology.[52] In the late nineteenth century, a host of new technologies restructured everyday life, such as the telephone, the streetcar, and the electric light.[53] Even as control over technology became the province of trained scientists, engineers, and planners, the products of mass production spurred enthusiasm for both technology and mechanical know-how among middle-class Americans with little technical training.[54] Personal technologies, from telephones to wireless radios, fostered an "almost unqualified enthusiasm" for technology among Americans in the 1910s and 1920s.[55]

As the artifacts of the machine age proliferated, technological discourse permeated American life from modernist literature to middle-brow magazines. The authors of American modernism embraced technology even as they critiqued it.[56] Sinclair Lewis's Babbitt, for instance, lived in a landscape irrevocably shaped by skyscrapers, telegraph wires, and electric razors. Wholly uncritical of technology, Babbitt thanked the "God of Progress" when he pulled on his BVDs or stepped into his automobile.[57] By 1929, cultural critic Waldo Frank declared that the machine in America had given rise to a cult of power based on technology; the machine had become an instrument of corporate power and a "household idol."[58] If the literary elite criticized technology, popular literature cultivated Americans' enthusiasm for new gadgets, machines, and electronic devices. Journals such as *Popular Mechanics*, serial fiction such as the Tom Swift books, and a host of other sources encouraged amateur ingenuity in America. President Herbert Hoover, "the Great Engineer," may have symbolized the social benefits of machine age rationality and, for some the hegemony of technical experts, but he shared the spotlight with Tom Swift—an amateur inventor who won fame and fortune through tinkering and who always stayed one step ahead of the engineers.[59] Thus, the automobile was embedded in wide cultural discourse that created a national enthusiasm for technology and praised those with technical and scientific knowledge as social leaders.[60]

Americans, eager to own new technologies and cultivate their own technical expertise, embraced the automobile.[61] The motor car, as historian Carroll Pursell observed, "reified deeply rooted values of individuality . . . free choice, and control over one's life. It was the perfect example of the nation's habit of trying to replace politics with technology."[62] Automobile ownership gave American consumers a part to play in the national dialogue on technology. Consumers did not simply drive the automobile, they repaired, tinkered with, and intervened in the design of the machine. Early automobile travel was difficult. Driving, and especially long-distance touring, required basic mechanical knowledge in order to run and repair the machine. The difficulties of early motor travel, when added to the middle-class expectations of economy and comfort, inspired travelers to learn something about mechanics and to tinker with the design of the car.

Drivers shared their automotive experiences with a national community of users through journals and magazines. Automotive journals that addressed users, such as *Fordowner*, flourished in the first decade after mass production of the auto. The growth of how-to literature, repair manuals, and journals such as *Popular Mechanics* nurtured a basic mechanical know-how among a wide swath of Americans. These texts gave consumers access to understanding, repairing, and tinkering with products of mass production and cultivated the image of an amateur expert.[63] Even more general magazines observed the growth of automotive know-how among average Americans in this period. By 1918, *Outlook* claimed that "So much as been said and written of the automobile . . . and it has become so intimately connected with the life and progress of the Nation, that the average man or woman is surprisingly familiar with its general construction and mode of operation."[64]

In the scholarly tradition of Leo Marx and John Kasson, this book is a cultural history of American's relationship to the emergent technology of the automobile between 1900 and 1939.[65] This project relies on the interdisciplinary methods of American studies, drawing together theories of popular culture, material culture studies, and the history of technology to decipher the cultural importance of one new technology, the automobile, for American consumers. I chose to focus on automobiles because the introduction of affordable, mass-produced cars made not only travel but also a larger discourse of ingenuity more accessible to the middle-class. Ownership of the means of transportation was key to popular modification. As the Women's Bureau of the Department of Labor explained in 1923, the "actual driving and care of cars," swelled the number of amateur patents because the automobile furnished "a greater opportunity for observing the conditions of efficient . . . operation of the mechanism."[66] Indeed, I argue that the hands-on operation of the automobile encouraged travelers to appropriate the means of transportation and reinvent it.

Seeking the voices of consumers, this study draws upon the rich body of popular writing on the automobile, from advice literature to travel narratives, published in the first third of the twentieth century. These travel stories invariably addressed the mechanical skill and ingenuity of the driver. In addition, to better examine popular design changes to the body of the automobile, I also rely upon an equally rich body of photographic evidence. Another kind of evidence, patent records for motor travel equipment, reveal that some consumers moved beyond tinkering with their cars to actively engaging the patent process in hopes of altering the standard design of mass produced cars and profiting from their ingenuity. To place the activities of middle-class consumers within a larger dialog on automobile design, marketing, and use, this book incorporates the voice of manufacturers through industry journals and corporate records, especially correspondence between the engineering department at Ford Motor Company and consumers.

Drawing on recent paradigms in the history of technology, this study argues that users were active participants in the social construction of new technologies.[67] The open road, the home garage, and the auto show represented what historian Ruth Schwartz Cowan has described as the "consumption junction," a place where consumers, engineers, designers and manufacturers met and where buyers ascribed cultural meanings to the automobile.[68] A highly charged artifact in the machine politics of the early twentieth century, the automobile had tremendous potential to reorganize existing social structures in the United States and mediate the relationships among various groups of consumers and between manufacturers and users.[69] Although the abundant advice and advertising that surrounded automobiles promoted the dominant designs and ideas of manufacturers, there was also ample space in the early twentieth century for consumers to participate in a dialog on automotive design. Tinkering with the car gave consumers a way to improve the fit between their desires and the mass produced machine.[70] This tailoring of the car, whether it was adding lights, electric starters, or an entirely new body, gave buyers some authority over design and a way to show off their technological savvy. Auto ownership also enabled various groups of consumers to challenge reigning ideas about who could claim mechanical know-how. Tinkering allowed them to participate in a larger discourse of technological enthusiasm and ingenuity.

Consumers were not all the same; they came from different communities, had different priorities, and indeed entered the consumption junction under "a number of different guises."[71] Consumers used mechanical knowledge to shift their positions in the network of production and consumption. Women, who were portrayed by manufacturers and their husbands as passive consumers, remade themselves into competent mechanics and active users. In turn, male consumers recast themselves as ingenious tinkerers and grass-roots inventors. Indeed the definition of the proper automobile consumer was up for grabs in this period, and constantly renegotiated along the lines of gender, class, race, and technological knowledge. Americans not only tinkered with the design of their automobiles but also with the definition of consumer.

Tinkering with the automobile was also an act of creativity and emulation. Consumers who tinkered, and especially those who became grass-roots inventors, relied on spatial thinking and "fingertip" knowledge rather than formal education or training in science and engineering.[72] Tinkering was a process by which amateurs with little or no technical training could imitate the lives and hopefully the recognition of famous inventors such as Henry Ford or Thomas Edison.[73] Tinkerers, like the popular portrayals of famous inventors, worked in their spare time and used trial and error to invent. Not only did emulation maintain an older model of apprenticeship, but, as historian Brooke Hindle has argued, by the mid-nineteenth century "technological emulation was most practiced in holding up the inventor, rather than the invention, as the model of emulation. Each popular invention was tied to an eponymic inventor, and inventors were, indeed, raised to the level of popular heroes."[74]

The popular magazines and advice literature of the 1910s and 1920s perpetuated the idea of emulation, encouraging middle-class readers to turn their experience as consumers into useful inventions by replicating the practices and character traits of nineteenth-century inventor-heroes. Tinkering offered consumers a measure of control over the automobile and was one of the ways in which they could claim authority in negotiating their relationships with manufacturers, marketers, and designers. By examining the ways in which Americans tinkered with the bodies of their cars, I explore automotive design from the bottom up, as a process that included manufacturers, engineers, designers, advice experts, and consumers in "various guises" from buyers to grass-roots inventors.

Recent theories of popular culture that posit audiences as producers of culture have also been particularly important to this project in analyzing how and why consumers remade the automobile.[75] As cultural theorist John Fiske has argued, "every act of consumption is an act of cultural production, for consumption is always the production of meaning."[76]

Scholars of contemporary popular culture have asserted that popular audiences make culture out of the commodities of everyday life.[77] Cultural production is centered on what Fiske calls "poaching," or using the products available on the market rather than starting from scratch.[78] Thus, modification of the automobile was a type of cultural poaching. I assert that tinkering was a form of popular culture that gave consumers some power over the archetype of mass production, the automobile, allowing them to tailor the machine to fit their needs as travelers.

Beyond changing the shape of the automobile, motorists used tinkering to redefine their cultural positions within American society. According to other recent theories of consumption, audiences use cultural commodities to "construct meanings of self, of social identity and social relations" sometimes in conformity with and sometimes in opposition to, the dominant discourse.[79] For instance, women drivers used the acquisition of mechanical knowledge to support their claims to greater physical autonomy. If a woman could drive and repair her own car, she could travel more freely and without a chaperone. Recent theories of popular culture, then, allow me to interpret the activities of drivers as not just fun or escapist but as a form of cultural politics. Yet, historically, users of technology, no matter how active, have had difficulty overturning entrenched social hierarchies and business systems that placed the user at an increasing disadvantage. Ultimately, tinkerers worked within, not outside of, the system of corporate capitalism which made a concerted effort to consolidate innovation in the hands of professional designers and engineers working for large corporations and eliminate the challenges of modification by users and innovations from independent inventors.

Changes in manufacturing and design, as well as increasing attempts by automotive corporations to manage consumer desire in the late 1920s and 1930s, made automobiles easier to drive but more difficult for amateurs to modify. Ultimately, the liberatory aspects of automobility were checked by emerging social and cultural hierarchies that constrained individual autonomy and limited attempts to change the design of the auto from the bottom up. Thus, this study of tinkering charts how Americans increasingly defined the boundaries of ingenuity along the lines of gender and technical expertise in the early twentieth century. The following chapters explore more closely the meaning of automobility and tinkering for consumers in the interwar years and consumers' ongoing dialogue and sometimes conflict over design with engineers and automobile manufacturers.

Chapter 1 investigates what middle-class consumers, and in particular motor tourists, wanted from the design of early automobiles. This chapter also considers the popular discourses of ingenuity that encouraged tourists to blur the distinctions between consumption and production and modify the bodies of their cars. Most middle-class motorists desired comfort, economy, and efficient use of space in their automobiles, and these priorities fueled a growing aftermarket parts industry and a culture of tinkering among enthusiastic drivers. Chapter 2 examines the gendered nature of technological authority in the early twentieth century. The automobile offered women a new space in which to tinker with the models of technological heroism and the boundaries of mechanical knowledge, reinventing, for a moment, definitions of female consumers as competent and autonomous users of technology. Although women motorists gained a greater share of public space through their use of the automobile, by the late 1920s women were increasingly excluded from the circle of consumers who could claim ingenuity. Chapter 3 takes a closer look at a smaller group of consumers, mostly men, who defined themselves not only as tinkerers but as inventors. In a vibrant dialog with advice experts and manufacturers, these consumers-turned-inventors tried to profit from their ingenuity by patenting and selling their ideas for the car. Chapter 4 presents one grass-roots inventor's story, that of Earl S. Tupper, to analyze the difficulties tinkerers faced when they attempted to cross the line between consumption and invention by patenting their ideas. Even though Tupper followed advice literature and worked diligently, his experiences exemplify the difficulties of redesigning the automobile outside a growing network of corporate research and production in the 1930s. The final chapter examines the auto industry's view of consumers and its response to popular ingenuity in the 1930s. At automobile shows and world's fairs, the automobile industry cemented its role as the leader of innovation and national progress through dynamic exhibits. Automotive exhibitions presented the history of the automobile as one in which corporations, not individuals, initiated change. Automotive exhibits of the 1930s instructed Americans that progress flowed from the top down, from corporate engineers to consumers, and attempted to turn tinkerers in to consumers.

Tinkering, in the early twentieth century, demonstrated that automobile design was part of a dialectical process that included consumers, engineers, advice experts, and manufacturers. As automobiles became more affordable and roads improved, Americans bought cars and ventured onto the open road. Many of these drivers were handy with tools and added trunks, luggage racks, and beds to their cars to render the vehicle more comfortable and economical on long-distance trips. Tinkering with the automobile became one way in which consumers demonstrated their technological expertise. In the early years of the automobile culture, tinkering blurred the lines between consumption and invention and gave consumers a measure of technological authority in a culture that valued ingenuity.

Chapter 1

What Consumers Wanted

"There was this about a Model T," wrote E. B. White in 1936, "the purchaser never regarded his purchase as a complete, finished product. When you bought a Ford, you figured you had a start—a vibrant, spirited framework to which could be screwed an almost limitless assortment of decorative and functional hardware. Driving away from the agency . . . you were already full of creative worry."[1] A veteran of early motoring, White recalled the popularity of tinkering with the Model T. In his sentimental eulogy for the archetype of Ford-style production, White demonstrated that early automotive design was not determined completely at the point of production, nor did it exclude consumers.

In the early years of the automobile, between 1900 and 1930, motorists actively and enthusiastically redesigned their motor vehicles. Automobile touring, in particular, provided fertile ground for middle-class consumers to become tinkerers and, occasionally, grass-roots inventors. In the first years of mass production, car manufacturers did not have the final word on design.[2] The Model T, for instance, may have been a homogeneous product when it rolled off the assembly line, but, in the hands of users, it did not keep its standardized body for very long. As Trevor Pinch and Ronald Kline have demonstrated, farmers remade the Model T into a multifunctional machine, often using the auto to run other machinery on the farm.[3] Travelers also had specific needs that prompted them to modify the automobile into a multi-purpose vehicle. According to social psychologist Donald Norman, tinkering is a common and often overlooked practice that increases the fit between a device and its users; it corrects design failures or shortcomings that engineers are often unable to anticipate.[4] The early mass-produced car could not serve the varied needs of all its buyers, and tinkering on the part of consumers helped tailor a standardized product to fit their diverse needs.

This chapter analyzes how consumers tinkered with the bodies of their automobiles in the first decades after mass production, by purchasing and building after-market accessories. Examining the consumer practices of motor travelers this chapter address three questions. First, what were the cultural motivations and rewards for tinkering with the automobile? Second, what did tourists want from the design of the auto and how did they adapt it to their own set of criteria? Finally, how did a growing cadre of advice experts on camping, motor travel, and automotive know-how help Americans navigate the field of automotive accessories and blur the lines between consumption and production by encouraging consumers to build and even invent their own additions to the car? Motorists did not work alone; they were aided by advisors who sold the notion of a consumer ethos, that consumption of goods could solve social and personal discomforts, and who promoted the notion that outfitting the car was not only a consumer activity but also an act of resourcefulness and ingenuity.[5]

Fueling a booming market for automotive accessories, motorists bought devices and modified the car to their own specifications. In doing so, drivers appropriated and reassembled the products of mass production, making do with whatever was at hand.[6] By modifying the bodies of their cars to meet specific criteria of comfort and convenience, the new ranks of motor tourists who hit the road during and after World War I used automotive accessories to reinforce a middle-class lifestyle that softened the practice of "roughing it" and maintained standards of comfort based on the private home.[7] Motorists in this period traveled on a tighter budget than their earlier, wealthier counterparts, but they also enjoyed enough disposable income and leisure time to engage in the growing consumer culture of the early twentieth century.[8]

Ingenuity

In the decades between 1900 and 1930, a wide cultural discourse of ingenuity inspired popular enthusiasm for technology and cemented the relationship between technological know-how, national progress, and the average American, and particularly the male consumer. For instance, a 1919 advertisement for *Scientific American* in *Outing,* a magazine for auto travelers, told readers that every man was a modern scientist.[9] Even as technological and scientific research became dominated by professionals during the interwar period, popular histories of invention, popular fiction, mass-market magazines, and travel narratives fostered a national enthusiasm for technology and praised all levels of ingenuity. The development of more affordable, mass-produced automobiles opened new and exciting possibilities for the American consumer to practice technological competency and demonstrate his, and occasionally her, own ingenuity.

Mass-market magazines portrayed tinkerers and their innovations as ingenious. *The Motorists' Almanac* in 1917 told drivers, "Much pleasure

Every Man a
Modern Scientist

Figure 1. A wide variety of popular print sources encouraged readers to engage in the larger discourse of technological progress after World War I. This advertisement for *Scientific American* appealed to motorists reading *Outing*, one of the central publications of the outdoor vacation movement. "Every Man a Modern Scientist," *Outing*, July 1919, 268.

and a great saving of energy can be derived from undertaking your tinkering yourself." Arguing that the owner's knowledge of his own auto was superior to all others, the editor enthused, "odd half hours expended in these humble jobs promote the brotherhood of man and the machine."[10] Journalists, motor touring experts, and advertisers found both the drivers who reshaped their automobiles and the accessories they built to be resourceful, smart, and imaginative. For instance, a Ford Motor Company publicity release in 1916 announced the introduction of a "clever telescopic apartment" for Ford cars. The advertisement, which ran in the *New York World*, announced, "Inventive geniuses are daily bringing forth new ideas for touring travel." Replacing the passenger seats, the compartment provided room for a bed, a dressing room, and a shower warmed by heat from the exhaust. *Outing* labeled another "Ford Auto-bed" an "ingenious contrivance." As for motorists, J. C. Long noted, "If the weekend camper is ingenious he may rig up a bed of his own" inside the automobile.[11]

Tinkering, whether it took place in the garage or autocamp, gave consumers a forum in which to show off their ingenuity. Popular commentator and vernacular humorist Marietta Holley commented on the cultural currency as well as the gendered nature of automotive know-how in her 1906 short story *Samantha vs. Josiah: Being the Story of a Borrowed Automobile and What Became of It*. Set in the fictional community of Mormon brethren, *Samantha vs. Josiah* featured Samantha, the wise and long-suffering wife of Josiah Allen, a boastful tinkerer. In this story, Holley satirized Josiah's attempts to invent an automobile accessory and impress the community with his knowledge of automobile mechanics. After announcing to his wife that he was "about to invent . . . an attachment to [automobiles] that will make us rich as Jews," Josiah spent long hours in his barn devising an attachment that would reduce dust and dirt created by the wheels of the car. Josiah's continual lack of common sense provided a foil for Samantha's wisdom. Samantha regarded tinkering with resignation as well as skepticism. She reflected, "I felt that though [the dust-laying attachment] might give him a drenchin', it would probable not kill him; he said he would make a preliminary trial with our old waterin' pot." The invention, however, did not prove successful: "With the first revolution of the wheel, the waterin' pot . . . emptied its entire contents on my pardner."[12] Failure, however, did not deter Josiah from tinkering or boasting.

Holley observed that the automobile gave men a way to show-off their mechanical know-how and thereby gain some authority within their families and their communities. Josiah's interest in the automobile was shared by many of the brethren. In public, men and boys gathered around the car as if the car "wuz lumps of sugar and they wuz flies," to share advice with Josiah. She criticized Josiah's desire to gain prestige through feigning an understanding of automobiles. "Nothin'" she observed, "pleased him more than to have over the outlandish names of the machinery, especially before me and the brethren, showin' off I spoze, how much more he knowed than we did."[13] Holley's critical humor reflected the connection between authority, even on a local level, and ingenuity. Although women participated in driving and some unescorted women motorists laid claim to technological competency, advice literature that encouraged tinkering addressed itself to a predominantly male audience. Both male and female drivers bought auto accessories to enhance the comfort and convenience of the auto, but tinkering and ingenuity became almost exclusively male activities in the interwar period.

Eleven years later, *Illustrated World* summed up the rewards of modification in an article entitled "Individualizing Your Automobile." The anonymous author related the scenario of a "novel-looking" car that drove into a garage. Men and women "immediately gathered about it in admiration, for it was trimmed with more than a dozen different things of unusual design." When asked what new model of car it was, the owner replied that it wasn't new. No, it was "the same old car painted up and individualized." Personalizing the car required not money but "only a little ingenuity." The featured attachments, which included curtains and wing-shaped fenders, were not purchased accessories but things of "individual design." Creating such accessories, the author reported, gave drivers great pleasure, for "it is an agreeable sensation indeed—having one's personal designs viewed with approval."[14] Traveler Kathryn Hulme confirmed that travelers took great pride in their equipment. She recounted the story of one man who "converted his car so that at night, by pulling out one seat, and pushing in the other, he had a perfectly elegant bed on which to unroll the hair mattress he carried. He was tremendously proud of the outfit and insisted on demonstrating it to all unfortunate campers who had to put up tents each night. . . . Listening to him, one had the impression that every delight of the open road began and ended with that springy mattress."[15]

Advice on equipment also reinforced the idea that outfitting the car displayed the driver's ingenuity. Packing and unpacking quickly was a sign that the motorist was efficient. Motor camping expert Elon Jessup, who frowned upon "slack methods," told tourists, "once a satisfactory outfit is collected for his particular purpose, this then becomes a standardized system so that he can always attach his equipment to the car and drive away on a moment's notice."[16] This was especially important for the middle-class weekender who, with a limited number of days in which to travel, needed to get the most out of his vacation time. Harry Shumway, auto touring editor for *Field and Stream*, told readers that the weekender who chose wisely and packed efficiently would not only enjoy the trip to its fullest and save money doing it but that his family would "rise up and call him a wise man."[17]

Early motor journals, such as *Horseless Age, Motor Age,* and *Fordowner* included amateurs in a national dialog on automotive innovation by inviting users to share their ideas. When these journals began publication between 1895 and 1913, motorists and manufacturers were practically the same group of people. Automobile journals in this early period were "written by and for devotees of the new 'sport' . . . self-acknowledged champions of . . . innovation."[18] All three published readers' comments and stories about improvements to the automobile.

Fordowner provided a national forum for drivers to share their own stories of automotive ingenuity. In the first issue, the editors asked subscribers to "cooperate with your fellow Ford owners in getting live news for your own publication. Send in photographs of your Ford, write of your Ford achievements, and tell of your Ford improvements." Under the heading "Help Build Your Magazine," the editorial staff prompted readers who had solved the problems of motoring to "pass on your discoveries to your fellow Ford owner."[19] Along with reviews for new equipment and hearty approval of owner modification, the magazine also featured relatively unknown inventors of automobile accessories such as L. F. Shilling, who patented his automobile bed and advertised in *Field and Stream*.[20] In this and numerous other stories, tourists sent in photographs and short descriptions of their equipment and how they built it. Within the pages of *Fordowner*, touring became a primary site for modification of the automobile by middle-class motorists.[21]

In its first six years, *Fordowner* created a national community of users. Like other populist motor journals in the mid-1920s, however, *Fordowner* shifted its focus away from users to the automotive industry. The growing gap between owners and the automotive industry was reflected in the changing names of the automobile journals. In 1920 *Fordowner* became *Ford Owner and Dealer*, and in 1925 the journal again changed its name to *Ford Dealer and Owner*.[22] By 1925, the journal seemed written solely for an audience of auto dealers. Indeed, *Fordowner* was the last of the three publications to exclude its audience of drivers; *Horseless Age* merged with *Automotive Industries* in 1918 and *Motor Age* ceased to include owner questions and advice after World War I.[23] Nevertheless, for a short time during the early twentieth century, such national publications offered a place for American motorists to exchange information, acknowledge the user's ingenuity, and transform consumption into an act of production.

Economy and Comfort: Middle-Class Design Criteria

In the first two decades of automobility, American motorists wanted amenities that manufacturers of low-priced, standardized vehicles often did not provide. Chief among the list of what drivers wanted were devices such as gas gauges, turn signals, tops to enclose open cars, electric starters, headlights, demountable tire rims, and trunks.[24] Mass produced cars before World War I were in many respects incomplete machines, and manufacturers like Henry Ford omitted many devices now considered essential, like gas gauges, to lower the production and the retail cost of the car.

Middle-class travelers, in particular, added a variety of accessories to make long-distance driving safer, easier, less expensive, and more comfortable. Popular additions included turn signals, interior heaters, mud guards, and devices to enclose the open touring car and protect its occupants from the weather, such as curtains and automobile tops. One historian of the early automotive industry noted that between 1916 and 1927, the "car of the American family," was an open touring car.[25] Intended for good weather driving and sightseeing, the typical touring car could seat as many as six passengers and did not have a top or any kind of enclosure that might obstruct the view. However, manufacturers, like Hupmobile, recognized the desire of tourists for closed cars and added optional cloth tops after 1916. Tops remained an accessory until the early 1920s. Before the enclosed and well-equipped car became affordable in the mid-1920s, with the introduction of the modestly-priced Chevrolet, motorists often designed inexpensive and creative devices for protecting themselves from the elements.[26] One anonymous driver, for instance, offered *Popular Mechanics* his idea for turning beach umbrellas into sturdy and inexpensive automobile tops.[27]

Consumers of Ford's Model T became famous for modifying the bodies of their automobiles.[28] In 1914, *Fordowner* noted that "to better adapt Ford quality and service to their individual requirements, many owners [construct] bodies of original design and add to the factory equipment."[29] A year later, Burt Reid, a contributor to *Illustrated World,* asserted, "the greatest new game of the day is getting a Ford, and then trying to see what you can make of it. . . . You simply can't express your individuality with a Ford in its original state, for Fords are all alike from their little squat wooden wheels to their little snub-nosed radiators." He noted that Ford owners added new steel fenders for safety and stream-lined style, tops, radiator hoods, and even entirely new bodies. Drivers could assemble or build their own racing car bodies to lend a "racy 'devil car'" style, or sedan bodies that turned the Ford into a closed car with "the same comforts as a limousine."[30]

Even as some manufacturers began to incorporate devices such as headlights and electric starters as standard equipment, the Model T, which dominated the auto market between 1913 and 1923, still lacked many of these conveniences.[31] One driver asked the readers of *Scientific American* in January 1917, "Why does the American manufacturer stop in the middle" of equipping the car? He complained that reasonably-priced cars or "what most motorists call a 'standard buy'" lacked things that made driving comfortable for the user. With a direct jab at the Model T, advertised as the Universal Car, the writer explained that, in their effort to standardize cars, manufacturers overlooked the "fact that the human race is not built on a universal plan." He concluded that standardized cars could not meet the needs of a diverse public and that the motor trade must "wake up to the fact that the *user* has a standpoint totally different from that of the *manufacturer.*"[32]

Users did not hesitate to share their point of view with manufacturers. Ford owners, who felt a close relationship to the creator of the Tin Liz-zie, wrote to Henry Ford telling him how to improve his product. In these missives, consumers based the legitimacy of their suggestions on their experience as drivers. "I drive a car, and know wherefore I write," declared J. C. Tucker of Pittsburgh, who wrote to Ford with his idea for improving the safety of their cars.[33] Men and women offered a multitude of changes to the Model T, including adding better seat cushions and

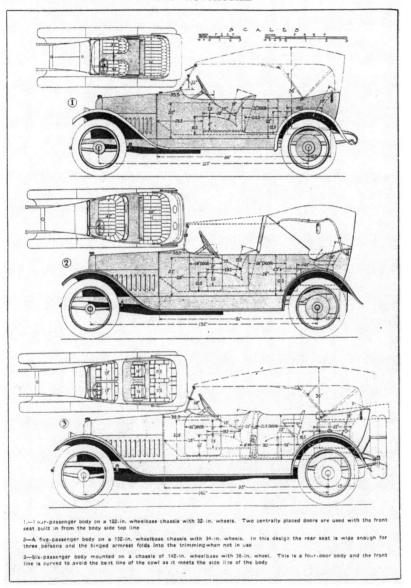

1.—Four-passenger body on a 122-in. wheelbase chassis with 32-in. wheels. Two centrally placed doors are used with the front seat built in from the body side top line

2—A five-passenger body on a 132-in. wheelbase chassis with 34-in. wheels. In this design the rear seat is wide enough for three persons and the hinged armrest folds into the trimming when not in use

3—Six-passenger body mounted on a chassis of 142-in. wheelbase with 36-in. wheel. This is a four-door body and the front line is curved to avoid the bent line of the cowl as it meets the side line of the body

Figure 2. Drawings of typical touring car bodies show a car open to travelers' improvements. Touring cars left little room for trunks on the back of the car because the rear seat was located over the back axel. Open top cars were good for sightseeing but provided little protection for passengers. *Automobile*, 8 July 1915, 68.

more gauges on the dashboard to inform drivers of levels of gasoline and tire pressure. Consumers with particular regional experiences wrote to Ford expressing their ideas on specific failures of the Universal Car to meet all environmental conditions. Although the Model T was rugged—lightweight, with a high body that made it durable in rural conditions—drivers noted that its design was far from ideal. R. H. Halton, from Hot Springs, Arkansas, wrote to Henry Ford in 1925, "I own a Ford car and have had it for a long time. I like it so blame well that is why I write you." Perhaps intimidated by Ford's stature, Halton noted that "Advice is out of the question and to suggest is foolish." But he told Ford that the Model T sedan did not perform well in the hilly country around Hot Springs and asked the manufacturer to provide more power in his cars.[34] In a similar request, a driver from Shelton, Washington, informed the engineers at Ford that their cars were ill suited to the wet conditions of the Northwest. V. E. Paul complained that the touring car body leaked, ruining tools and upholstery. "This is a wet country and nearly all cloth parts are ruined during one rainy season. Many people think you are using poor material. . . . If this suggestion is worth anything to you, you are welcome to it."[35]

Motor tourists, who logged long hours on the road, had much to say about the discomforts of their cars. Automobile touring grew significantly during World War I and placed new demands on automobile design.[36] Advice on how to equip the car for travel flowed into the Engineering office at Ford Motor Company. Letters arrived from thrifty "tin can" tourists who wished to economize by turning their autos into temporary hotel rooms or vehicles resembling private Pullman cars. Other writers, some of whom did not own cars, saw potential profits in catering to a growing market of motor tourists in the early 1920s. And some correspondents were merely enthusiastic about tinkering. One observer wrote that although he was not an engineer, he did have an important design idea for the 1923 models of the four-door sedans. "As a family car it seems near the ideal. Only in one way," wrote Einar Lund, "this car, like other automobiles, has little in convenience, namely for camping. Many people do not like to sleep on the ground even if they have a tent." He suggested that the sedan would make the "ideal camping car" if Ford would only make the front seats convertible, allowing them to recline by hinging the backs and provide mosquito screens for the windows.[37] When Ford refused to incorporate specialty accessories, consumers bought and built their own equipment. In 1921, motor expert Elon Jessup remarked that a great number of tourists reconstructed their cars, converting the seats into beds, adding trunks, and attaching a variety of other equipment. Jessup declared that tinkering with the automobile body was "warranted to strike a responsive chord in both the imaginative and practical strain of most any motorist."[38]

In 1914, *Motor Life* reported that the market for cars and accessories had become solidly middle class. The editor of the magazine noted that automobile owners were less affluent and more interested in economizing. Understanding the fundamentals of automobile mechanics could save drivers money; if drivers repaired their own cars, they freed themselves from expensive and, possibly, dishonest roadside mechanics. The *Motor Life* editor portrayed the middle-class driver as involved in the maintenance of the machine and as possessing significant mechanical knowledge. "The motorist is too wise, and wants too much for his money," the author asserted. "If [the driver] has anything out of order, he sees how it is fixed so he can attend to it the next time and save the repairman's fee."[39] *Fordowner* noted that its equipment page reviewed "devices to provide extra comfort and some to save Ford operators money."[40] Travel authorities presented equipping the car for sleeping as one important way to economize.

Just as the automobile promised freedom from railroad fares and schedules, motor accessories offered middle-class travelers a way to avoid hotel costs.[41] Autocamping advocates denounced hotels in the name of greater economy and independence for middle-class families. From his editorial desk at *Field and Stream*, Harry Shumway, wrote that adding camping equipment to the car could liberate the tourist from hotels.[42] With sleeping and eating equipment, tourists could stop anywhere, at any time of day. In 1918, *Outing* reported that the magazine received letters daily expressing enthusiasm for autocamping. The tourists who sent "dozens of letters," inquiring about motor touring equipment, "didn't want to know where they can find hotels. They want to know where they can get away from them."[43] Historians of auto touring have argued that this desire for independence stemmed from a sense of American individualism.[44] This was certainly true, but many middle-income tourists slept in their cars to lower the cost of vacationing.

Magazines promoted the belief that equipping the car for camping would save money.[45] One writer for *Ford Owner and Dealer* declared that sleeping and cooking accessories actually made family travel a possibility.[46] In the brief economic slump after World War I, *Outing* observed, "Anybody who can afford a car and a vacation can afford a motor camping trip. With this much [equipment] at your disposal, such a trip is the most economical way in which you can . . . vacation—and we are thinking a good bit about economy these days."[47] "As thousands learned last summer," said *Motor* in 1922, "the freedom from dependence upon hotels . . . which the camping outfit gives cannot be reckoned only in dollars and cents."[48] This writer argued that motor travel would improve the mental and physical health of the middle-class American family.

Many middle-class motorists believed they could measure the value of motor camping in dollars and cents. Travel narratives included budgets that confirmed the idea that the automobile provided the cheapest form of tourist transportation. Emily Post, for instance, included a lengthy budget in her travel narrative carefully itemizing each day's expenses.[49] Elon Jessup observed in 1921, "Almost every motor camper keeps an expense account. On the slightest provocation he will exhibit it, and this with gloating pride." He added that autocamping was the least expensive way to travel: "I have been assured many times that the total expenses of an all-summer trip are no greater than living at home. . . . Certainly a goodly proportion of . . . the motor campers now touring the . . . land are people who but for this inexpensive form of traveling would not be able to go at all."[50] Yet, as one commentator observed, motor travelers who opted to economize by camping shared a "self-imposed sacrifice of some of the modern conveniences."[51]

Although motorists praised the virtues of roughing it, they worked hard to maintain middle-class standards of material comfort. As early as 1910, one writer for *Harper's* noted that the proper outfit provided motor tourists with not only economic independence but also physical comfort. "It gives you on land the freedom that a yacht gives you at sea, and much more. In many ways, a touring car can be made even more comfortable than a yacht."[52] Discussions of motor travel often focused on the preservation of material comfort, making the built environment as important to the motor traveler as the natural environment. Emily Post confessed, "the way I like best to see anything is comfortably." Post, who camped out only once during her 1915 cross-county tour, spent most of her nights in urban hotels and admitted that mud and blowouts gave one an "appreciation for Pullman trains."[53]

Ten years later, artist James Montgomery Flagg, a close friend of Post, concurred. He wrote, "For me, who . . . likes to be extremely comfortable, to lash my determination to the point of actually starting on a transcontinental drive is funny." In his memoir of the trip Flagg noted, "There is a freedom about motoring across the continent that is lacking in the train ride. You have no schedules." He did acknowledge one drawback to train travel: "The galling monotony of the stifling Pullmans is less exhilarating." And yet independence was not adequate compensation for all the hardships of motor travel. Upon reaching the West Coast Flagg quipped, "if anyone told you to turn around and drive back, you would leap at his throat and strangle him to death."[54] Like Post, he traveled back to New York via Pullman car. Flagg and Post represented the most privileged motor travelers. Members of the leisure class, they embarked on motor touring as an adventure but not as a regular way of travel.

The desire for comfort was not limited to the upper classes. Motor camping expert J. C. Long wrote that the average man and his family could not afford "Statler service nor meals created by Oscar."[55] Nevertheless, Long observed that "Mr. Average Man . . . will not care to overdo in the way of roughing it."[56] As a testament to their desire for comfort, middle-income families, or "weekenders," converted their cars to maintain standards of physical comfort that they associated with the private home. Travelers and advisors alike used the phrase "comforts of home" to describe both the attributes of touring equipment and the motivation for adding it to automobiles.[57] Frank Brimmer, writing for *Outlook*, wrote that "old-style camping was not popular because few liked to go forth and play Spartan." Brimmer noted that Americans liked motor camping because it enabled them to take all the "comforts ordinarily ascribed only to a permanent domicile."[58] Elon Jessup agreed that motor camping distinguished itself from earlier forms of outdoor leisure because it was "camp life with as many of the comforts of home life as are conveniently possible."[59] Motorists' repeated references to comfort demonstrated their interest in maintaining a middle-class lifestyle reliant upon material goods.[60]

When applied to motor accessories, the term comfort drew upon traditional ideas of domesticity. Historian Katherine Grier argued that the desire for material comfort represented a "distinctively middle-class state of mind" and embodied a complex set of meanings that went beyond the physical to include notions of security and familiarity associated with a domestic ideal and ideas of social progress.[61] As other cultural historians have observed, progress for the middle-classes in the 1920s meant smoothing away the physical discomforts of life.[62] The automobile fulfilled these requirements perfectly. Consumers believed that the automobile would allow them to travel with a degree of personal freedom and privacy found only at home. Motor tourists saw equipment as the key to realizing their goals of economy, comfort, and privacy.

Ingenious Consumption: Buying Auto Accessories

As motorists set out to make the automobile more comfortable, they confronted the problem of whether to buy after market accessories or to build their own accessories for the car. Facing the accessory market could be daunting; consumers could choose from an almost endless array of specialized equipment. In addition, because motor touring was a new leisure experience, motorists turned to a growing field of experts for advice on equipment. These experts presented economy and comfort as problems to be solved through a combination of consumption and ingenuity. Jessup observed in his advice book on motor camping: "The call of the open road is a difficult matter clearly to define but the manner in which our gasoline caravans may be equipped to answer the call is a real and extremely definite problem. There is nothing intangible about this."[63] Experts like Jessup identified particular challenges—bedding, eating equipment, and storage—and agreed that a pleasurable vacation depended on assembling the right equipment.[64] *Popular Mechanics* observed, "motor camping is fun . . . if you have assembled an outfit that makes for comfort." Similarly, a midwestern traveler advised women motorists in particular, "If you would like a summer of rare enjoyment, get proper equipment. . . . You will never regret it."[65] Testimonials such as this helped create a market for automobile accessories and encouraged motorists to tinker with the bodies of their cars. One commentator on the auto industry, Harold Shertzer, wrote, "Careless and short-sighted policies of manufacturers have brought protest from the automobile public in the form of accessories, accessory dealers, and accessory advertisements." He noted the accessory market was open territory, with many companies and individual entrepreneurs, inventing and marketing a range of goods.[66]

After-market accessories grew as a distinct business within the automotive trade between 1910 and 1920. Accessories included parts like spark plugs, belts and tires; non-standard items like heaters, signals, and headlights; and novelties, such as trunks and tourist equipment. An early edition of *Automotive Industries* described accessories as "clocks, speed indicators, . . . vulcanizers, trunks, horns, . . . and [lap] robes."[67] The accessory business grew out of early production methods when car manufacturers built automobiles from component parts manufactured by other industries such as body makers, tire manufactures, and tool companies.[68] In 1915 business leaders who traded in the wholesaling of accessories formed the Automotive Equipment Association in Chicago to fight pirate (cheaply-made) parts and accessories, adopt a code of ethics, and promote the distribution and sale of after-market auto goods.[69] Accessories were sold through jobbers and trade catalogs to various retail outlets. Consumers purchased such equipment at their local garage or repair shop, from national catalog stores like Sears, Roebuck, from five-and-dimes, department stores, or a growing number of chain stores that sold automotive parts, such as Western Auto.[70]

As the automotive industry expanded, accessory manufacturers vigorously promoted advertising strategies and retail sales to capitalize on consumer enthusiasm for traveling and tinkering. At the National Annual Convention of American Garage Owners' Association in 1916, W.S. Smith encouraged garage owners to include displays of accessories

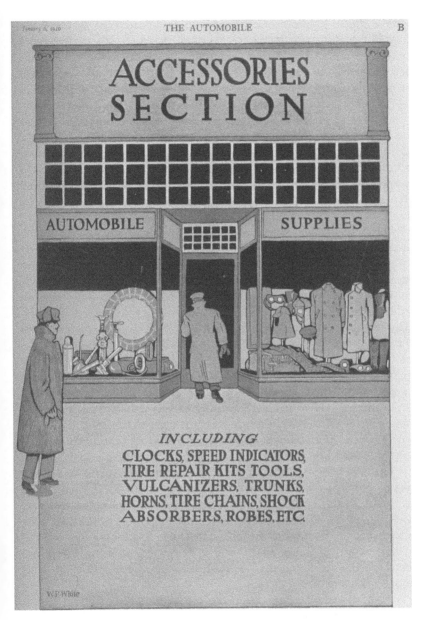

Figure 3. A growing industry of aftermarket parts and accessories catered to tinkerers who not only repaired but also wished to enhance the comfort and convenience of early automobiles. Automotive Accessories Page, *Automotive Industries*, 6 January 1910.

in their shops. Emphasizing the profitability of attractive seasonal displays, Smith instructed garage owners that they were the perfect retail outlet for accessories: "As the garage man is nearer to the auto owner than the dealer or catalogue house, there is no reason why he should not have the auto owner's accessory business if he wants and deserves it."[71] Merely including a case of accessories in the front office of the repair shop was not enough to move the increasing numbers of auto novelties, however. In the advertising age of the 1920s, the Automotive Equipment Manufacturers encouraged sellers to adopt the advertising techniques of other retailers and create attractive window displays. To encourage creativity, the Automotive Equipment Association sponsored a national contest for the best displays, awarding cash prizes to the winners.[72]

By the mid-1920s, retailers like Morris Ellis, also known as "Ellis, The Rim Man," made healthy profits from stores that only carried auto accessories. Ellis started in the after-market auto business in Boston as a tire rim salesman (hence the nickname) and built his business into three automotive accessory stores between 1918 and 1926. Ellis noted that he had done well at the accessory business because he advertised and merchandized like other novelty retail stores. *Automobile Trade Journal* wrote of Ellis in 1926: "The successful retail distributor of automotive merchandise—whether he is a garageman, service station proprietor, automotive store keeper or in any other branch of the motor trade, must know and apply up-to-the-minute merchandising methods to this end of the business." Current merchandising meant diversifying stock and using add-on sales techniques to get consumers to buy more than one item at a time. Ellis was successful because he moved beyond automotive parts to feature tourist equipment in his store, including large items like "trunks, camping beds, bumpers, etc., which were not ordinarily stressed much by accessory stores."[73] Western Auto was perhaps the most successful discount chain, growing from a tire store in 1909 to twenty-six stores across the nation in 1926. Like Ellis's stores in Boston, Western Auto diversified its stock to include almost all accessories on the market, including tourist equipment. In catalog advertisement from 1926, President Don Davis claimed that Western Auto was the largest store of its kind, serving one in five drivers.[74]

Tourist accessories, those items favored by long-distance and leisure travelers such as beds, trunks, lamps, dining equipment, and tents were specialized. Nevertheless, *Automobile Trade Journal* told its readers that tourists comprised a lucrative market. In January 1925, *Automobile Trade Journal* exhorted accessory sellers to capture tourists while they were dreaming of summer travels. The journal explained, "They're dreaming now of touring; show them how much more comfortably they can tour with proper touring equipment."[75] And in 1927, the editor declared, "Tourist money is profit plus" in the accessory market.[76] At the height of vacation season in 1926, according to the American Automobile Association, "fully nine million cars hit the highway on vacation tours . . . carrying thirty-six million people." The journal estimated that these tourists spent at least $3 billion and "swelled the profits of tens of thousands of merchants in the automotive trade."[77] Based on these astonishingly high numbers, the editor told members of the automobile trade to plan early seasonal selling campaigns for tourist accessories.

Touring accessories came from different manufacturing sources that predated the automobile industry, such as luggage manufacturers and sporting goods companies. A complete motor tourist or autocamping outfit contained a constellation of non-automotive equipment including: a water-proof tent, cots, sleeping bags, water bags, cookware, gas stove, metal furniture, and perhaps even a percolator or refrigerator that ran off the car's engine. Sporting goods companies manufactured and sold some of the first tourist accessories for the autocamp, building on earlier equipment that they supplied to the military, trappers, and nineteenth century campers.[78] For instance, Wilson Sporting Goods made water-resistant bedding for campers.[79] Tent and awning manufacturers also developed lines of camping equipment that could be adapted to motor touring.[80] Lean-to tents (a tent that used the automobile as a supporting wall) became favorites of autocampers. Manufacturers of waterproof canvas and tents, such as Utica-Duxbak and J. F. Burch, began selling auto tents and a host of other products in 1914.[81] Burch advertised its specialized lean-to auto tents as a "durable, practical, comfortable and easy-to-carry" means of shelter that aided motorists in converting their automobiles into sleeping quarters.[82]

Hoping to capitalize on this new leisure market, the Coleman Lamp Company advertised its products as necessities for motor campers.[83] Using a style of advertising pioneered by sporting goods companies, Coleman tried to create a feeling of club membership through rule books and advice.[84] In 1926, Coleman issued an autocamping guidebook with a list of rules that declared autocamping a sport and instructed consumers that they needed the right equipment to play the game.[85] Coleman hired automobile-touring authority Frank Brimmer to endorse its products and make them part of the proper way to autocamp. Brimmer told motor campers that camp fires were old-fashioned and dangerous. In comparison, Brimmer said that Coleman stoves met requirements of compactness and ease and made cooking "exactly like it is at home."[86] Whether the stoves were safer or easier than cooking over an open fire was debatable.[87] Yet, by 1928 Coleman reported its total sales at over six million, and attributed their success to the motor camping market.[88]

Figure 4. In a common solution to the sleep problem, tourists attached lean-to tents with cots to the side of the car. This one used the car for support and prevented the tourist from getting too close to nature. *Outing*, May 1921, 75.

Motorists purchased automobile accessories from a variety of retailers. Some automobile dealers sold touring attachments but they did not see these accessories as their primary stock in trade.[89] When motorists wanted to buy auto-touring equipment, they rarely went to an automobile dealer. Rather, mail-order catalogs served as one of the primary suppliers of motor accessories from the 1910s through the early 1930s. Sears, Roebuck, for instance, carried Ford attachments, general automotive hardware, and camping goods in the 1910s and 1920s.[90] Department stores entered the market briefly between 1910 and 1915 and traded on name recognition, convenient locations, and knowledgeable salespeople. In the early 1910s, Marshall Field in Chicago converted a section of the fifth floor "Store for Men" into a showcase for automobile accessories.[91] Describing the variety of their automotive attachments, a Field's catalog noted, "It has been our aim to include in our stock everything that would prove of practical use to a motorist in the efficient driving of his car."[92] Marshall Field sold a great variety of accessories including tires, motor clothing, auto tents, camp stoves, kitchenettes, water buckets, tow lines, and battery testers. They also carried a special assortment of equipment exclusively for Ford cars.

Like sporting goods companies, department stores hired experts on outfitting to sell their goods and promote confidence in the store. In Nina Wilcox Putnam's 1921 travel narrative *West Broadway*, the protagonist Miss Latour lamented her scant knowledge of auto touring equipment. In preparation for her motor tour Miss Latour visited the automotive counter at Bushman's, a fictional department store in New York City. "I almost ran there," said Latour, "because I began to realize I was . . . green. And it being the age of specialists, I determined to allow the specialist on Bushman's top floor to practice on me and pull my ignorance out by the roots." At Bushman's the ultimate salesman, Mr.Hiyou, confronted Latour and her lack of experience. Although she informed the salesman that she intended to stay in hotels on her cross-country tour, she left the store with a load of convertible motor camping equipment. She noted, "He sold me a suitcase which turned out to be a kitchen cabinet when you opened it up, with dishes and knives and forks and a vacuum bottle and everything but the kitchen stove in it, and then he sold me the kitchen stove in condensed form."[93]

Miss Latour was not the only traveler who bought excessive amounts of equipment.[94] Every travel narrative written by touring motorists during this period included a section on outfitting, usually with a list of equipment. Motor travelers with a sense of irony pointed out that despite their intentions to travel light, they packed too many things. Surveying her luggage, Post exclaimed, "Never in the world did people have so much luggage with nowhere to put it." Traveling by car left tourists with a greater demand for the comfortable necessities and less room in which to pack them. Post lamented, "Everything we have with us is the wrong thing and just so much to take care of without any compensating comfort." Like others of her class, Post eliminated extra weight en route by shipping spare luxuries home and sending nonessential clothing ahead to her destination.[95]

The proliferation of specialized equipment inspired a momentary backlash against the number and practicality of after-market motor devices. As early as 1916, *Motorist Almanac* told automobile owners, "Beware of the 'auto novelty,' for out of ten thousand such devices but a handful is of any value except to the advertising man and the manufacturer."[96] Even the promotional voice of *Scientific American* took on a note of caution in its review of accessories for 1920: "The number of automobile accessories that are devised every year is legion and while many have a real field of usefulness, there is an equally large number that have no real reason for being and are of doubtful utility, except as ballast."[97] This was stern criticism from *Scientific American*, which published annual lists of hundreds of new automotive accessories and openly promoted them all as useful.[98] By 1924, a commentator for *Motor* ridiculed the inflated accessory market and observed that "the most fun one gets out of owning an automobile is duding up a car with all the new fangled gadgets." Jokingly, the author characterized the acquisition of accessories as an addiction: "When you begin buying gadgets it is like eating water cress or smoking opium—the more you get the more you want."[99]

Do-It-Yourself Advice: Solving the Sleep and Storage Problems

Perhaps to counter the decadent influences of purchasing too much auto equipment, literature on outfitting the car for travel, and especially autocamping, stressed that motorists construct their own accessories. Touring experts routinely told motorists not to rely on the outfitter or a department store but on their own ingenuity in solving problems that were part of motor touring. Elon Jessup wrote, "no article of equipment ever built answers all requirements. Outfitting for a motor camping trip is a matter which requires individual judgment."[100] *Motor Life* and *Ford-owner* heartily agreed and instructed motorists not to "depend upon the outfitter" for all of their equipment needs, but to build, and even, invent their own accessories.[101] The do-it-yourself advice declared that all forms of modification demanded ingenuity, whether drivers purchased or built their own accessories, and encouraged consumers to solve various problems with a combination of equipment and tinkering. The heady enthusiasm for modifying the automobile led some consumers to try their hand at inventing their own equipment. Sleep and storage represented two of the most pressing problems for motor travelers before the development of motor hotels and the addition of the trunk as standard equipment on automobile.

Middle-class motor tourists often did not feel completely equipped until they had converted the car for sleeping. Redesigning the interior of cars to accommodate beds enhanced travelers' independence from urban hotels. As early as 1909, *Motor Car* featured photographs of tourists who slept and ate in their specially equipped cars. The author noted that "an automobile in which one can cook one's food, eat, sleep, and dress . . . without setting foot on the ground, is the latest addition to the long list of inventions for the convenience of travelers."[102] Some of these elaborate conversions turned the automobile into a multipurpose vehicle that stored camping equipment and provisions, provided sleeping accommodations, and offered a place to cook and eat inside the car.[103] This continued interest in taking as much comfort on the road as possible inspired some travelers to convert their vehicles into ever more elaborate camp cars and eventually self-contained trailers.[104]

Prior to the development of motels and trailers, however, modifying the auto for touring often meant constructing beds within the interior of the standard touring car or sedan.[105] From the beginning of motor touring, travelers had built beds in their cars. For instance, in July 1911, Mr. and Mrs. Newton "turned gypsy" and drove their Franklin touring car cross-country. They "remodeled" their Franklin to provide sleeping accommodations by "detaching the front seat and substituting one built with a hinged back that would drop backward to the rear cushion, forming a level, cushioned surface over which we could place a pneumatic mattress for a bed."[106] Taking tinkering for granted, the Franklin Motor Company used the Newtons' story as publicity, praising them for this novel conversion of their auto.

Popular magazines confirmed that sleeping accommodations loomed large as the most daunting problem confronting the automobile tourist. *Sunset* noted, "To most vacationists the sleeping question is the big one."[107] A tourist who requested advice on beds from *Field and Stream* wrote: "One of the things which interests me about auto camping is the problem of beds. As about one-third of our time is spent in bed it would seem that this item should receive careful thought." The editor replied: "I am almost tempted to say that a camp bed is more important than one's home bed, owing to the fact that the camper on the move gets mighty weary and if his night's rest is not comfortable he comes home a wreck." The editor offered criteria for constructing the proper bed and commented, "no bed or cot is going to be restful if it sags down with the sleeper's weight. It makes you feel like a pig in a bag and is darned uncomfortable." Finally, he recommended to his readers that all accessories and conversions must "meet your demands for comfort."[108] In the very early years of motor travel, sleeping in the car was sometimes a necessity, especially in the western states where hotels were few and far between.[109] Yet, even after 1914, redesigning the automobile for sleeping allowed growing numbers of middle-class families to avoid hotels and travel more economically.

Solutions to the sleep problem took different material forms. Designs ranged from tents that affixed to the exterior of the car to convertible interiors. Tourists who preferred the safety and shelter of the automobile could read pages of advice on how to reconstruct the interiors of their cars. There were two ways of creating a sleeping compartment. Motorists could buy or make a cot and lay it over the tops of seats to create a makeshift bed. Or, in a more radical act of tinkering, some motorists cut the supports on the front seats of the car (which were made of wood on the Model T) and added hinges so the seats would recline into an upholstered bed. In 1915, *Motor Life* featured Mr. and Mrs. Lawlor, two "modern" gypsies who traveled in an automobile that "except in the matter of space, . . . has been fitted up so that it is like a private [rail] car on a small scale, with comfortable sleeping accommodations."[110] In 1920, *Popular Mechanics* told cost-conscious travelers that they could "billet" the whole family in a touring car with a few simple modifications of the car's interior. In this case, the proposed design included hinging the front seats so they would recline and adding a camp cot to the space between the seats and the top of the car to create an upper berth.[111] Sleeping inside the car became so popular during the auto-touring boom between 1914 and 1920 that a few auto manufacturers, like Jackson and Overland, added beds to their autos in an attempt to capture the niche market of motor tourists.[112]

Interior beds drew upon notions of luxury and privacy associated with Pullman sleeping cars. Although motorists openly criticized the high fares of railroad cars, they regarded the Pullman as the standard of travel comfort. Articles in the 1920s asserted that sleeping in an auto-bed offered the comfort and privacy of a Pullman car and the freedom and economy of traveling by automobile.[113] An advertisement for Line's Auto Sleeper claimed that travelers could "roost high and dry" because the Line's bed "makes a Pullman of your Auto."[114] The comparison between Pullman cars and auto beds remained viable even into the late 1920s. The 1928 trade catalog of auto beds from Modell's Camp Outfitters in New York City advertised several products that continued to use the Pullman car as a standard of comfort.

Although they attempted to provide comfort and privacy, these designs were constrained by the spatial limitations of automobile interiors. Thus auto accessories, and in particular auto beds, were often convertible, solving two or more problems at once. Historian Sigfried Giedion has attributed convertibility to an economy of space and has defined multipurpose designs as uniquely middle-class.[115] Convertible automobile bodies were inspired not only by Pullman cars but also by metamorphic furniture that had its roots in the middle-class parlor of the nineteenth century. Metamorphic furniture was designed to perform several functions in households with limited space. For example, Murphy beds disguised themselves as desks or armoires by day. Multipurpose furniture allowed a new class of apartment dwellers to gentrify small domestic spaces.[116] Giedion concluded that "patent furniture arose in America . . . from the demands of an intermediate class that wished, without overcrowding, to bring a modicum of comfort into a minimum of space."[117] Similarly, converting the car for sleeping turned the automobile into a multipurpose machine.[118]

Convertibility embodied tourists' desire for efficiency and signified the ingenuity of the inventor. Telescopic, collapsible, and compact items also became the material expression of a national interest in efficiency.[119] As *Motor Life* observed of both motoring and automobile design in 1914, "the whole tendency of the day is toward greater and greater economy and efficiency."[120] As manufacturers employed new methods to render production more efficient, such as assembly-line production and time-motion studies, the weekend traveler adopted material

Figure 5. A comfortable night's sleep became one of the chief problems tackled by motor tourists turned tinkerers. Nurturing middle-class standards of comfort, popular magazines gave advice on building and buying auto beds that mimicked the privacy of railroad berths. Auto beds from three companies, the McMillin Auto Bed Company, the ABC Manufacturing Company, and the Peoria Auto-Kot Company. "When the Car Becomes Your Bedroom," *Outing*, April 1921, 25.

goods and systematic methods to conserve both time and space. Automobile accessories needed to be compact and simple. Accessories that unfolded and collapsed easily allowed the tourist to set up camp quickly and to get back on the road with minimum delay. Compactness followed the dictates of traveling light and, in the case of motor tourists, left room for more accessories.

Travel commentators praised convertibility as a sign of automotive progress and popular ingenuity. Frank Brimmer wrote, "Some of the most interesting, not to say surprising, motor gypsy accessories . . . look innocent enough, but . . . are quickly metamorphosed into spacious picnic tables with benches or chairs." Brimmer noted that quick transformation time and small size differentiated modern motor equipment from its nineteenth-century precursors, patented furniture. He denied that automobile accessories had any of the "idiosyncrasies" of "some folding furniture of ancient vintage," and pronounced the multipurpose goods on the motor camping market to be thoroughly modern.[121] From the traveler's perspective, Winifred Dixon confessed her vulnerability to buying anything collapsible. "The charm of an article which collapses and becomes something else than it seems," she wrote, "I cannot analyze or resist. Others feel it too."[122]

As the consummate modern consumers, motor travelers also wanted more storage space in the automobile for all their equipment. Few cars at this time, however, had trunks. Although some manufacturers of expensive touring cars, such as Pierce Arrow, integrated trunks into their body designs before World War I, built-in trunks were not standard equipment on inexpensive cars until the mid-1930s. Most automobiles had little room on the back for trunks because body makers placed the back seats of the auto over the rear wheels and a spare tire on the back of the automobile. For instance the typical touring car models of 1915 sat four to six passengers but had little room for luggage.[123] Most auto manufacturers considered trunks to be an accessory, something that drivers could purchase from an after-market supplier or dealer.[124] A 1915 article in *Automobile* noted that manufacturers studied the needs of tourists and determined, "the conditions which such tourists meet are abnormal and it is of course not to be expected that the car driven about the city streets will ever be called upon to carry the amount of baggage necessary for a tour through the unsettled country." Manufacturers like Franklin felt that it was unnecessary to add trunks as permanent features. A spokesperson for Franklin argued that a standard "baggage boot" constructed as part of the rear of the car would look irregular and the general public would not buy the car. He suggested that tourists use the ample running boards of the touring car as the place to store luggage. Indeed, even Ford Motor Company agreed with this idea and provided luggage racks for the running boards and extra space inside the body of the auto as after-market accessories.[125]

Luggage carriers and trunks did catch on, and became popular accessories for a variety of motorists.[126] Itinerant salesmen, housewives, and tourists wanted a protected space in the car to transport goods, groceries, and luggage. A writer for *Ford Owner and Dealer* observed in 1920 that carrying luggage was of interest to tourists and "to commercial travelers,

Figure 6. Grass-roots inventors used national magazines to advertise their specialized accessories for the car. These advertisements often referenced the more luxurious Pullman sleeping car while assuring auto campers of the economy of avoiding trains and urban hotels. "Lines Auto Sleeper," *Field and Stream*, May 1921, 105.

to picnicers, and for general utility use."[127] If auto manufacturers would not offer storage compartments as standard equipment, then aftermarket suppliers were ready to do so. Industry journals and popular magazines were filled with advertisements for trunks, racks, and others devices to solve the baggage problem. *Scientific American*'s annual review of new auto accessories for 1915 displayed a great variety of patented trunks and running-board luggage racks.[128]

As with other types of equipment, the popular press advised motorists to build luggage carriers themselves and even highlighted the handi-work of tourists who successfully added trunks to their cars. One writer for *Outing* told readers that with "a few simple tools and a small outlay in money" they could construct their own "practical Flivver trunk rack" that would be both "serviceable and cheap."[129] In 1917, *Popular Mechanics* provided tourists who wanted to build their own luggage racks with detailed plans for a suitcase holder that could be constructed simply by bolting strips of metal to the running board. A later article in *Popular Mechanics* offered a rack that solved two storage problems simultaneously by using tent poles as part of the rack to hold luggage.[130]

Addressing the baggage problem, a writer for *Fordowner* encouraged motor tourists to assemble their own luggage racks. "Just as the railroad car is not complete unless there is a baggage car to haul the luggage, so the Ford car is really not a complete touring car unless . . . adequate provision is made for luggage carrying."[131] The author advised tourists that the construction of storage space was "an important detail of comfort," and added, "a little ingenuity will work wonders." In the same article he suggested readers assemble their own storage racks and trunks for Ford cars. This advice suggested that consumers use individual creativity rather than buying accessories.

Tourists stowed luggage anywhere they could find room on the automobile. Optimal places included hanging baggage in front of the radiator, or placing it on running boards, on either side of the hood, under the folds of the collapsible top on touring cars (when the top was down), and in the back of the car over the spare tire. Luggage holders came in two general design types, the rack and the trunk. Manufacturers and inventors elaborated on these designs and consumers assembled them in various combinations to suit their own requirements. Luggage carriers featured straps and racks and attached suitcases, boxes, picnic baskets, and duffel bags to the exterior of the car. Advice on building luggage carriers put a high premium efficient use of space and neatness. Advice experts told drivers not to strap too many suitcases and bundles to the exterior of their Model Ts because this would make the Ford "look like a tramp car." An article in *Fordowner* suggested using the space under seats as compartments for luggage and offered readers diagrams for building these as well as a rear luggage carrier and braces for the running boards.[132]

Luggage racks did not do a good job of protecting clothing, bedding, and other important items from dust, rain, and the occasional large pothole that jolted bundles completely off the car. In a 1922 review of luggage racks, *Motor Life* observed that the racks were a "boon to humanity" for they increased the "capacity of a car considerably and they do it without crowding the occupants." Yet there was a design problem. "Motor-

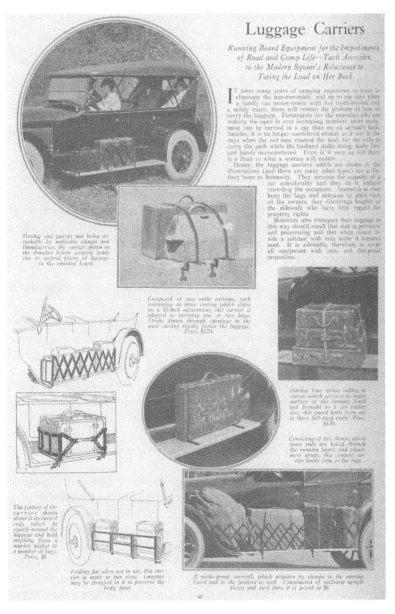

Figure 7. Before trunks became standard on all cars, travelers tinkered with designs for carrying the comforts of home efficiently and without crowding the passenger compartment of the car. These designs placed luggage along the running board where it would not be jolted off the car by bumps, but where it unfortunately blocked access to the car doors. "Luggage Carriers," *Motor*, May 1922, 46.

ists who transport their baggage in this way should recall that dust is pervasive and penetrating and that when mixed inside the suitcase with rain water it becomes mud," reminded the author, who advised using dirt-proof tarpaulins.[133]

Trunks, in contrast, offered more protection for motorists' things, since they were leather or metal boxes that usually hung on the sides or the back of the car.[134] Serious autocampers, however, built elaborate cabinets, in addition to trunks, to store food supplies and cooking utensils.[135] As *Field and Stream* noted in 1929, "There are many odds and ends to be carried on a [motor] camping trip—dish and bath towels, soap, carving knife, light ax, and staple provisions." In order to store these necessities, the magazine advised drivers to "build a box the entire length of the right side running board, and as high as possible and still permit the doors to open. Any handy man can build such a box." Once the trunk was built and the car packed, the writer declared, "The autocamper is now quite completely equipped."[136]

A More Complete Car

By the mid-1920s, travelers' desire for a fully outfitted car encouraged auto manufacturers to adopt many after-market accessories as standard equipment. Trunks—the tourist accessory with the widest appeal to a range of drivers—were standard equipment on all General Motors automobiles in the mid-1930s.[137] Beds, in contrast, did not have as wide a market. However, small and mid-sized automobile manufacturers offered auto-beds and convertible interiors between 1910 and 1930. The Willys-Overland Champion, for instance, was marketed as the "most versatile car in America" in 1923 and included, through "unusual foresight" (in the words of an advertisement), a bed. Promotional literature told dealers to "play up the feature of indoor sleeping comfort and no hotel bills.[138] The auto-bed was not a big seller and the 1924 Champion body was discontinued the following year.[139] The permanent auto-bed was no longer made by any automobile manufacturer by the late 1920s. In the 1930s, however, two mid-sized companies, Nash and Hudson, reintroduced the auto-bed in an effort to attract cost-conscious customers. The advertising for these beds drew upon earlier themes of economy, efficiency, and independence to appeal to tourists who did not have the money to stay in hotels or invest in trailers.[140] The effort was too late, and these ventures were short-lived. Motels and trailers had effectively dispensed with the need for automobile bodies that could be converted into beds.

As other automotive historians have shown, by the late 1920s the Model T seemed antiquated, uncomfortable, and lost some of its market

share to better-appointed, more stylish Chevrolets.[141] Ford owners like
C. F. Booher of Celburne, Texas, wrote lengthy letters to Henry Ford
describing the numerous and frustrating shortcomings of the Model T.
"While it seems as useless as carrying coals to Newcastle or as ludicrous
as . . . exporting macaroni to Italy," he began, "perhaps I may be permit-
ted to offer a suggestion to assist the Ford organization in meeting the
competition offered by recent additions to the cheap, light car field."
Booher claimed to be a loyal Ford owner tempted away by the low-priced
competition and advised the manufacturer: "Why not let it remain for
Mr. Ford to be the first to put the most completely equipped car on the
market. The factory can do this at less expense than the individual and
it has been by experience that, regardless of the Ford price, people take
the cost of necessary accessories into consideration when comparing the
prices of cars. It would seem to me the better policy to utilize the saving
in manufacture to more fully equip the car than to radically lower the
first cost."[142]

Similarly, a physician who signed his letter to Ford Motor Company
"A. Medicus" chastised Ford in March 1927 for not keeping up with the
competition. He wrote that he was about to buy a Chevrolet and wanted
to suggest a list of "improvements, the lack of which led me and other
physicians and business men . . . to turn away from Ford." The writer
listed more than fifteen upgrades to the body of the Model T, including
an automatic windshield wiper, speedometer, oil gauge, stop lights,
horn, shock absorbers, front bumper and an overall redesign of the
body so that it looked "less abrupt." He concluded, "It is these refine-
ments which are today making the Chevrolet supreme, and gaining for
it the ascendancy over Ford."[143] In May 1927, Ford Motor Company shut
the factory doors and ended production of the Model T. The subsequent
Model A would feature all of the improvements suggested by "A. Medicus," including shock-absorbers, windshield wiper, combination tail
and stop lights, bumpers, and an instrument panel with speedometer,
oil, and gas gauges.[144] The complete auto would give many consumers
what they wanted, but it also effectively limited tinkering with the body
of the automobile and narrowed the opportunities for consumers to
design and build accessories and demonstrate grass-roots ingenuity.

*   *   *

In the first decades of automobility, consumption became an act of
production as motorists bought and assembled after-market accessories
and added them to their automobiles to make travel more comfortable
and cost-efficient. When tinkering with the cars, travelers also engaged
in acts of ingenuity, as articulated in mass-market magazines such as *Pop-*

ular Mechanics and *Scientific American*. Through outfitting, modifying, and rebuilding the bodies of their vehicles, drivers influenced the design of the auto; consumer demand led to common aftermarket accessories becoming part of standard production. Tinkering also enabled middle-class travelers to demonstrate their technological skills and claim status in a culture that valued individual ingenuity.

For women motorists, technological skill with automobiles influenced larger social arguments about women's spatial autonomy in the early twentieth century. Women who drove their own cars and often traveled unescorted by men were interested not only in outfitting and modifying the automobile to meet middle-class standards of domestic comfort. Many were also interested in redefining the boundaries of both mobility and technological know-how to include women. Women drivers tinkered with the car and, by extension, with their gender roles. Stories of motor travel written by and for women in the period between 1910 and 1920 revised the dominant discourse of ingenuity to include women as technological heroines. These stories encouraged women to cultivate mechanical skills and self-sufficiency. Motor heroines who were knowledgeable and often independent provided valuable, if short-lived, role models for a new generation of women drivers.

Chapter 2
Women's Ingenuity

> "It certainly is great, Ruth the way you crank up your own car,"
> Grace declared. "It must take an awful lot of strength, doesn't it?"
> "Yes," admitted Ruth, as she jumped back into her automobile and
> the car plunged on ahead. "But I've a strong right arm. . . ." Father
> says it takes skill . . . as well as strength to drive a car. . . . Girls could
> do a lot more if they tried harder. "Sometimes . . . gumption counts
> for more than brute force."
>
> —*Laura Dent Crane,* The Automobile Girls at Newport *(1910)*

In the first decades of motor travel, young women like Ruth and Grace
emerged as popular heroines for women drivers.[1] Alongside the many
stories of technological heroism for boys and men, such as Tom Swift,
motor girls represented one of the few examples of technological skill
and ingenuity for women. The introduction of the automobile in the
United States coincided with debates about women's changing relationship to public space and technology, and the emergence of the motor
heroine marked a seminal period for the popular discussion of women's
use of the automobiles.[2] Women motorists not only remade the automobile to fit middle-class notions of efficiency, comfort, and convenience;
they also used the automobile to help revise their relationship to public
space. In these accounts of motor travel, women became capable drivers
who were not intimidated by hand-cranked ignitions nor confined to
less-powerful electric vehicles marketed specifically to women.[3] Women
motorists spoke with familiarity about the mechanical systems of the car
and the internal combustion engine, creating a new kind of heroine,
one who possessed what had been thought of as "male" mechanical
know-how.

Women's narratives of motor knowledge contributed to "liberatory
fantasies" surrounding the introduction of the automobile. Such fantasies represented "a powerful and persuasive means of social agency, and
. . . their source to some extent lay in real popular needs and desires."[4]

These stories of mechanical competency opened a cultural window for women to imagine their technological potential and their possible equality with men. Women's narratives of automobility combined the New Woman's desire for greater physical freedom with the acquisition of mechanical knowledge.[5] This chapter examines the cultural construction of the technological heroines as an attempt to redefine, or tinker with, women's relationship to technology and public space. Popular accounts of automobile travel challenged the notion that women lacked mechanical skill and instead portrayed them as technically competent consumers of the auto, equal to men.

Despite their heroic characteristics, the cultural power of the motor heroine proved difficult to sustain as the woman's movement faded and as male drivers asserted their exclusive authority over the automobile in the 1920s and 1930s. Men as drivers, mechanics, advice experts, and journalists challenged women's claims of gender equality in tinkering and as potential motor authorities. Motor advisors often argued that women, as a group, knew nothing about driving and even less about mechanics. Simultaneously, family travel narratives dominated motor travel stories in the 1920s, replacing the earlier tales of youthful women's autonomous motor adventures. Motor travel advice reinforced women's traditional roles as wives and mothers in the 1920s and 1930s. With the emergence of the companionate vacation, women drove less frequently and turned repair work over to their husbands. Yet, in the early years of automobile travel and in the midst of a coordinated woman's movement, middle-class women advocated their mechanical skill, their equality as drivers, and their claims to greater independence on the open road and through the automobile.

Motor Girls: Technological Heroines and Popular Feminists

Women's depictions of automobility appeared in two forms, fictional adventure series intended for a commercial audience of adolescents, such as the Motor Girls (1910–1917), the Automobile Girls (1910–1913), and the Motor Maids (1911–1917), and autobiographical travel narratives which acted as advice literature for women motorists. The Stratemeyer Syndicate produced the most successful of the girls and automobile series, the Motor Girls, along with a host of adventure series aimed at adolescents such as the Motor Boys, Tom Swift, and, later, Nancy Drew.[6] Lillian Garis, journalist and wife of Harold Garis, author of the Motor Boys series, authored the majority of the stories under the pseudonym Margaret Penrose.[7] As literary scholar Sherrie Inness has argued, the series mediated and interpreted the new technology for the first generation of women consumers.[8] Although the books promoted consumption, these stories also provided role models for the acquisition of mechanical knowledge and promoted tinkering among female users of the car.[9]

In the Stratemeyer series, the automobile was not merely an evocative modern detail but an engine of change; it gave the fictional women drivers a measure of independence based on their technological skills. Knowing how to drive and repair an automobile distinguished the adolescent motor girls (about sixteen to eighteen years of age) from an older generation of aunts and mothers, described in the books as unfamiliar with technology.[10] Motor girls were transitional figures with mixed identities; as characters they maintained a feminine ideal by occasionally accepting the help of boys, traveling less widely than their male counterparts in the Motor Boys series, and always returning home at the end of their adventures.[11] Serial fiction offered different meanings for a variety of audiences and contained political "accents" or popular political desires.[12] I argue that the retelling of mechanical triumphs that praised women's competency, whether sane driving or a bit of savvy repair work, contained feminist accents; they spoke of women's desire and capacity for both mechanical skill and physical autonomy. These fictional series meshed with motor narratives written by real women in the same period. In both cases the stories created occasions that demonstrated the technological potential of women drivers.

Rational, clever, and, above all, mechanically adept, the "motor girl" represented a new kind of cultural heroine, one who mixed an interest in technology with what historian Susan Ware has termed "popular feminism."[13] Although women's narratives of automobility did not consistently advocate for formal political involvement, their heroines promoted a form of feminism. Historian Virginia Scharff has argued that female drivers "hoped to appropriate the social and spatial possibilities of motoring without taking the risks of doing so on feminist grounds."[14] Women motorists advanced early feminist Frances Willard's notion of a "wider world for women." Willard took up bicycle riding, she said, to "help women to a wider world."[15] The automobile, like the bicycle, embodied feminists' desire for greater mobility.[16] Automobile travel allowed middle-class women to momentarily expand their geographic and social boundaries in the realm of public leisure and demonstrate independence from the social structures designed ostensibly to protect them.[17]

The "experimental" and daring activities of women drivers also fit what historians have defined as a "third arena" of the women's movement in 1910. Unlike social service or woman's rights, the third arena of political action "included more amorphous and broad-ranging pronouncements and activity toward women's self-determination via 'eman-

Figure 8. Illustrations in the Automobile Girls serial fiction embodied the enthusiasm of young women for autonomous travel by automobile. Laura Dent Crane, *The Automobile Girls at Newport* (Philadelphia: Henry Altemus, 1910), frontispiece. Reproduced from Special Collections and Rare Books, Jackson Library, University of North Carolina at Greensboro.

cipation' from structures, conventions, and attitudes by law and custom.''[18] These popular heroines articulated an informal and more amorphous political agenda that argued for spatial emancipation by virtue of woman's mechanical competency. In this way, women's stories of automobility represented an appropriation of the dominant role model of the male inventor-hero.

Stories about male inventor-heroes dominated the popular culture surrounding the introduction of the automobile, and indeed almost every other technology of the nineteenth and early twentieth century. Whether ham radio operators, crack mechanics, or ennobled engineers, technological heroes offered viable role models for boys and men to control emergent technologies and use them to gain fame and fortune.[19] Indeed, at least one historian has called the early twentieth century "the long summer of boy engineering." The growth of "countless books, stories, advertising images and increasingly movies" defined the engineer as "the masculine ideal of America," and placed political and social authority in the hands of male engineers.[20] The early literature on the automobile extended many of these larger discourses of technological enthusiasm, ingenuity, adventure, and a respect for inventors to a new generation of modern men. Instructional books taught boys the principles of gas engines, and in serial fiction like the Motor Boys, boy readers could identify with the mechanical skills, the inventiveness, and the manly ambitions of the main characters.[21]

For a brief moment, however, popular representations of automobile use also included New Women as equal participants in the machine age. As the press debated women's suitability for driving, women's advocates noted that they had special, innate skills that made them worthy of the privileges of automobility.[22] In 1910, one male expert argued that "most women have the nerve and can acquire the skill, but they lack the strength that is sometimes necessary."[23] Most early automobiles required hand cranking to start the engine because they lacked the electric ignition (The electric ignition, called by some the "ladies aid," was developed by Charles Kettering and available after 1912 on more expensive cars.) Hand-cranking demanded upper-body strength that many critics claimed women did not have, even though male drivers also found the hand crank dangerous.[24] Once the car was started, a driver frequently had to jack up the car to replace flat tires and push or pull the car out of mud holes. Women answered such charges with the assertion that they possessed the strength as well as the caution, determination, and skill to drive and repair automobiles. The new athleticism of the second generation of New Women as well as their nerve, made them competent drivers. Indeed, some women also took the position that intelligence and intuition gave them an advantage over male drivers. One of the fictional motor girls told her male friends, "You boys are well enough where only muscle is concerned . . . but when it comes to a matter of brains you're not in the same class with us."[25]

As role models, fictional motor girls combined gumption with good behavior. Motor girls stuck to the speed limit, except when chasing a thief or saving a life, and unlike the motor boys, they did not engage in recklessness driving for sport. (Motor boys, in contrast, were risk takers who broke the speed limit; hit dogs, cows, other cars, and challenged the authority of the police.) Ruth Stuart, the leader and driver of the Automobile Girls, was described as "a good little chauffeur who never allowed her attention to be distracted from running her car, no matter what was being talked of around her, nor how much she was interested."[26] Even when an emergency arose, Ruth drove with "a steady hand and steady eyes."[27] On one of their adventures, Ruth's ability to drive was tested even before she left the driveway. As Ruth drove her large car into the street, a young child "flung himself out in the middle of the road." Ruth swerved around the baby and avoided an accident, highlighting her skill as a driver. The narrator remarked, "Mr. Stuart's 'Bravo, daughter!' was lost in his throat. But the little group of waiting friends gave three cheers for the girl chauffeur."[28] Cora Kimball, head of the Motor Girls club, also displayed both rationality and determination whether driving her motorcar or her motorboat. Although she pleaded with another chauffeur to "conform to the regulation speed," the narrator noted that it was "rather unusual for her to show such timidity"; Cora had nerve.[29] Ultimately, the author of the Motor Girls series characterized the ideal woman driver as "quick-thinking and emergency-acting."[30] A motor girl did not succumb to nervousness. Rather her caution, quick reflexes, and "gumption" put her in control of the machine.

Journalists sympathetic to women drivers agreed that good reflexes and a dedication to safety made women not only suitable consumers of the car but better drivers than men.[31] In 1910, the *New York Times* described women as "careful" drivers, having fewer accidents than men.[32] Driving instructor Miss D. Chilton told *Motor* that women were "quicker to learn and less liable to lose their heads than men."[33] Another expert, Mary Mullet, observed in 1906 that women's sense of caution made them better drivers than men. She wrote, "'Women often show a lot more sense about [driving] than the men do. . . . Did you ever hear of a woman running over anybody? I never did.'"[34] Additionally she noted that women's swift reactions refuted the notion that women were unsuited to driving. Racing enthusiast Mrs. Andrew Cuneo agreed that gumption as well as caution worked to her advantage. Although Cuneo asserted that women drove "more gently" than men, she could

Figure 9. Barbara, one of the central characters of the Automobile Girls, demonstrates her nerve by confronting a highwayman with a gun. Automobile girls represented women drivers as fearless, ingenious, and self-sufficient. Laura Dent Crane, *The Automobile Girls Along the Hudson* (Philadelphia: Henry Altemus, 1910), 67. Reproduced from Special Collections and Rare Books, Jackson Library, University of North Carolina at Greensboro.

not help noting that she had more nerve than some male drivers. She admitted that once she drove so fast she made racing star Barney Old-field yell "Slow down!"[35]

Beyond a sense of caution and nerve, women's understanding of technology was central to the debate over equal access to automobility and a larger discourse of ingenuity. In the same interview, Cuneo observed that women's true gift for handling the new machine arose from a "natural intuition [that] puts her into closer touch with her car than man seems to be able to get with his. She acquires the 'feel' of the mechanism more readily, she detects more quickly the evidence of something out of adjustment."[36] Driving in the first two decades of motor travel was difficult; bad roads and unreliable engines meant drivers needed to change tires, adjust carburetors, replace spark plugs, and dig themselves out of the mud.[37] Basic mechanical knowledge was a prerequisite to driving, even if a professional mechanic performed the more complicated repairs.

As women traveled and laid claim to automobility, they wrote narratives that emphasized women's ability to tinker with the machine. For instance, Ruth Stuart, of the Automobile Girls, "talked as familiarly of an emergency brake and a steering wheel, of horse power and speed-transmission, as most girls talk of frills and furbelows." Her father had to pull her away from a circle of admiring boys to whom she explained the principles of running an automobile.[38] Cora Kimball, in the Motor Girls series, maintained the engine of both her automobile and her motorboat. The author credited Cora's mechanical knowledge to practical experience: "with a quickness born of long experience, [Cora] ascertained that there was plenty of gasoline and oil in the craft." Just before embarking on a long trip, Cora "tested the vibrator and found the current good, though at times . . . the engine had been known to start with the magneto. But it was not safe to depend on it."[39]

The fictional heroines' interest in mechanics echoed the experiences of real women drivers, who argued that motor travel required a willingness to tinker.[40] These writers acknowledged that few women were born with mechanical inclinations, but that an intimacy with machinery would come through a combination of lessons and experience. Technical knowledge of the car included changing the oil, keeping grease cups filled, and adjusting the carburetor. One anonymous author for *Ladies' Home Journal* instructed women to acquire an instruction book on motor mechanics prior to buying a car and to "study it." The journalist warned that the basic principles of auto mechanics "will look terrifyingly unintelligible at first, but bring to bear upon it your modern, alert woman's mind for a few evenings, and it will become as simple as rudimentary arithmetic." The author concluded that there was great pleasure in understanding how to perform routine repairs, "for, after all, not the entire joy of motoring is in simple driving; a lot of it is in knowing your car."[41]

For women, mechanical skill, unlike physical strength, offered an even playing field on which they could claim equality with men. Just as the fictional heroine Ruth declared that gumption counted for more than brute force in mastering the car, automotive editor for *Outing* magazine, Robert Sloss, told his readers, "Unusual physique is not necessary for the woman motorist. Neither sex needs extraordinary muscular development in automobiling, and almost any woman . . . can master its mysteries quite as well as a man, provided she has the will and patience to acquire the know-how."[42] Sloss ventured the "surprising statement" that women already possessed the mechanical ingenuity to run and maintain an automobile based on their experiences with machines in the home. "Did you ever see a woman fixing her sewing machine?" he queried. There was little difference, asserted Sloss, between sewing machine and automobile except that the latter was larger and women drivers needed encouragement and experience before they could diagnose automotive problems with confidence.[43] Supporting the idea that women could gain mechanical know-how as easily as men, the *New York Times* noted the women in 1910 were "as well equipped in knowledge of the mechanism of an automobile as many of the men, and it is no longer a curiosity to see a woman on some country road pumping a tire, timing valves, or fixing some part of an engine." Hence, once women became "familiar with the principles of construction, care, and operation of each part of their car . . . they derive much pleasure in being able to operate their own machine."[44]

For their part, women argued that whether or not skill with machines and ingenuity was an innate characteristic, technical expertise could be learned through experience or lessons.[45] For instance, Blanche McManus, journalist for *Harper's Bazaar*, related the story of a young American woman determined to care for her own car. "Juliet, in feminized overalls approached the . . . chassis with that diffidence and distrust that all women have toward machinery. But familiarity breeds knowledge as well as contempt." After a few lessons, Juliet "was able to talk glibly of 'lean' and 'thick' mixtures, learned the wires, and forgot to jump when she saw a spark. . . . 'Ignition', 'circulation,' and 'timing' became household words." McManus claimed, " 'knack' was the open sesame . . . as in most things and easily within a woman's grasp."[46] Almost a decade later, when travel writer Winifred Dixon described her cross-country motor trip, she noted the value of experience. "What I knew of the bowels of a car" had been gained, not from systematic research, but from bitter experience with mutinous parts in ten years' progress through two, four,

Testing a Battery With a   Always Keep the Radiator   Any Woman Can Fill the
Hydrometer   Filled With Water   Grease Cups

Figure 10. Illustrations like this one advised women on how to maintain their cars without the help of husbands or male mechanics, and underscored the notion that women could be adept at working on the car. "Little Things About the Car," *Ladies' Home Journal,* March 1917, 32.

and six and finally eight-cylinder motors." Dixon continued, "I had taken no course in mechanics. . . . [But] I had a smattering of knowledge of . . . defective batteries, leaky radiators, frozen steering wheels, cranky generators, wrongly-hung springs, stripped gears and slipping clutches."[47] Similar to male drivers who had little training in mechanics, women could learn to maintain and even modify their cars through hands-on operation of the vehicle.

Women motorists who traveled alone and in single-sex groups unescorted by men challenged the reigning ideology that women travelers needed male protection on the road.[48] Women drivers reinvented the late Victorian image of the lone woman traveler[49] that had emerged in the pages of numerous women's magazines.[50] These women rode trains, stayed in hotels, and ate in restaurants without male companions, and in doing so extended the boundaries of women's public sphere. In 1906, *Cosmopolitan* ran a series of articles on the growing numbers of unescorted woman travelers in which columnist and playwright Eleanor Gates argued that "the problem reaches into every household where there are girls to safeguard."[51] Articles observed that women fell prey to disease, nerves, and the sexual advances of strange men, especially in the public space of the train station or hotel lobby. Women's magazines also counseled that women could protect themselves through a combination of modesty, knowledge of the systems of travel (understanding train schedules), and consumption, or buying the right goods. And they argued strongly that idea of autonomy for women in public space. Gates asserted that the traditional rules designed for women's protection prevented them form sharing equally in public leisure space.[52] The automobile fit neatly into these arguments because it allowed women more control over both transportation and public space.

Long distance travel by automobile provided the perfect venue in which women could prove their autonomy. In 1909, as women's magazines debated the ability of women to travel unescorted, Alice Huyler Ramsey became the first woman to drive cross-country from New York to San Francisco. Carl Kelsy, sales manager for the Maxwell-Briscoe automobile company, which sponsored the trip and provided the automobile, dubbed the adventure a "female reliability run." Ramsey later reflected that Kelsy was "a natural for seeing opportunities in special advertising stunts."[53] Yet promoting the Maxwell gave Ramsey an opportunity to demonstrate women's potential as good mechanics, for the story focused on her technical skill. She did not need a chauffeur or male escort because, in most instances, she could repair her own car. As her story reached local newspapers across the country, Ramsey became a role model for other women. In one instance, a farm woman waited all day at the edge of the expected route to meet the daring woman driver.[54] At a moment when male drivers raced over the continent testing automotive design, women and automotive manufacturers hoped long-distance runs by women would demonstrate the suitability of women as drivers.

Less famous women conducted their own "reliability tours" under the guise of leisure travel. Devoid of sponsorship and lacking national news coverage, these tours nevertheless fostered mechanical authority and autonomy among a wider group of women. For instance, Vera May Teape, a young rural woman, drove from Ohio to Colorado with her mother in 1907 and noted her pride in maintaining and repairing her car, the Baby Bullet. Using impromptu solutions to mechanical problems, Teape recorded in her diary her ability to diagnose engine trouble and solve it without the help of an expert. After replacing a nut on the sprocket wheel, Teape reflected proudly on her ingenuity: "We wasted lots of time and I was horribly dirty, but I rather think most men would have had the machine hauled to a repair shop." She reported that her repair held so well that there was no need to stop at a garage.[55]

Fictional travel stories also showcased the technical authority of motor heroines by placing them in dangerous situations that they could overcome only through ingenuity. For example, a 1911 pulp novel entitled *Patty's Motor Car* placed a young woman in the familiar situation of a breakdown on a lonely country road after dark. Patty and her beau,

Philip, both examined the engine. Patty "didn't understand fully all the complicated parts, but she had a fair working knowledge of its main principles, and she, too, was unable to discover anything wrong or out of order." Although not an expert mechanic, Patty was Philip's equal; they were both amateurs. While waiting for help to arrive, the two had ample time to discuss the engine trouble. Philip decided the problem lay in battery; a small crack in the casing that interrupted the current, but did not know how to repair the problem. Patty cleverly produced a solution and fixed the car. Fulfilling the chapter's title, "Patty's Ingenuity," she unwrapped a piece of chocolate, folded the tinfoil wrapper into a long strand, and stuck it in the crack. The tin became a conductor and fixed the battery. Philip exclaimed, "Patty, you're a genius!"[56] Unlike later stories that emphasized men as mechanical authorities, this early work sketched an ingenious heroine. Similar to *Patty's Motor Car,* other auto narratives showed men and women working together as partners.[57] Other early motor heroines demonstrated their ingenuity by altering machines to fit their needs. In *The Motor Girls on Crystal Bay,* the girls rigged the galley of their motorboat with an elaborate system of electrical appliances run off the main battery. In addition, they redirected outgoing hot water from the engine to wash their dishes.[58] Unlike the Motor Boys—who built at least one machine, a combination airplane-dirigible, from the ground up—the Motor Girls never built new machines, but they did become ingenious consumers by modifying their existing vehicles.[59]

Autobiographical accounts of driving provided detailed examples of women tinkerers.[60] In 1923, *The Motor* featured Miss Chilton, a racecar driver, who related her triumphs including her "best repair." During a competitive race in Britain, a "water joint burst" in Chilton's car and she repaired the hose "with a strips torn from a mackintosh, the radiator being then filled up from a mountain stream." Chilton lost only a few minutes in the race, a credit to her mechanical as well as her driving skill, reported the magazine. The article noted that although Chilton was "now an expert in diagnosing trouble, she had to learn in the hard school of experience."[61] In an equally dramatic account of tinkering, Pauline Bell, a sixty-year-old woman who piloted her car from Ogden, Utah, wrote to *Fordowner* in 1920 providing careful instructions on how she upgraded her 1918 flivver for long-distance driving.[62] She outfitted her Model T with multiple after-market accessories, including demountable rims (which made changing tires quicker), an electric starter, and shock absorbers. She also had the "front seat cut" to provide a convertible bed so that, like many motorists, she could economize by sleeping in the car. These accessories made driving easier, more comfortable, and less dangerous. And she constructed a trunk to carry sleeping equipment and kitchen supplies. Reflecting on the experience, Bell wrote that her skill as a tinkerer had helped her conquer the hardships of long-distance motor travel.

Adopting some of the tropes of male travel adventure stories, women's travel narratives dramatized repairs making women drivers into heroines. Bell recalled an incident when she mended a tire just in time to outrun a thunderstorm. "We could see the storm coming," she recalled. "I had several blow-outs, and had used all my inner tubes, so I had to vulcanize a tube before I could change. I got one ready and lighted the gas in the vulcanizer." The wind became so strong that Bell removed the engine cover and constructed a temporary shelter to protect the flame of the vulcanizer, a device for welding rubber.[63] Hammered by wind and rain but undaunted, she repaired the rubber and replaced the tire just in time to escape a lightning strike. The drama highlighted Bell's expertise and her ability to take care of herself on the road.

Like Bell, Winifred Dixon retold her tinkering stories with a sense of theater. In her book, *Westward Hoboes*, Dixon proclaimed, "I love to tinker! In the old two-cylinder days, when the carburetor flooded I would weigh it down with a few pebbles and a hair pin." Dixon recounted one instance when she and her female traveling companion, Toby, and a Chippewa Indian repaired their automobile using only intuition and a nail-file. Driving through the Northern Plains, Dixon reported that they had trouble with the ignition. After breaking down, Toby and Dixon began a methodical examination of the engine in search of the problem. Fifty miles from the nearest mechanic, the two women had no choice but to take the car apart and tinker until they fixed the problem. "All Toby knew was that Bill of Santa Fé [an excellent mechanic] had taken it apart, done something to it, and put it back together again, and it ran. So we decided to follow Bill's procedure as far as we could, and began taking it apart." Adding to the sense of adversity, Dixon noted that someone had stolen their tool kit leaving only a "monkey wrench and a pair of pinchers." After hours of unscrewing parts using only the pincers, a group of male tourists stopped to offer advice. "'You took it apart without knowing how to put it together again?' said one of them. They exchanged glances which said 'How like a woman!'" Dixon asked if they could explain the principles of the ignition system. She recalled: "The man muttered something . . . and drove off. Like most men, he was willing to stay as long as he could appear in a superior light, but no longer." Fortunately Dixon and Toby met another traveler, a Chippewa Indian, "whose knowledge, combined with our own, was just sufficient" to repair the car. She wrote, "I do not believe Albert really knew a fuse from a switchbox, but he did remember one essential we had forgotten,—that the points should be a sixteenth of an inch apart. He said without tools he could do nothing. So we proffered a nail-file, by happy inspiration, with which he ground the points." The happy ending came with the hum of the engine. "A prouder moment neither Toby nor I ever had, when by grace of a Chippewa and a nail-file we monkeyed with our ignition fifty miles from a garage,—and conquered it."[64] Dixon's story demonstrated the skill of two groups of amateurs outside the dominant narrative of ingenuity, women and Native Americans. She related the sense of triumph at disproving the idea that women should not "monkey" with their cars.

Many other women joined Dixon in arguing that they were mechanically competent enough to travel alone. When asked if she was nervous about traveling without a man in her party, Pauline Bell replied, "We do not need a man along as I know all about my car."[65] In fact, Bell and other women drivers often related incidents in which the male motorists they met on the road knew little or nothing about mechanics.[66] In 1915, an *Illustrated World* article on women drivers featured Kathryn Williams, a "Mecanicienne." The author noted, "when a carburetor [sic] gets choky or a tire blows our Miss Williams, scorning masculine aid, goes after it herself."[67] New Women such as journalist Kathryn Hulme, who drove cross-country in 1928 with her female friend Tuny, purposefully avoided accepting assistance with automotive repairs. Faced with repairing their car, Hulme and Tuny reported that they drove off the road and out of sight of other travelers. "We always like to do our tinkering in lovely and lonely spots," remembered Hulme. "We had many experiences with the 'assisting' man camper who thinks that when a woman gets anything more complicated than an egg-beater in her hand, she is to be watched carefully." Hulme met so many interfering men that it was difficult to repair the car unless they "retreated to the desert where there was nothing more chivalrous than a stray steer to impede our progress."[68]

Women motorists found that repairing their own machines brought the pleasure of self-sufficiency, the same things male motor travelers sought in the new frontier of the open road. In 1907 Vera Marie Teape confessed to her diary, "the sensation of traveling swiftly and yourself controlling the machine, whose every sound you understand, is something only those who have experienced can at all conceive."[69] If women could change tires and perform general engine repairs, they could travel unescorted. Home economist and travel advisor Christine Frederick remarked as well that "learning to handle the car has wrought my emancipation. . . . I am no longer dependent on tricksome trains, slow-buggies, . . . or the almanac." She wrote that the automobile linked her suburban home to the city allowing her to commute to the city on her own schedule.[70] Ruth Stuart, of the Automobile Girls, remarked to her father, "Isn't it well that I have a taste for mechanics, even though I'm a girl? Suppose I hadn't studied all those automobile books with you until I could say them backwards. . . . You never would have let me go on this heavenly trip, would you?"[71] Heeding a larger call for women's independence, the Motor Girls ruled out the presence of boys on their first automobile adventure. Cora observed, "If we had boys along . . . they would claim the glory of every spill, every skid, every upset and every 'busted tire.' We want some little glory ourselves."[72] Yet in many of the stories a group of friendly boys was never far off, and often appeared at a moment of trouble. Self-reliant in theory, the Motor Girls cautiously negotiated a new role for young women.[73]

Nevertheless, the stories emphasized a growing desire for independence. Ruth of the Automobile Girls explained why she learned to drive: "All my life I have longed to travel by myself; at least with the people I want, not in a train, or a big crowded boat. Dad knows the feeling; it's what makes him run away . . . and get out on the prairies and ride . . . ! I'm a girl, so I can't do that or lots of things. But I can run an automobile."[74] The final book of the Motor Girl series, *The Motor Girls in the Mountains* (1917), more explicitly connected new transportation technology and the popular feminist goal of a wider world for women. A large portion of this story explored Cora's encounter with a female aviator, who was crossing the country in an attempt to set a record. The drama in this final story centered on Cora becoming lost in the woods. After spending the night alone in the forest Cora saw a lone airplane. Separated from her car, Cora coveted the technology of flight and the possibility of freedom that it offered. She envied the aviator, who she assumed was male, "No forest held *him* in its iron clutch. He was free as the bird whom he resembled in his flight. He could choose what path he would." When the aviator revealed herself, Cora broke down with relief—she was saved, and safe with this new stranger. In one of the most overtly political conversations in the series, Cora discussed the issue of gender equality with the woman pilot. On a cross-country flight from Chicago to New York, the woman was "bent on beating the best record ever made for the distance by either man or woman." Cora exclaimed, "I don't see how you dare to take such risks,. . . . It must take a tremendous amount of courage." And the aviator responded, "There's a lot of satisfaction in beating the men at their own game." Cora acknowledged that was true, saying, "We women all owe you a lot for doing it."[75] Women aviators and drivers made each of these new technologies seem safe for public consumption and they also embodied the goals of New Womanhood to make new space for women outside the home.[76] Two decades later women drivers still enjoyed the thrill of self-sufficiency. As Eleanor Roosevelt told *American Motorist* in 1933, "I like the sense of doing the thing myself that driving my own car gives."[77] However, by that time, Roosevelt would represent a minority of women motorists.

No Vacation for the Motor Wife

By World War I, the growth of family motor travel and the role of the "motor wife" challenged, and eventually supplanted, the image of the independent, capable motor heroine. Drawing on changing notions of marriage and family relations that emphasized domestic partnership or "companionate marriage," touring experts devised the companionate vacation as a way to bring men and women together in leisure.[78] Indeed, motor touring experts as well as historians have argued that the automobile and the affordable vacation known as autocamping reunited the family in its leisure practices.[79]

Yet the rise of the companionate vacation limited women's access to mechanical knowledge and the automobile. Historian Christina Simmons has noted the companionate marriage, based on ideas of equality and partnership at the turn of the century, "represented the attempt of mainstream marriage ideology to adapt to women's perceived new social and sexual power" while at the same time trying to curb women's independence from men.[80] Similarly companionate narratives of automobility attempted to contain women's spatial and mechanical autonomy by reasserting women's traditional roles in the family and by deskilling the woman driver, arguing that she was dependent on men.

In 1919, Sinclair Lewis lauded the ideology of companionship in his motor novel, *Free Air.* Published two years after the Motor Girls series ended and as family motor narratives flooded popular magazines, *Free Air* bridged the transition between stories of female autonomy and those of the companionate couple, by marrying the motor girl to the technological hero. In the novel, Claire Boltwood, a young woman motorist, drives cross-country with her ill father seeking freedom from upper-class "respectability" and a lesson in self-sufficiency. Claire is a good driver who wants to see the country from behind the wheel of a car. Physically stronger and more mechanically minded than her father, Claire does all the driving. A few miles after embarking on their westward trip and at the exact moment that the car broke down for the first time, Claire meets Milt Daget, a skilled mechanic escaping the confines of small-town America. Milt repairs her car's distributor and begins a friendship with Claire. Also on his way to Seattle, Milt follows Claire and her father providing mechanical expertise and male protection. In exchange, Claire offers Milt a taste of high culture and encourages him to study engineering at a university. As the motorists traveled west, Claire and Milt build a friendship that defies class and regional differences, and that eventually deepens into romance. As confirmation of their equality, Claire announces, "we already know we are partners! We've done things together." Claire notes that they had experienced life together in a deeper way than most young people of her class. By the end of the book, they marry.[81]

In spite of Claire's growing independence from parental authority, she gave up her autonomy and her authority as a driver when she became Milt's partner. Over the course of the novel, Claire's mechanical skill diminished as she gave control of the machine to Milt. Crossing the Rocky Mountains proved an insurmountable task for Claire as a driver. "She had the feeling of the car bursting out from under control . . . ready to leap off the road, into a wash. She wanted to jump. It took all her courage to stay in the seat." Claire lost her nerve, refused to drive over another mountain, and waited for Milt to provide a solution. Claire "waited reverently while the local prophet [Milt] sat in his [car], stared at the wheels of the Gomez [her car], and thought. . . . She did not even try to help him while he again cleaned the spark plugs and looked over brakes, oil, gas, and water. She sat on the running-board, and it was pleasant to be relieved of responsibility."[82]

Eventually, Claire relinquished complete control of the car, including the driving, to Milt and experienced what the author, Sinclair Lewis, called a feeling of "freedom unbounded." Under the guise of partnership, Milt and Claire assumed traditional gender roles in relation to the technology; Milt was the acknowledged expert and hero. In fact, his expertise made him Claire's equal in terms of social class. In college, Milt's knowledge of the automobile gained him respect and promised to make him wealthy. The upper-class members of his fraternity "found that he knew more about motor-cars than any of them, and as motor-cars were among their greater gods, they considered him wise." Claire, on the other hand, decided to join Milt at the university to develop her domestic expertise. She explained that she wanted to "learn a little about food and babies and building houses."[83] Here the motor girl retained some of her interest in modern ideas of science and technology, but only as they might be applied in the more traditional space of the home.

The advice literature on autocamping echoed Lewis's vision of companionate travel.[84] In the 1920s, the family motor vacation placed women firmly within the confines of domesticity and ultimately gave them less opportunity to gain and maintain their skills as drivers. Motor camping expert Elon Jessup observed that in the recent past men and women had traveled separately; when he went camping in 1900 he invariably saw only other men. By 1921, Jessup wrote, "Today when I go to the woods, the sight which . . . greets my eyes is a khaki clad mother seated in front of a tent holding a nursing baby . . . and turning flapjacks with her free hand. . . . Father is setting the table." He concluded, "Camping is no longer exclusively a man's recreation. It has become a family affair."[85]

As affirmation of the family vacation, advice experts told women that motoring with their husbands was the romantic ideal.[86] For instance, Vivian Gurney, contributor to *Sunset* magazine, wrote that a motor honeymoon allowed her to be "alone together" with her new husband away from the social demands of a resort hotel.[87] Men were encouraged to include their wives in their outdoor activities to show equality. Camping expert Frank Brimmer began his book *Motor Campcraft* with a family portrait and dedicated the volume to "The Missus and the kids always my confederates along the Open Road."[88] In a letter to *Outing* magazine, a reader endorsed Brimmer's vision of companionate travel by prompting his cohorts to include "friend wife" in their outings: "in this new day our women are entitled to an every-increasing share of our activities, whether they be work or play. Surprise Her with an invitation on your next trip."[89] Women could also make life on the road easier, argued one contributor to *Fordowner* in 1916, "If the Ford owner enjoys motor camping and is blessed with a helpmate . . . he possesses the primary necessities for a successful trip."[90] Ostensibly, men and women participated equally in autocamping. Historian Warren Belsaco has argued that autocamping was a return to pioneering; husbands and wives worked together in the common effort of survival, setting up sleeping quarters, preparing food, and cleaning up.[91]

Family auto vacations thus provided an ideal space for the practice of "masculine domesticity." According to historian Margaret Marsh, in the years before World War I middle-class men gained the financial security and added leisure to spend more time with their families and notions of marriage shifted to emphasize the role of fathers as partners rather than patriarchs. Marsh defined masculine domesticity as "a model of behavior in which fathers would agree to take on increased responsibility for some of the day-to-day tasks of bringing up children. . . . A domestic man would also make his wife, rather than his male cronies, his regular companion on evenings out. And . . . he would take a significantly greater interest in the details of running the household . . . than his father was expected to do."[92] Motor travel provided the perfect venue in which middle-class men could tinker with their roles as fathers and husbands. Touring authorities such as Frank Brimmer wrote that men shared in domestic responsibilities such as cooking, and provided snapshots of him cooking and taking care of the children on the road.[93] At best, autocamping husbands, including Brimmer, claimed their wives as

Figure 11. The cover of *Motor Camper and Tourist* depicted the ideal family motor vacation in 1925 and the gendered division of labor many women motorists wrote about in their diaries. Reproduced from the Collections of the Library of Congress, Prints and Photographs Division, Washington, D.C. LC-USZ62-662726.

friends, spent more time with the children, and performed some domestic tasks.[94]

Yet, mediators like Brimmer generally divided the work of autocamping based on technological know-how and physical strength, which put men in control of the car and recommended women take responsibility for the "lighter" domestic chores. For instance, Herbert Ladd Towle suggested that women—who, he argued, lacked mechanical skill—should turn driving over to their husbands. Towle observed that "most tours are family affairs and I fancy that the average woman will generally yield the responsibility [of driving] to stronger hands." However self-reliant when alone, he argued, she "likes to be taken care of' when she may." In his scenario women would oversee the packing of, "the hampers and personal belongings rather than . . . the actual management of the car."[95] Indeed, assigning labor based on traditional gender roles may have made the trip go more smoothly because everyone knew what to do and how to do it. A contributor to *Field and Stream* suggested that tasks in the camp be divided along traditional gender lines to improve efficiency. He wrote: "Roughly speaking the heavy work (except biscuit making) is entrusted to the men and the gentle tasks, such as washing dishes and the like, are performed by the fair sex."[96] This division of labor tied women more closely to domesticity and denied the earlier promise of automobility to include women and to allow them to tinker not only with modern technology but also with the boundaries of their gender roles.

Many motor wives lamented the lack of freedom and the unequal partnerships of traveling with husbands and children. For women the family motor vacation did not provide an escape from daily routine. Wives and mothers often performed the same ceaseless chores they did at home but without the conveniences available there.[97] Gula Sabin, who drove from Wisconsin to California with her family in 1926, described women's work in auto-camps as dirty and tedious. For instance, one night after her husband wrestled unsuccessfully with their portable gas stove, Sabin cooked dinner in the community kitchen of their camp. She described the kitchen as an exclusively female domain: "A long row of women stood before the stoves in this commodious structure. Old women, young women; thin women, fat women; short women, tall women; homely women, pretty women." Sabin found that women, regardless of class or educational level, did most of the cooking, cleaning, washing for their touring families. And these tasks were accomplished with less than optimal equipment. She remembered making camp after a very long day on the road and then having to cook over an open fire: "The only stove in this camp-site was a brick one, consisting of a chimney and an open space below, covered with an iron grating.

Figure 12. Women autocampers performed domestic work even while on vacation, and often without the help of their male companions, making women writers declare that the family motor travel was not a vacation for women. Mammoth Public Auto Camp, 1923. Reproduced from the Collections at the Library of Congress, Prints and Photographs Division, Washington, D.C. LC-USZ62-66079.

Over this smoky stove, by the light of a candle, I cooked our dinner, and shortly after this repast we retired to our tent." While lying in their tent, her son exclaimed: "'Oh! This camp life is just great, isn't it, mother?' . . . He was lying on his cot, gazing up at the stars. . . . I pretended to be asleep—it would spoil his fun, were I to answer truthfully."[98] Sabin was not alone. In her history of women and the automobile, Virginia Scharff briefly noted that "putting the family on wheels did not necessarily mean getting away from housework. . . . Jobs that had been performed with familiar equipment in customary surroundings could become problems requiring extra energy and creativity." Scharff quoted popular novelist Mary Roberts Rinehart as saying: "The difference between the men I have camped with and myself, generally speaking, has been this: they have called it sport; I have known it as work."[99]

Diaries of women auto campers confirmed the notion of women's labor as anything but light.[100] Mary Crehore Bedell, who motored with her husband for three months in 1924, wrote that her marital partner never cooked, at least not until she contracted ptomaine poisoning.[101] Another woman remembered traveling in a family caravan during the interwar period and recalled the "primitive" equipment her mother used to feed ten people daily. "It was some job to feed ten of us! I know my mother had more than her fill of it before we got back home."[102] In the stark language of a daily "itinerary," another diary from the same period recorded women performing domestic chores while the rest of the family enjoyed leisure activities, such as fishing and sightseeing. An entry from 1919 noted: "Monday. The women folks washed and ironed. The men folks went into Denver."[103] A diary from 1932 reported: "July 4 Rainy. Mother washed in the electric machine of the filling station's wife. Dad took us down to the 4th of July celebration." This was one of many instances in which the mother and adult aunt did domestic work while husbands and children played.[104]

Tourist photographs, which captured the daily routines of motor camp life, illustrated women doing the domestic work in camp. Mary Bedell had herself photographed doing the dishes with the thick forest of Yellowstone National Park behind her in 1924 to illustrate the primitive equipment used by women in camp.[105] A photograph from 1923 depicted a group of men gathered in one of the public camps watching two women do the laundry.[106] Just as the companionate marriage did not fulfill its promise of providing the "equality women deserved" by creating a bond of "creative companionship and interdependent cooperation," neither did autocamping create a new kind of domestic environment where men and women participated equally in the daily work of maintaining home on the road.[107] Rather, motor travel helped establish what Ruth Schwartz Cowan called the feminine mystique of the interwar period. She wrote, "Whatever it was that trapped educated American women in their kitchens . . . the trap was laid during the . . . [19]20s."[108] Ironically, automobility and the family motor vacation became part of this trap.

In 1927, New York journalist Frederic Van de Water published his account of the companionate vacation, writing extensively on the division of labor in the auto camp and the different experiences of men and women on vacation. Dubbing his wife the Commodore and himself the Engineer, Van de Water worked hard to present a picture of "matrimonial equality" in the auto-camp. His descriptions of camp life, however, also captured the dissatisfaction of women motorists. Relating the events of a typical Sunday afternoon in camp, Van de Water wrote, "So we rested each Sabbath, though the Commodore resented the term 'rest' with some justification." While Van de Water "pottered about [the car] trying to discover what made [it] sound that way, the Commodore did the family wash. For some reason, she never looked forward with particularly bright anticipation to our Sundays."[109] Whether or not Van de Water perceived the irony, he observed the gendered nature of "shared" work in the auto-camp. Similar observations made other male advisors "soberly wonder whether we had been doing our share of the camp work . . . to help our matrimonial partner to enjoy her vacation too."[110]

These motor advisors, Maurice Decker and Winfield Kimball, included a cautionary tale for husbands who did not share the work equally in their travel advice book. In this story, "friend husband had skillfully and swiftly packed the tent and the cot in the car and considered his work done. He sat behind the wheel and punctuated the moments with impatient honks of the horn while the light of his life vainly tried to catch up with her tasks." The authors, who were present, noted that the wife called on them to witness her declaration of inequality: "Every morning he folds up the tent and hops in the car, hollerin' for me to hurry. He thinks he's done his share of the work. He keeps tellin' me to hurry or we won't make the next camp ahead. He don't do a third as much work as I do."[111] After seeing other vocal wives who commiserated with the Commodore about the rigors of keeping house on the road, Van de Water speculated: "The problem of whether man or woman bears the heavier burden of labor in motor camping never will be settled. It is a question too deeply entangled with the emotions for sober solution. Each sex is secretly convinced that it carries the heavier end of the load and at times will defend its belief with a surprising vigor. The Engineer never met a husband who was not certain that all the onerous duties fell to him, but he never heard one express this conviction within earshot of his wife. . . . Women were not so reticent." Van de Water explained discontent among women as the result of gender differences: "men, as a rule, relish camp life and the days filled with motoring more than women."[112] Statements like Van de Water's helped establish a hierarchy of knowledge on the open road that assigned authority to men.

At least one female author acknowledged this hierarchy and instructed women to support it as a way to stroke their husband's ego. In *The Car Belongs to Mother*, Priscilla Hovey Wright observed that the success of any "conjugal trip" lay in the husband's disposition. To this end, she wrote, "The wise woman takes her hands off the wheel physically, but never relinquishes it mentally for a moment." She noted, "The husband drives of course, although the wife gently and sweetly tells him she stands ready to relieve him at any time so that he, too, may look at the scenery. This brings out his masterfulness as he says he guesses he can drive and look at the same time." Giving over the wheel to one's husband for the entire trip would result in greater control for women once they returned home, reasoned Wright. By the time the trip was over, the man "has had his fill of driving and gladly relinquishes the wheel to the woman—who the very next day may start off with the girls for a little jaunt of a few hundred miles!"[113] The author concluded that husbands would then view their wives with new respect and wonder. However, this formula did not work for the majority of women who ceded authority to men, either willingly or not. Even though most middle-class suburban women, as Wright recorded in her book, used the car more regularly than their husbands to chauffeur children to school and complete daily errands such as shopping, they no longer garnered respect as competent drivers or mechanics.

Undermining Women's Skills

Although middle-class women were acknowledged consumers who possessed domestic skills and a history of leisure travel, and therefore brought a variety of knowledge to the auto camp, male experts dominated the advice literature on motor camping in the 1920s and 1930s, and many sought to undo women's advances in experience and know-how.[114] Writing about what equipment to take on the motor tour, journalist Adelaide Ovington noted that she relied on her husband, catalogs, and a "reliable authority," Horace Kephart, to outfit the car and prepare for the motor vacation.[115] Ovington attributed Kephart's reliability to his superior outdoor experience. She wrote, he "teaches us real woodcraft, which is knowing how to do without the appliances of civilization rather than adapting them to wild life."[116] Men like Kephart became feature writers on motor touring for national magazines, such as *Outing* and *Field and Stream*. *Outing*, which supported the growing cultural dialogue on auto touring in the 1910s and 1920s, published six summer issues of 1919; only five of the forty-three authors were women. Additionally, none of the women appeared more than once, whereas male authors such as Elon Jessup wrote features that spanned several issues or edited monthly columns. In 1919, Jessup edited the "Outing Services Departments" on motors, equipment, services, and advice. In the same year, Horace Kephart edited an advice column on "problems that crop up in camp and along the trail."[117] Monthly features and the regular publication of advice manuals established the authority of experts like Brimmer, Kephart, and Jessup. Between 1920 and 1926, Brimmer published at least three books, edited a monthly section on autocamping for the *New York Evening Post*, contributed to various magazines, and promoted Coleman stoves.[118] These same experts spoke directly to women in *Woman's Home Companion, Country Life, Designer,* and *Motor Life.*[119]

Camp advice undercut women's claims that domestic chores on the road were drudgery. When male experts published advice on cooking, they assured motorists that meal preparation was easier than women claimed.[120] One advice columnist declared that one could prepare meals in twelve minutes.[121] Other male advisors reasoned that if women thought cooking over an open fire was difficult, it was because they lacked experience. Stewart Edward White, a camping advisor, wrote, "Mighty few women I have ever seen were good camp-fire cooks; not because camp-fire cookery is especially difficult, but because they are temperamentally incapable of ridding themselves of the notion that certain things should be done in a certain way."[122] In White's estimation, women were too rigid for camp cooking because it called for experimentation. For men, cooking represented not a daily activity but "a new sport which promised thrills and adventures."[123] Cooking also offered the men another opportunity to demonstrate their skills as tinkerers. White wrote in 1915 that camp cooking was a form of invention; it required ingenuity. He noted, "the secret of successful camp cookery is experimentation and boldness. If you have not an ingredient, substitute the nearest thing to it . . . cut loose . . . and invent."[124] With a proliferation of articles by male authorities, men became more than equal partners. They defined the experience of auto camping, dispensing advice on how to solve the problems of re-creating home on the road and assigning responsibilities for daily tasks. One female journalist complained in 1925 that "entirely too many articles have been written on motor-camping, the new national pastime, without taking into account the woman's point of view."[125]

Women did not appear as regular columnists on motor travel until the mid-1930s, when trailer travel eliminated autocamping and separated the car from the living space. The interior of the trailer, which looked more like home (albeit a scaled-down version), was considered women's domain. The "trailer wife" emerged as an authority on trailer life in the two leading trailer publications of the 1930s, *Trailer Caravan* and *Trailer Travel.*[126] In an effort to market trailer travel to women, these female advisors promoted domestic science, modern technology, and the skillful use of canned goods to convince women that housework on the road with a trailer would be easier than cooking over an open fire.[127] Yet the use of appliances and the application of domestic science changed women's work but did not reduce the amount of time spent in domestic labor.[128] Cooking advice in trailer magazines, in fact, suggested that women prepare elaborate meals.[129] In addition, by the 1930s, women motor travelers were portrayed as more interested in romance and domesticity than in technology and independence.[130] In November 1936, *Trailer Caravan* magazine ran a story entitled "Patent Applied For" about two young women who had invented an improvement for trailers, but gave up their patent for romance and marriage. At the end of the story, one heroine decided to marry the hero and spend her life in a trailer for two. She explained with a sigh: "I'm so tired of being self-reliant."[131]

Popular ingenuity, once open to women, became almost wholly the province of male drivers, consumers, and tinkerers by the early 1930s. As women performed domestic duties, male drivers claimed authority over the car, asserting that women were mechanically unskilled, poor drivers and, ultimately, dependent on men.[132] Articles on driving written by male experts equated masculinity with technological skill. As early as 1914, *Motor* noted that the "early life of men gives them co-ordination of eye, brain, and body; knowledge of road rules . . . reserve strength." In contrast, the magazine charged that women's domestic life resulted in a "lack of mechanical and transportation experience [which] handicaps her in solving roadway problems; her average physical strength is less—in short, the life of the average woman unfits rather than fits her for safe motor car operation."[133] Articles in the mid-1920s and 1930s assumed women, as a group, lacked the ability to repair or even drive their cars. Herbert Towle, a writer for *Scribner's,* called women "chronic amateurs" who did not understand the simplest controls on the car, such as the spark advance. One writer, who identified himself simply as a "mere male instructor," in 1923 concluded, "Mechanically, women have no sense, and they are more likely to turn a screwed part in the wrong direction than in the right."[134] On the road in 1926, Frederic Van de Water described not only his wife, but women in general, as technologically incompetent. He observed, "Some women, our transcontinental experience has led us to believe, are not at their best behind a steering wheel." Women autocampers, in Van de Water's estimation, were dangerous because they had only the "most elementary knowledge of camp craft or motor lore."[135]

In contrast, men were often portrayed as mechanically proficient, good outfitters, and ingenious.[136] Auto touring allowed men to show off their resourcefulness through the practice of tinkering. Herbert Shumway, editor of *Field and Stream*'s "Camper on Tour" column wrote that wives would "rise up and call [their husbands] wise men" for assembling ingenious motor outfits.[137] Indeed, Beatrice Massey and Emily Post seemingly deferred to their male companions on all automotive matters from outfitting to modifying the automobile.[138] The lack of evidence for women's ingenuity in these narratives further underscored the cultural understanding after 1920 of women motorists as technologically inferior. Women rarely appeared as featured innovators in user magazines such as *Fordowner,* and they held few patents for automotive accessories. As Nancy Barr Mavity, journalist for *Sunset,* observed, "Despite [women's] mastery of the intricate mechanism of the sewing machine, and their ability to repair the household plumbing with a hairpin and a button hook, they were told with many reiterations that they were inferior in mechanical ability."[139]

Driving lessons in particular gave men a chance to practice automotive authority and portray women as technologically illiterate.[140] In 1920, *Literary Digest* ventured that "Woman's right to vote . . . is admitted in practically all quarters to-day . . . but a good many masculine backnumbers still deny her right to have her own way with a new . . . car." The editor implied the latter was a wise idea; teaching "friend wife" to drive, he noted, was difficult business which would arouse "a twinge of sympathy" in many men. In the magazine one husband related the "tale of how his marital tranquility suffered a blowout as a result of his attempts to initiate wifie into the mysteries of spark plugs, clutches, brakes and accessories." No matter how many times the husband explained the mechanical processes of the car, his wife could not learn to drive.[141]

According to Murray Fahnestock, editor of *Ford Owner and Dealer,* women did not possess the mental capacity to understand the automobile. Fahnestock wrote that it was the "mentality of the woman driver that gives the most trouble" when teaching them to drive.[142] Fahnestock, an expert on the Model T, maintained that women were both stubborn in their lack of knowledge about cars and ornery about asking "dumbbell" questions. In this editor's mind, any questions were an indicator of ignorance. Fahnestock also denied the complexity of the Model T's transmission, saying it was simple to operate. The Model T's planetary transmission was typically composed of a shifting pedal to change gears, a pedal for reverse, and a foot brake. A rudimentary form of automatic transmission, the planetary was quite different from the other standard forms transmission at the time, and it was notoriously difficult to operate.[143] E. B. White feared the Model T's planetary transmission, saying that it took skill and nerve to operate the odd configuration of pedals and the spark lever (accelerator) on the steering column.[144] Ford Motor Company also acknowledged that the operation of this transmission required instruction and published a book intended for all drivers, men and women, explaining how to operate the transmission.[145]

Fahnestock mocked the woman who critiqued the design of the planetary transmission and told male driving instructors to talk down to women when explaining the system. "'Three pedals—when I have only two feet!' exclaims the woman driver who is apt to think that three pedals make the control more complicated," wrote Fahnestock. He instructed male drivers teaching their wives to drive: "Don't go into the technicalities of the planetary transmission—simply try to talk [women's] language and show them that the middle pedal is the 'back-up' pedal, and that they only need use this . . . when they wish to back the Ford into someone else's car." Fahnestock concluded, "When one tries to explain the interdependent action of spark and throttle levers to the average woman driver—the result is madness." To preserve male sanity, he suggested separating mechanical know-how from driving. One could teach a woman to drive even if she never understood how the car worked. He also advocated simplifying the mechanisms of the car for the woman driver. "In preparing the car for dumbbell driving," he wrote, "we should endeavor to make the car as fool-proof as possible."[146] Automotive experts within the industry would apply this same logic to all consumers, male and female, in the 1930s.

When women did write about the car, they confronted a hierarchy of knowledge that portrayed them as technologically inferior to men.[147] In 1927, a woman told Nancy Mavity that she hated the "fool proof" machine that her husband bought for her because "I don't enjoy being classified with fools." Her husband would not teach her to drive his car, saying that she was "too nervous." The rationale of nervousness, she said, allowed him to maintain the myth that women could not learn car mechanics. "To save himself the bother [of teaching her to drive] and still keep the myth of nervousness intact, he finally bought this for my . . . use. That kept him safe on his pedestal." After telling this story, Mavity offered advice for women who wanted to "avoid the burden of the inferiority complex in its subtler form." She wrote: "Never let your husband teach you to drive. . . . In fact, if it is at all possible, be the one to teach him. That will even things up psychologically. But if you reinforce his ingrained sense of masculine superiority with the authority of a teacher, if you let him be the expert . . . you will never catch up— never!"[148] Stories of driving lessons illustrated the establishment of a technological hierarchy that placed men in a position of power and expertise over women.

Finally, motor advice from the interwar period asserted that women motorists, whether traveling alone or with their husbands, were ultimately dependent upon the greater mechanical expertise of men. Lone women travelers, in particular, were portrayed as silly, nervous, and mechanically incompetent. Viviane Gurney, in her honeymoon travel narrative, offered a vision of women travelers who lacked the nerve to travel unescorted. On the outskirts of Yellowstone Park, Gurney wrote, "We met four women in a Ford half way up the grade, all crying because they could not go up and were afraid to turn round and go back."[149] Frederic Van de Water charged that women motorists did not approach the problems of motor touring in a serious manner and depended upon the chivalry of men. They seemed to "take touring with a certain light-heartedness, a serene fatalism regarding the future, an abiding trust in Chance. . . . Certainly, in the chivalrous West, the problem of motor or tire repairs is simplified for a purely feminine expedition." Van de Water told several stories of unescorted woman motorists who, through lack of mechanical know-how and poor driving, got themselves and other drivers into trouble but who were always helped by knowledgeable men. He explained, "All you have to do is to sit still and look appealing and the next car that passes will come to your aid."[150]

Traveling in the mid-1930s, author Winfield Kimball recorded similar experiences with single women. He wrote that he met many women "unattended or unhampered" by men who got along just fine without husbands. However, these same women, in Kimball's view, were still dependent on male assistance. They might have motored unescorted, but "when something does turn up that requires the strong assistance of the male, there are plenty of representatives ready to lend a hand." He illustrated this point with a story about "two school-marms who were hitting the South Dakota trails in lone-wolf fashion." The two women trolled the autocamp looking for help with their car and passed over Kimball when his wife appeared. Eventually, the author noted, the young women found the help of two single men. The men repaired the teachers' car and set up their tents. Witnessing the scene, Kimball's wife exclaimed, "'Humph! . . . They were just looking for somebody to tag along and do their work."[151] Commenting that women did not need mechanical skill, a writer for *Motor* asked, "Why should attractive women bother mastering mechanical details? After all, there is no need for an attractive woman to master mechanical details so long as she has a pair of eyes and uses them when in distress—as she will, without any advice."[152] Such stories undermined women's claims to autonomy by arguing that, even if women motored alone, they were still dependent upon men.

Small numbers of women continued to express their dissatisfaction with these stereotypes and portrayed themselves as capable and ingenious users of technology. In 1939, Priscilla Hovey Wright concluded that there was "some obscure, psychological reason" behind the myth that women could not handle machines like the car. She wrote with an edge of sarcasm, "Man is the acknowledge master of the machine. . . . Yet, Man, the master and inventor, is forced by the economic and social conditions of daily living, to turn the darlings of his brain over to Woman, who, knowing nothing about them . . . nevertheless makes them go." By her own admission, Wright was "bitter and frustrated" with the idea that women were unmechanical. She asserted that women were intuitive tinkerers who had an "uncanny, unscientific ability to make things go" with only the help of simple household tools like the "hairpin, razor blade, nail file, and embroidery scissors." Women were masters of the machine, Wright assured her audience, especially the growing legions of suburban "matrons" who drove the family car on a daily basis.[153]

In the same year, *Independent Woman* encouraged women to drive to gain autonomy. Writer Geraldine Sartain told women that there was a "consciousness of power that comes with successful handling of an automobile. The driver's consciousness of power offsets inferiority complexes." Sartain further instructed her readers, "Don't let the sneering masculine commonplace, 'a woman driver,' deter or frighten you. An entire generation of men drivers and even men who have never sat behind a wheel have perpetuated the myth that the ability to handle machinery is a secondary sex characteristic." She concluded by reminding women drivers, "After all, an automobile is the largest piece of machinery that we women currently operate. It can make us feel infinitely more important than managing an electric egg beater."[154] Owing to its size, mechanical complexity, and its ability to provide personal mobility, the automobile became perhaps the most important consumer technology of the early twentieth century. Although the definition of who could be a mechanically skilled driver or tinkerer narrowed after 1920 to exclude women, women themselves still saw automobility as an avenue to respect and independence.

*   *   *

With the introduction of the automobile came tremendous opportunities for various groups of consumers to redefine their relationship to technology and public space by asserting their ingenuity and authority with the new machine. New Women used the opportunity to extend their autonomy and define women as equal to men in their claim to the automobile. Motor heroines in the 1910s defined women as not just potential purchasers of cars but as rational, brave, independent, and mechanically skilled drivers. This definition of the woman consumer included technological skill and ingenuity. The window of opportunity for women to claim equal authority in driving and repairing or modifying the automobile, however, closed as male advice experts asserted that woman's place was not behind the wheel but in the passenger seat next to her husband, the real mechanical expert. Women continued to drive, outfit, and occasionally repair the car, but they would not become tinkerers, or more important, grass-roots inventors in the same numbers as men. Their authority over the design and use of the car was effectively limited. Some motorists, mostly men, would attempt to capitalize on their ingenuity and cross the line between consumption and invention by patenting their modifications to the automobile. Consumers-turned-tinkerers may have been able to modify their own individual vehicles but they had little luck as inventors. As the following two chapters demonstrate, amateurs had difficulty selling their ideas to the large corporations that dominated production and design by the 1930s.

Chapter 3

Consumers Become Inventors

In the spring of 1926, as many Americans dusted off touring equipment and began tinkering with their autos, *Scientific American* told its readers to put their ingenuity to work, not just for fun but for profit. Milton Wright, editor of *Scientific American*'s Commercial Property News, which counseled readers on the "dos and don'ts" of invention, reminded would-be inventors that "little things count." Wright was convinced that "one of the most encouraging things about inventing is that it generally is the simple little ideas, ideas that any of us might have thought of, which make the most money."[1] He noted that small inventions, in particular novelties, could reap big rewards because they cost less to manufacture and often had large sales volume. What could be smaller, simpler, and seemingly more promising than gadgets for the automobile? Automotive accessories fit this advice perfectly, and between the beginnings of mass production and the early 1930s many consumers-turned-tinkerers pursued the twin promises of cultural recognition and financial reward by inventing auto accessories.

Ironically, at the same time, the opportunities for grass-roots inventors on a national level shrank significantly, as innovation shifted away from independent inventors to university-trained engineers and scientists working in corporate research laboratories.[2] Historian Thomas Hughes observes, "after World War I, industrial scientists displaced the independents as the principal locus of 'research and development activity,' the new name for invention." Hughes made a distinction between the work of "grass-roots" inventors, tinkerers with only one patent, and a "singular band of independent inventors," like Bell and Edison, whose inventions had tremendous influence on innovation. Although he declared that "the era of technological enthusiasm reached its apogee" in the 1920s, at the same time, America saw the decline of independent inventors who could profit from their patents.[3] In many ways the automobile industry was at the center of this change. Although the beginnings of the automobile were characterized by the work of independents, such as Henry Ford and Charles Kettering, by the mid-1920s

Figure 13. *American Motorist,* the magazine for the American Automobile Association, included tinkering as one of the rites of spring and standard preparation for summer vacation. "Springtime," *American Motorist,* June 1934, 4.

the future of the machine and the industry seemed to rest on the model of corporate research set forth by Alfred Sloan and General Motors.[4]

Nevertheless, the popular discourse of ingenuity thrived in the interwar period, as did tinkering with the automobile. Historian Peter Whalley has argued for a re-examination of the decline of independent or grass-roots inventors and the rise of corporate research and development laboratories after World War I to better understand the "social embeddedness of the innovation process." Independents were a diverse group, "from the person with the single invention, to the inveterate amateur, to the budding technical entrepreneur, to the professional independent inventors." They were often "self-employed, or if their primary employment was in a job where they were not rewarded for their inventions, then they fell under the rubric of 'independent.'" All began inventing to "solve a problem of which they had direct experience."[5] Although Whalley examined late twentieth-century inventors, his ideas help explain the popularity of tinkering with the automobile body in the interwar period and the desire among some tinkerers to enter the ranks of grass-roots inventors by patenting and selling their ideas.

Automobiles opened a new space in which American consumers could tinker with machinery and become grass-roots inventors. Fueling the desire to patent were patent lawyers and popular authorities who dispensed advice on the process and rewards of invention in magazines and journals. Such cultural mediators exhorted tinkerers to move their good ideas beyond the garage by sending them to the U.S. Patent Office and to some of the nation's largest manufacturers, including General Motors and Ford Motor Company. However, patent records alone do not provide an accurate picture of invention in the United States because many grass-roots inventors worked in anonymity and never patented.[6] Drawing on advice literature, patent applications, assignment records, and letters to Ford Motor Company, I sketch a picture of consumers who became grass-roots inventors, their motivations, and their struggles to profit from their modifications to the car. While popular advisors maintained the democratic nature of invention in the 1920s and 1930s, the forces of corporate capitalism defined invention and innovation quiet differently, limiting the opportunities for both grass-roots inventors and automobile consumers to initiate change from the bottom up.

Always Room for Improvement: Advice on Patents and Invention

Advice literature on invention, and in particular on the patent process, capitalized on popular enthusiasm for technology and encouraged average Americans to tinker with the mass-produced products of everyday life. This literature told consumers that they could cross the line between consumption and invention if they cultivated their powers of observation, devised simple improvements to existing machines, and patented their ideas to make them commercially valuable. Disseminated through advice manuals, magazines, and journals like *Popular Mechanics* and *Scientific American,* advice on invention taught amateurs the criteria for gaining a patent and defined grass-roots invention as democratic and simple. Advice books written and published by patent attorneys from the late nineteenth century through the interwar period followed an almost standard format offering guidance on the patent process from initial record searches to filing final claims. They also included an explanation of legal fees. In 1927, Munn & Company (the patent law firm that published *Scientific American*) reported fees that ranged from $10 to file a copyright to $125 for the total cost of patenting a mechanical device.[7] Most important, for this discussion, advice in the form of books and articles proliferated in the early twentieth century and helped define the boundaries of ingenuity.[8]

Patent advisors argued that there was always "room for improvement" in existing products, as long as would-be inventors used their powers of observation and drew on their practical experiences with technology. Simon Deutsch wrote in 1911, "Often the greatest inventions . . . are lying close by. . . . It is well to cultivate the home field first, and try to improve things with which we are most familiar, and not those of which we have only vague knowledge."[9] Advisors also encouraged inventors to improve upon existing machines and devices. Attorney Charles Labofish devoted several chapters of his advice manual to "Improvements on Improvements" and advised readers that small but valuable ideas where "always in demand."[10] Many advisors used the invention of the pencil and the hairpin as examples of "good trifling ideas" that were tremendously successful.[11] The advice remained the same throughout the 1920s. *Scientific American* instructed the "outside" inventor: "If you are seeking a field in which to exercise your talent for invention, you will be more likely to succeed if you select one about which you know something. This is especially true if your invention is an improvement or an attachment, rather than a device of a pioneer nature."[12] Most popular advice emphasized the value of improvements over new inventions. The "average" person could spend years working on complicated machinery or pursue foolish inventions such as the perpetual motion machine and never patent or earn money from the idea. Improving on existing commercial goods promised the quickest reward.

Popular advice dating to the nineteenth century lauded invention as good for both the individual and the nation. The rhetoric that praised inventors as superior lasted well into the first decades of the twentieth century and contributed to "progress talk"—the notion that technology and science have been the forces for the advancement of American society.[13] Progress infused discussions about amateur invention with the benefits of technology for the individual and for society at large. For example, one article entitled "The Mechanism of Progress: A Theory of Inventiveness" began with the idea that "Progress depends first of all on human inventiveness." The author estimated that ingenuity demanded some degree of leisure in which to "accumulate the special knowledge which may serve as the raw material for invention."[14] He might well have been describing middle-class tinkerers.

Between 1900 and 1930, a wide group of voices from patent attorneys to sociologists contended that anyone with some leisure time and a desire to acquire mechanical know-how might pursue this higher calling of becoming an inventor. In fact, advice experts exhorted tinkerers to invent as part of productive leisure. In 1929, patent attorney Adam Fisher began his advice manual with the assertion that "Invention is the basis of wealth and industry. The faculty of invention is the highest evidence of man's intelligence; it is the golden sign of his oneness with God—Inventor of the Universe." Fisher offered the idea that God could have made the world perfect, "complete and fully equipped at the outset, served by absolutely perfect machinery, methods, and equipment in every possible field of activity." If that were the case, he observed, "Man would have nothing to do except to eat and sleep and keep posted on baseball scores." Fisher insisted, "the Creator has preferred to let man 'work out his own salvation' and to compel him to gradually better his condition through the exercise of the faculty of invention."[15] The themes of social Darwinism and self-improvement ran through popular advice like Fisher's and echoed the scholarly literature on invention.

Historians and sociologists in the interwar period identified the "average" man as a potential inventor and a contributor to national progress. This rhetoric persisted into the late 1930s when corporations came to dominate patent activity.[16] For instance, in 1927 patent examiner Simon Broder asserted that "every man is a potential inventor, albeit a very humble one." He noted, "inventions that have greatly affected the world differ only in magnitude, and not in kind, from the countless ingenious departures from current practice that are daily made in the ordinary course of scheming [and] designing."[17] Social psychologists used invention as a measure of group intelligence and social potential.[18] Joseph Rossman, a social psychologist and patent examiner, evaluated the social potential of women and African Americans based on their technological ability.[19] He concluded that these groups had promise as equal contributors to society based on the evidence that they had inventors among their ranks.

This inventive discourse stated that anyone who adhered to the virtues of hard work and study could participate in the social and technological progress of the nation. However, advice experts addressed themselves primarily to the white, middle-class and largely male subscribers to popular magazines devoted to science and technology. Popular literature updated the virtues of hard work and success for a twentieth century audience and made them an integral part of the persona of the modern man.[20] Cultural mediators, such as patent attorneys and advice columnists, instructed readers that invention was not a matter of genius but rather the product of careful observation, practical experience, hard work, and the occasional lucky break. Henry Robinson, engineer and inventor, defined the steps to successful invention as built upon the moral virtues of the nineteenth century: "earnest application, constancy, self-sacrifice, frugality, temperance." He noted that these steps could help the widest possible audience become a successful inventor. "A very large number of people in and out of the mechanical profession," he wrote, "are intensely eager to know how to become successful inventors. Wealth, honor and glory are the reward of the successful."[21] These were the familiar qualities of the self-made man, popularized by Horatio Alger's stories of luck and pluck, but with the addition of mechanical ingenuity.

Although experts defined these virtues as essentially male, some advice manuals printed in the late nineteenth and early twentieth centuries, during the rise of the New Woman, admitted women to the circle of aspiring inventors.[22] Similar to the automobile stories in which women could become technological heroines, patent advice briefly included women as potential inventors. Patent attorney Joseph Minturn devoted a small section of his advice manual to women inventors in 1895 and acknowledged that few doors where open to ambitious housewives and women of leisure. Although he noted that few women had applied for patents, in comparison to men, he declared, "invention admits her to a wide field of useful employment where she is on absolute equality with men." Minturn encouraged women to patent and equated invention with the "Divine act of Creation" and the "highest type of earthly happiness."[23] A report by the Women's Bureau of the Department of Labor in 1923 illustrated that women lagged behind men all fields of invention and lacked the money, time, and facilities that were open to men.

Charles Labofish, a Washington, D.C., patent attorney, felt that invention was essentially a democratic process open to both sexes. In 1911, Labofish wrote an unusual book that couched his advice on invention within a story of "despondent youth," love, and adventure worthy of a dime novel.[24] Two of the characters were young men with limited pros-

THE STEPS BY WHICH HE IS REQUIRED TO CLIMB AND MOUNT
THAT DESIRED EMINENCE

Figure 14. Advice to grass-roots inventors emphasized nineteenth-century ideals of self-sacrifice and earnest application. "The steps by which he is required to climb and mount that desired eminence," T. M. Flemming, illustrator, in Henry Robinson, *Inventors and Inventions* (New York: privately printed, 1911), 14. From the National Museum of American History, Behring Center, Library, Smithsonian Institution, Washington, D.C.

pects for economic success. The other was a quick-witted female stenographer, Miss Sharp, who also wanted the social benefits of invention. On one hand, Miss Sharp provided the model for the woman inventor who matched the men in terms of ambition and creativity. On the other, she also acted as an incentive for the men to achieve the virtues of hard work and, for the lazy character, to make the "transition from puerility to manhood" and become a successful inventor. At the end of the story, Miss Sharp became the companionate wife and inventive partner of Mr. Swift, the more successful of the two men and nephew of the patent attorney. Much like motor travel narratives, images of independent women inventors faded from the pages of advice manuals by 1920. Although the advice stated that all Americans had access to invention, advisors equated the independent inventor with the self-made man.

Discussions of genius versus hard work centered on the "inventive faculty." The "inventive faculty" resided in the human brain and represented innate genius. Advice manuals regularly raised the question of innate genius only to refute it. Minturn, for instance, addressed the issue in a chapter entitled "Invention not Genius, but Hard Work," wherein he contended that "the inventive faculty is common to all mankind and the capacity to invent improves with effort, precisely as one may learn to play a musical instrument by continued practice." He also debunked the idea that Thomas Edison was a genius, claiming that if the "so-called" Wizard of Menlo Park had really been a genius, he would have developed the phonograph as a young boy and he wouldn't have made so many mistakes along the way. Why did Edison succeed where others failed? He worked harder and honed his mental power through practice and constant tinkering.[25]

In *How to Win a Fortune by Inventing*, Labofish argued that invention was the key to social mobility; invention allowed those with nothing but brains to capitalize on their ideas and achieve success. He wrote, "The inventive faculty is as much a part of every human being as every other faculty in the human mind."[26] In that same year, attorney Richard Owen declared emphatically, "EVERYONE IS AN INVENTOR." He defined the inventive process in the most accessible terms: "You use your brains, devise a simple little device that removes the difficulty, that enables you to do better, quicker work. . . . It happens every day."[27] All one needed to do was rely on his or her instincts and experience, and seize the opportunity.

Advice experts also made invention accessible by emphasizing that improvements were the products of keen observation of existing technologies. As Labofish told the despondent youth, "Practical inventing requires not flurried genius, but habits of calm and calculative observation." It also took, according to Labofish and other attorneys, a lawyer who could help them turn ideas into commercial property with a patent. "With a fair knowledge of the rudimentary principles of governing patents and inventions," noted Labofish, "a person of moderate temperament and studious habits has a fair chance to educe something new and . . . of intrinsic commercial value."[28]

During the interwar years, this rhetoric on the accessibility of invention remained consistent, accentuating the value of small improvements over revolutionary new technologies. Another attorney reiterated the central idea of this advice: "Possible inventions are present everywhere and in almost everything. The inventive mind is really a mind of perception, the ability to look at everything with a view to improving it or replacing it with something better." He exhorted readers to recognize their powers of observation.[29] Even into the 1930s, patent attorneys reminded Americans that anyone could be an inventor. To the question of genius, one attorney replied, "Most men are inchoate inventors and as such may hope to develop their ideas and produce devices beneficial to mankind." He confirmed that good inventions were products of "observation, attention, perception, imagination, comparison, and judgment."[30] One did not need a degree in engineering, but only the qualities of a savvy consumer. In their attempt to reach the broadest possible audience, patent attorneys like other cultural mediators reaffirmed the idea of invention as democratic terrain.

Popular histories of invention illustrated this advice with famous inventors who emerged out of humble or anonymous beginnings. These stories also established an older generation of independent inventors as role models at a time when invention and innovation shifted away from individuals to corporations.[31] *Popular Mechanics*, in a characteristic portrayal of "typical" inventors, offered an etching of Charles Goodyear vulcanizing rubber using only the cast-iron stove and washtub available in his own kitchen.[32] *Scientific American* ran several series on less well-known independent inventors, as well. In a series entitled "Inventors Who Have Achieved Commercial Success," Milton Wright asked a variety of independents how they got started. Many members of the sample used "fingertip" knowledge, while others were professional engineers. William F. Mangles, carousel inventor from Coney Island, New York, revealed that he "grew into" invention. As a young man with no capital and little education, Mangles used his spare time to "work over an invention" in his mind. Several years and numerous patents later he claimed $300,000 a year in royalties by licensing his machines to dozens of parks.[33] Mangles became an independent inventor in the nineteenth century before large corporations dominated technological innovation. Nevertheless, his story was offered a model for grass-roots inventors of a later generation who also lacked advanced education or wealth.

For the patent attorneys, advice manuals acted as national advertisements for their services. Minturn's *The Inventor's Friend* included a graphic advertisement that used the attorney's name six times.[34] Attorneys used a variety of strategies to advertise their services in the nineteenth century, including exhibition wagons that traveled to state fairs.[35] Patent attorneys in the twentieth century advertised in mass-market magazines such as *Scientific American* and *Popular Mechanics,* as well as in more specialized auto journals. In order to establish the credibility of the writer, patent manuals often warned would-be inventors of patent "sharks" or unscrupulous attorneys who wanted only to line their pockets with the dollars of naive inventors.[36] Unethical attorneys charged hopeful inventors for unnecessary record searches and patent applications for ideas that did not merit the Patent Office stamp of approval.[37] Labofish insisted, "The ultimate fate of the inventor is largely dependent upon the skill and integrity of his patent attorney."[38] Patent attorneys appealed to tinkerers' sense of ingenuity and encouraged them to patent their ideas for improving machines like the automobile.

These advisors, ethical or not, insisted that patenting was essential to profiting from a good idea. A patent conferred cultural authority by recognizing that the idea was "new, useful, and non-obvious"—the basic criteria for granting a patent.[39] In fact, a patent was the ultimate signifier of ingenuity; it awarded the holder a monopoly over their idea, device, design, or process and carried the imprimatur of the U.S. Patent Office. Minturn articulated the lofty social position of inventors: "Invention is the top round of the ladder of human attainment and the American inventor occupies that." The image that accompanied this statement underscored the nationalism inherent in much of the discussion of invention by placing Uncle Sam, as inventor, on the top rung of achievement.[40] Several decades later, A. F. Gillet, vice president of the Jubilee Manufacturing Company in Omaha, Nebraska, lauded the role of independent inventors in a speech to the Inventors Association. He claimed that no other association had the right "to any higher claim on society than our own."[41]

Cultural prestige offered one set of rewards, mostly through recognition, but many aspiring inventors also wanted to make money. One advisor cut right to the heart of many inventors' motivations in his advice manual: "One thing certain is that the invention will not pay unless it is patented."[42] And another commented that the motivations for most grass-roots inventors lay not in recognition or in the benefit of mankind, but in the possibility of wealth. He observed, "Naturally the inventor is not so anxious about how much his invention will advance civilization, or build the nation, or administer to the wants and pleasures of mankind generally as he is about how much it will net him in dollars and cents."[43] Articles in popular magazines reinforced the notion that wealth was within the grasp of home tinkerers.[44] In another typical example, *Popular Mechanics* instructed in 1925, "Don't Throw Away Your Ideas." Author Leo Parker reiterated the common wisdom that "most valuable patents have been issued on little things, experts having held that simplicity is the highest trait of genius," and therefore all ideas, even those born of hobbies and home tinkering, were worthy of patent protection. He encouraged tinkerers to ignore doubts of family and friends, because almost all great inventions had been the result of some "kindly soul tinkering around [with what] the neighbors were pleased to call a 'crazy idea.' "[45]

By the 1930s this rhetoric had acquired a harder edge. One advice manual in 1933 noted that "inventions are not made for fun, or simply for fame . . . but primarily for profit in a commercial way." The author, A. F. Gillet, assured readers that patents "offer protection to the humblest and enable them to capitalize on the fruits of their brains."[46] Popular advice in manuals and magazines, then, told amateur inventors that good ideas and simple solutions to common problems could garner fame and fortune, if they patented their ideas.

Patenting Auto Accessories

Motorists needed little encouragement to patent their home-built motor accessories. Early motor travelers had firsthand experience and ample time on the road to "observe and study" the shortcomings of automobiles, and many motorists were eager to design, patent, and profit from improvements to the car. Drivers were not only consumers; they built equipment from scratch and entered the accessory market as grass-roots inventors.[47] By patenting their modifications, tinkerers contributed to the explosion of automotive accessories in this period. The number of patents for automotive accessories, and in particular devices related to motor touring, rose sharply after 1915 as more Americans purchased automobiles and began to travel. One hundred patents for auto accessories were surveyed for this chapter.[48]

Between 1915 and 1930 hundreds of improvements and devices were invented for the automobile.[49] A decade before the first consumer surveys, patent records reveal drivers' contributions to design.[50] In addition, the area of automobile tourist accessories provided a space, outside of the workplace, in which average Americans could become innovators.[51] Many of these patents pertained to the mechanical systems of the car, such as the transmission or the ignition, or improved the safety and comfort of the car, such as bumpers, windshields, and anti-rattle devices.

Among these numerous automotive accessories, the *Patent Index* also listed touring improvements, such as auto beds, auto tents, and other devices to convert the interior of the auto for sleeping, eating, and storage. These patents for tourist accessories document motorists' intervention into the design of the car and the accessory market, and reveal a larger national discourse that encouraged ingenuity.

Inventors of tourist accessories came from the growing ranks of the white-collar workers. The patent holders studied for this chapter were not professional inventors or engineers, and they did not work in research labs or engineering departments of automobile companies or after-market parts manufacturers. They were tinkerers who invented as part of their leisure time and made little or no money from their patents. Thirty-nine of the one hundred inventors surveyed for this chapter were identified in city directories. Of these thirty-nine inventors, twenty-one (or slightly more than one-half) worked in white-collar jobs unrelated to automobile industry or accessory manufacturers. Studies of invention have often focused on the nineteenth-century shop-floor innovations and changes to industrial machinery.[52] Motorists, in contrast, provide a picture of amateur invention in the twentieth century as a largely leisure time activity.

In the 1920s, journalists extolled the variety of middle-class professions they saw on the road. The employment backgrounds of the accessory patentees fit these descriptions perfectly.[53] The occupations of the amateur inventors I surveyed ranged from clerks and secretaries to small-business owners and professionals such as doctors and dentists. For instance, Siegfried Shirek worked for a brief time as the manager of the Dinkelspiel Company, a wholesale dry goods concern in Portland, Oregon. In 1921, when he patented his combination auto bed, the Portland city directory listed him as the president of the Maxam Shirt and Garment Company. As the manager of a retail clothing firm, Shirek may have had the money to patent his idea but not the skills to build it. Therefore he worked with a carpenter named Fenton with whom he shared the patent rights. Although the sample included a handful of carpenters, one cabinetmaker and one mechanic, skilled and semi-skilled trades were limited among accessory patentees.

Designs produced by grass-roots inventors attempted to reconcile the competing desires for economy and comfort expressed by motor travelers. Inventors offered two basic designs for auto beds, one type converted the seats so they would recline and form beds; the other added cots or stretcher beds that could be laid over the interior seats or extended from the running board. Both of these designs sought to use the car as a sleeping compartment, thus eliminating the need for a tent or the disagreeable option of sleeping on the ground. These designs

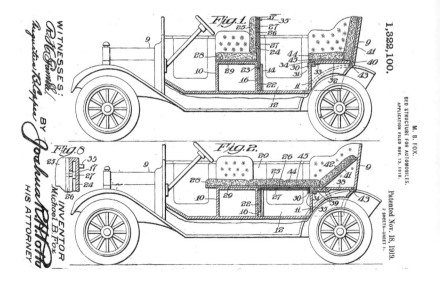

Figure 15. Patent by Michael Fox for an auto bed demonstrated a common modification among drivers who wanted to sleep in their touring cars. This ingenious conversion resembled convertible parlor furniture and railroad sleeping cars of the nineteenth century. Patent Record, M. B. Fox, Bed Structure for Automobile, 18 November 1919. Patent 1,322,100, U.S. Patent Office.

also seemed more efficient than camping outside the car because they eliminated the work of unpacking and setting up a tent, enhancing the feeling of individual freedom associated with motor travel.

Convertible designs lightened the tourist's load and sped the process of making camp by using the upholstered seats of the car as a mattress. For example, Michael Fox's patent showed reclining upholstered seats that were similar to the seats in a railroad sleeping car.[54] However, convertible seats required serious modification of the automobile and some mechanical skill; the seats could not be sold in stores. The driver, often with the help of a carpenter or mechanic, had to take apart the seats and reconstruct them to form a flat bed. This usually meant sawing in two the supports for the seats and then hinging them so they would recline.[55] One observer commented that "the desire of many motorists occasionally to sleep in their cars has brought to custom shops numerous jobs. . . . In camping sections of the country, these conversions sometimes attain a considerable volume of business."[56] Nonetheless, these patents had a limited market. It is difficult to determine how many individual travelers converted their cars into sleepers using this method, but about half the patents submitted for automobile beds used the seats as a foundation.[57]

Inventors of stretcher beds, on the other hand, claimed that their designs were superior because they eliminated the "mutilation" of the automobile's seats, thus protecting one's investment in the automobile.[58] Stretcher beds or cots were formed from a piece of canvas drawn tight over a frame. The frame was then laid on top of the seatbacks, creating a bridge between the front and rear seat and a level plane on which to sleep.[59] No other interior modifications were needed. One patentee wrote that he had invented "a bed that may be mounted within an automobile . . . where comfortable and stable sleeping accommodations may be provided without disarranging any portion of the car or its contents."[60] With a growing market for used automobiles in the mid-1920s, tinkerers who planned to resell their cars built stretcher beds to preserve the integrity of the automobile interior.

The final common design was for spring beds, which extended from an exterior point on the automobile (usually the running boards or back end), and combined with tents to preserve the privacy of sleeping motorists. As one patentee wrote, "The objective of my invention . . . is to provide a bed which will be roomy and comfortable and will be thoroughly protected by the car top from the weather."[61] Herrick Cole's 1917 design for a folding automobile bed featured a canvas tent that offered ventilation but also covered the bed completely. A year later, Otis Cook of Fort Dodge, Iowa, patented a much more elaborate version of the exterior attachment. His apparatus used the automobile as the center support for a canvas tent that completely covered the sleeping tourists and the car. Cook explained that his design allowed the beds to be "suspended above the ground by the body of the automobile and the supporting structure of the tent."[62] The tent provided tourists with fresh air, yet screened them from the elements and the prying eyes of fellow travelers. All these designs for sleeping equipment addressed consumers' demand for privacy.[63]

Faced with the spatial limitations of the car, grass-roots auto inventors tried to make their designs as multifunctional as possible. Interested in comfort and efficiency, they tried to utilize every inch of space on the car. For instance, inventors James and Elma Kippen, a husband-and-wife team, created a convertible automobile body that offered not only a bed but also extra storage space.[64] Inventors, in general, aimed to make touring accessories dual-purpose and interchangeable. Samuel Donnell of Seattle, for instance, patented an attachment that could "be used either as a bed or as a dining table and connected to the vehicle so as to be folded when unemployed." Thus, Donnell answered the need for equipment that solved several problems.[65]

As in travel advice literature, explanations of accessory designs highlighted efficiency and convertibility. Compactness was greatly valued.

Elvira Fischer wrote that her auto bed "folded into such a small compass that it may be easily carried in the tool compartment."[66] Charles Putnam wanted to give tourists a device that furnished "the maximum overhead room and the greatest degree of comfort with the smallest amount of labor."[67] Inventor Marjorie Steel said it best, however, when she described her patent for convertible beds as "convenient and comfortable." She stated, "a folding seat and bed structure of my improved construction possesses superior advantages in point of simplicity, durability and general efficiency and affords comfort and convenience to persons driving their cars on extended trips or tours."[68] Grass-roots inventors promised that their motor equipment would lower the cost of travel and improve the lives of travelers.[69]

After receiving a patent, inventors had to figure out how to make it pay. Advice experts offered much guidance on this issue, coaching amateurs on how to market their newly patented designs. Milton Wright at *Scientific American* wrote that the critical question for new inventors was: "Can it be sold?"[70] Patent holders could do one of several things to profit from a patent: form a company to manufacture and sell the device; sell or assign the rights outright; license the rights to a manufacturer and sell on a royalty basis; or contract with a manufacturer to produce the accessory in lots and then sell the finished product through a store, a traveling salesman or advertisements in magazines and newspapers.[71] Of these, forming a company to manufacture was certainly the most challenging, especially for grass-roots inventors who often lacked financial and business resources. The most direct and least expensive strategy for the patentee was selling the patent outright. Advice expert Adam Fisher advised patentees in 1929 that if they could not manufacture the item themselves "there remains but one other thing . . . , and that is to sell his invention outright for cash or to place it on a royalty basis." He observed, "We have finally arrived at that knottiest of all problems for the inventor: just how to sell his invention."[72] Fisher was right; selling took work and the "business sense" to find the right buyer and convince them of the market potential for the patented device.

In the case of amateur auto accessory inventors, very few assigned their patents, sold their products, or profited from their ideas. They invented during their leisure time and lacked the industrial connections and business skill to make a profit. A small number of auto bed inventors (roughly 15 percent) in my survey assigned or sold their patents to manufacturers.[73] The majority of these patentees assigned at the time of application to accessory companies that made autocamping equipment, such as the Tento Bed Company of Chicago, the Handy Auto Bed Company of Oregon, and the Auto Bed Camp Company in Kansas City, Missouri. In fact, the Auto Bed Camp Company occasionally featured

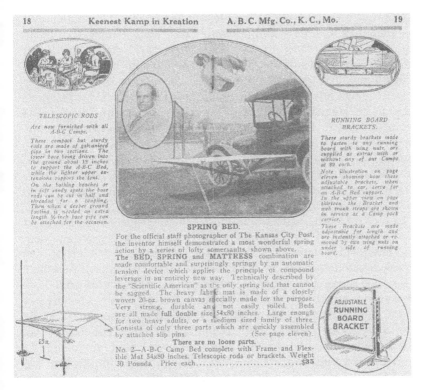

Figure 16. The ABC Manufacturing Company, which manufactured and sold touring equipment, celebrated the ingenuity of the grass-roots inventor and encouraged other home tinkerers in their efforts to patent and market their modifications to the car. "Keenest Kamp in Kreation," ABC Manufacturing Company, Kansas City, Missouri, Trade Catalog, 1922. From the Collections of The Henry Ford (G3793).

inventors and their patented auto accessories in their trade catalog.[74] Other inventors sold their ideas after applying for a patent. Clifford Aldrich, an architect, offered one of the best examples. A month before Aldrich received his patent he sold his idea to Joseph Wittman, owner of the Auto Bed Company. Aldrich did not make much money from the initial assignment, however. He sold his rights to the patent for one dollar and any profits from the sale of the product. Some inventors, but not many, did quite well financially. Lonza Windsor, for instance, sold his patent for a foldable tourist bed to one Charles August Wingblade of Fort Scott, Kansas, for $500, and Lester Ike parceled out his patent to several of his neighbors in Nebraska for $250 a share. However, there was no evidence that either bed was ever manufactured.

Only one inventor from my sample assigned his idea to an automobile manufacturer. Claude Eaton, a doctor from Flint, Michigan, sold his auto bed to the Inland Automobile Company of Indiana. For a year prior to receiving his patent, Eaton ran his own auto bed company out of his home. The venture attracted the attention of Inland and convinced them to buy the patent in 1922. Eaton then returned to his medical practice. He maintained partial interest in the patent, however, and five years later, he brought suit against the Inland Auto Company, winning back full rights to the patent. His future profits were cut short, though, when he died in 1928, only twelve months after winning the suit. Eaton's lawsuit was unique among this group of grass-roots inventors; most never assigned their patents, much less sued for infringement or repossession of rights.

Eaton's earlier home-based business, however, represented a strategy shared by some of his contemporaries. A few auto-bed inventors went into business for themselves, selling to a local market. The majority of accessory patentees were concentrated in the Western states, where high rates of car ownership and motor tourism made selling accessories possible and potentially profitable.[75] Inventor Burton Haney sold his patented auto beds from his home in Portland, Oregon. In 1926, he advertised his auto bed in the Portland city directory. For the price of $10 and the assurance that the Haney bed was "made for comfort," tourists could sleep in their car while visiting the northwest coast. Sigfried Miller, a foreman from Oakland, California, also started his own auto-bed business in that city in 1918. He advertised in the Oakland city directory until he went out of business in 1933. John M. Line, as well, sold his beds at his grocery store in Springfield, Missouri. Prior to receiving his patent, Line broadened his search for customers and bought advertising space in *Field and Stream* in May 1921 (see Figure 6). His hand-drawn advertisement illustrated the versatility of the auto bed. The text declared the bed to be comfortable, lightweight, and small, and instructed interested parties to "see your dealer" or write to Line personally in Missouri.[76]

Advertising in mass-market magazines provided a way for amateur inventors to reach a national market.[77] Magazines that promoted motor touring reviewed new accessories and provided advertising for various patented goods. *Field and Stream* reviewed new equipment, carried advertisements from large and small firms, and published comments and questions from readers.[78] *Outing* magazine collaborated with small manufacturers by providing direct advertising through their "Service Honor Roll." The magazine published a list of branded products and assured potential buyers that the products had been "tested and approved by *Outing*."[79] Drivers were also invited to contribute their ideas and innovations to the journals. However, as reflected by the less than 15 percent of the total patentees surveyed actually assigning, advertising, or selling their auto beds, profiting from patents for auto accessories proved difficult for amateur inventors.

Appeals to Large Manufacturers: Sales Letters to Ford Motor Company

Patent attorneys strongly advised new patentees to contact manufacturers directly as one of the easiest, cheapest, and most important steps in promoting their patents. This strategy was intended to supplement other efforts such as advertising in magazines and journals. Most advice manuals contained specific directions on how to choose appropriate manufacturers and how to compose a winning sales letter. In 1911, attorney George Kimmel simplified sales strategies for patents by boiling them down to two methods of procedure: personal solicitation and personal correspondence with manufacturers.[80]

Twenty years later, this advice had changed little. Adam Fisher's *Plain Talk* stated that inventors should target manufacturers near their home because they could follow up the letter with a demonstration (personal solicitation). He also urged inventors to select manufacturers that made products similar to the patented object.[81] If this failed, he advised inventors to contact larger corporations, securing the names of these companies from trade journals and standard business directories.[82] By the 1930s, patent advisors like Raymond Yates stressed the importance of finding the right manufacturer, assuming that few grass-roots inventors had the means to manufacturer their own products. "There are many inventors, so called," wrote Yates, "who think that any manufacturer, merely because he is a manufacturer will be interested in their inventions. . . . Hundreds of inventions die a sad death merely because their exploitation was bad and the inventions were not brought to the attention of the right people."[83] For instance, Yates advised patentees of automobile inventions not to "write to Mr. Alfred Sloan, President of General Motors, concerning a new gadget for automobiles." Rather, he directed them to General Motor's New Devices Committee, which considered letters from outside inventors and users who had patented and unpatented ideas to sell.[84]

Aspiring inventors followed this advice and sent thousands of letters to General Motors and to Ford Motor Company, which by 1920 produced three-quarters of all the automobiles sold in the United States.[85] Charles Kettering, head of research at General Motors and a one-time independent inventor himself, received what he described as a daily flow of letters from tinkerers inevitably beginning with the phrase: "I have an idea!" In 1933, Kettering noted it seemed "that over half the inventors introduce themselves in this fashion and unwittingly, perhaps, they are giving the manufacturer insight into what to expect."[86] Recognizing that the input of amateur inventors could result in new ideas, good public relations, and give the manufacturer a window into what consumers wanted, Alfred Sloan established the New Devices Committee in 1925.[87] With an eye toward public relations, Sloan wrote: "It is most important that the Corporation get the reputation of dealing sympathetically, as well as constructively, with new ideas and developments."[88] In the first few years of its existence the committee advertised in newspapers and openly solicited ideas. In 1926, *Automotive Industries* endorsed the New Devices Committee as proof that the automotive industry gave amateur inventors a "fair shake."[89] Whether inventors agreed with this statement was unclear.[90]

Ford Motor Company, with its universal car and populist founder, also received innumerable letters from users and aspiring inventors alike hoping for the same fair consideration of their ideas. Historian Reynold M. Wik has claimed that Ford owners sent almost one hundred letters a day to Henry Ford and the Ford Motor Company during the height of the Model T's production, between 1920 and 1927.[91] Wik has detailed the popularity of Henry Ford and his status as a folk hero in the 1920s among rural Americans.[92] Ford Motor Company used a range of mass-market media, from newspapers and magazines to films, to promote the Model T as everyman's car and the folksy image of its creator Henry Ford.

Ford's popularity was part of a larger age of celebrity and personal-ity.[93] Skillful use of the media helped make Ford a household name and he traded on his image as honest, fair-dealing, common man, someone who understood rural Americans. But his appeal was much broader. As self-made millionaire, he found fame among Americans from many regions and classes who wanted a square deal and who admired ingenu-ity. The press may have portrayed Ford as a country rube, but he and his staff knew how to use the media. A short-lived bid for the presidency of the United States in 1923 for the 1924 election and a spate of articles and books about his life, including the publication of his ghostwritten autobiography *My Life and Work* in 1922, cemented his status as a national personality.[94]

In the 1920s, hundreds of tinkerers wrote to Ford to sell their acces-sory ideas. After all, he was an independent inventor who had made good; many writers reasoned that he would treat them fairly. For instance, B. H. Snape sent Ford a letter in 1928 offering his patent for a running-board luggage rack. Although Snape had never owned a car and admitted he could not drive, he said he was "forcibly struck with the need of some means of transporting hand baggage upon a car. "I notice hundreds, I might say thousands of cars this last summer . . . with all kinds of makeshift racks on the running board piled with baggage." So he developed a "neat-looking" rack and offered it to Ford because he believed "I could expect a straight and honest courtesy by applying to you . . . instead of some of the smaller companies and accessory people."[95] Similarly, Dr. Charles Boyd, an osteopath in Long Beach, California, sent his idea for an improved bumper to Ford Motor Company with a note saying, "After having known somewhat of your business principles. I am sure that you would say: If we had anything better, we would have it on the market." Boyd admitted that although he had a wonderful new concept for bumpers he was "not in a position to experiment, manufacture or market this idea." He proposed that Ford take the idea, experiment and get the patents, and "give me a royaly [sic] that you would consider fair."[96]

Others, like Frank Beach, an unemployed accountant in Tampa, Florida, wanted to hold Ford to his honest reputation. Beach said he had worked out a heating system for the car in 1903, while still in grade school, and had sent a letter to Henry Ford sharing his idea after the development of the Model T. The company had sent him a rejection letter. But according to Beach, Ford had adopted the heating system. He wanted Mr. Ford to compensate him for his idea or give him a job. Like many writers, Beach felt a personal connection to the manufacturer. "Why should I have a hard time getting by when I can think of ideas that you can use to make you rich," he reasoned. "Why can't I go on thinking of ideas in your factory. Can you help me get to Detroit and get into your factory. I am not a fanatic or a nut but I need help right now. I gave you an idea solely to help you. [Now] I need help so lets go."[97] This kind of personal appeal reflected Ford's stature as a public personality in the 1920s.

Letters containing ideas for improving the Model T did not reach Henry Ford, however; they were forwarded to and answered by the staff of the Experimental Engineering Department. The engineering department at Ford had a reputation for being less bureaucratic and less systematic than its counterpart at General Motors, and Henry Ford remained head of the department into the early 1930s.[98] The company kept the letters from inventors and consumers, and the correspondence often had notations from members of the engineering staff that indicated they recorded what the public wanted in terms of design changes. Between 1923 and 1928, the period covered by the engineering correspondence files, Ford lost business to the inexpensive and more completely appointed Chevrolet. The company made some design changes in this period to address the sparse design of the Model T, and these improvements culminated in the conversion to the Model A in 1927.

The engineering correspondence provides insight into the fluid definitions of consumer and amateur inventor in this period because many
of the writers identified themselves as long-time Ford customers who
based their improvements on their experience as drivers. Most important, the letters offer a glimpse of the conversations between amateur
inventors and engineers at one of the world's largest auto manufacturers.

The engineers at Ford Motor Company received letters from a range
of people selling automotive accessories. These included patent lawyers
writing on the behalf of clients and manufacturers who wanted Ford to
adopt their products as standard equipment.[99] However, much of the
mail came from consumers, tinkerers, and grass-roots inventors with patented and unpatented ideas.[100] This group of amateur inventors shared
the class and gender characteristics of the auto-bed and tourist accessory
patentees. Most were men, although a small percentage of women also
sent letters. Out of the two hundred letters sampled from the Ford Engineering Department files, only sixteen were from women, two of whom
held patents. Writers hailed from all over the United States and lived in
cities as well as rural areas. Of the eighty writers who identified their
occupation, the majority were white-collar workers outside of the automobile industry. In addition, some identified themselves as having
ample leisure time owing to unemployment or imprisonment. Four writers declared themselves to be full-time inventors. Although some writers
did not own cars, this was rare. Finally, like consumers who wrote simply
sharing ideas or complaining about defects in the Model T, grass-roots
inventors claimed that their inventions grew out of direct experience
with the automobile as consumers.

Following the advice by patent attorneys, writers often explained that
first-hand observation led them to design improvements to the automobile.[101] Inventors like M. A. Zielinski, a tailor from Trenton, New Jersey,
included personal stories of driving and problem solving in their letters.
Zielinski wrote to Ford Motor Company in October 1926 promoting his
patented gasoline gauge. Adopting the language of advice manuals, he
noted that the design was simple. He also explained why a tailor would
invent a gasoline gauge. "It may be surprising to you as you see my letter
head that a tailor should worry about a gasoline gauge for motor cars.
As a Ford owner my carborator [sic] went wrong and I used ten gallons
of gasoline [over] ninety miles, it was dark and I was stuck many miles
from any gasoline station. From that time I have been wondering why
some one did not invent a gauge for a Ford car. That is why I made
one."[102] A representative of the engineering department answered Zielinski's letter, saying that the department had received multiple patents

for gas gauges and that they were considering adding a gauge to the Model T.[103]

Amateur inventors also appropriated the language of advertising, describing their improvements as convenient, inexpensive, and commercially appealing. Some inventors like D. J. Carrell, manager at Kate and I Candy Supply Company in Bay City, Michigan, noted that the process of invention was easy. He wrote: "The idea came to me in a simple way as all good inventions do."[104] Others described their inventions in terms of the therapeutic ideology of modern advertising: convenience.[105] New goods promised to make various aspects of modern life easier and less complex. Auto accessories were among these new conveniences, and their inventors hoped to convince manufacturers and consumers that they would make driving easier. One inventor asked Ford engineers to "please note the simplicity" of his signal device.[106] Another from of Los Angeles depicted his convertible tourist bumper as "compact and easy to operate," and as having great appeal to "tourists, the owners of cars without garages, and laborers whose cars are exposed to all kinds of weather."[107] A tinkerer from Seattle called his oil gauge "very simple and rugged," and an oil drilling contractor from Smackover, Arkansas, described his antiglare windshield was "very simple" and could be mounted in "four seconds or less."[108]

Some accessories defied simplicity. Yet, lacking other rationale for their usefulness, inventors adhered to this explanation of utility. J. C. Long, who worked as a general building contractor in Charleston, South Carolina, designed and patented a device that operated the automobile's horn from a button on the clutch pedal on the floor of the car. The convenience of this device begged explanation, and Long noted, "in such a position that the horn can be blown by simply extending the toe forward," thus allowing the driver to keep both hands on the wheel.[109] Ford engineers were not impressed and rejected the device as impractical. As if in response to Long's patented device, another driver commented, "I know all the little fool devices any one patents are sent to you asking consideration." He described his own signal device as truly ingenious and useful: "the intelligence of mine is inside and very simple to be so effective." He claimed that other accessories were used only occasionally but his signal was "used at every turn."[110]

Many solicitors hoped for the simplest path to profit, the outright sale of their patents. Grass-roots inventors put the lessons of advice literature to work and asked Ford Motor Company for various forms of compensation. Inventor Vera Wells wrote to Ford in 1924 asking whether the company would purchase her patent outright or "take it up on a Royalty basis." She hoped Ford engineers would let her "know at once and we can then get at particulars." Following the advice of experts, her letter was brief and to the point.[111] Ralph Simmons assured Ford that his compensation for allowing the company to use his signal patent would be small, and he was ready to give a demonstration of the accessory to the Ford agent in Pittsburgh at any time.[112] Some writers who were down on their luck asked Ford for new cars. In 1928, Riea Krug offered her patent for an electric clothing brush for cars and explained, "I am a [tenant] farmer's wife with limited means, so any thing you can do will be greatly appreciated.[113] Another correspondent wrote, "If you buy the patents, I expect to use a part of the money that I receive to pay for a new Ford," thus allowing Ford to benefit in two ways. He was reluctant to share the drawings for the patent, which had not been filed at the time he posted the letter in 1926, because "someone may try to get ahead of me."[114]

Some small inventors were wary of revealing their ideas to Ford without a firm commitment on part of the company. Typical of some letters, Edward O'Donnell, of Brooklyn, refused to share even the name of his accessory but emphasized that it would "save the people of the United States millions of dollars every year at practically no expense." He noted, "This thing is so simple a way that I dare not tell as it could be universally practiced immediately and I would get no benefits."[115] These writers trusted Henry Ford over the staff in his engineering department, addressing their letters to him directly. Rudolf Weirup began his letter to Henry Ford with the declaration, "I am an inventor," and assured Ford that his accessory was "a paying proposition, so if I can make a bargain with you let me know." In a more formal letter, a tinkerer from Newark, New Jersey, wrote to Henry Ford after submitting his idea for an "improved automobile seat" to the Lincoln Motor Company, a division of Ford. Lincoln had replied positively asking for blueprints and specifications, but he remained wary of the engineers at Lincoln. He told Mr. Ford, "I do not think it would be safe for me with no protection to submit the same to the Engineering Department. As I do not think all men are as honest as Henry Ford."[116] The worry that manufacturers might take ideas without paying for them illustrated amateurs' fears that they were at a disadvantage when dealing with large corporations. Indeed, by the mid-1920s, amateur inventors of both genders faced multiple challenges in patenting and marketing their ideas.

Women, in particular, encountered greater obstacles to inventing and marketing improvements to the automobile than did their male counterparts. Even though auto-touring experts portrayed motoring as an activity shared by men and women, when it came to modifying the car, women were seen as less innovative. In 1923, a survey of women inventors addressed what Mary Anderson, director of the Women's Bureau of the Department of Labor, called a "widespread unbelief in women's inventive ability."[117] The writers of the report emphasized women's contributions to transportation and noted the "increasing share taken by women in the operation of motor cars." Despite the growing numbers of women drivers, however, women submitted far fewer automotive inventions to the U.S. Patent Office than did men in 1923. Anderson attacked structural inequalities in the patent system and women's confinement in the home as reasons for the lack of recognized ingenuity on the part of women. The bureau's report observed that "woman's work keeps her in the home, or even if she is a 'woman in industry,' she has not the freedom of movement in the world of business that is accorded a man. As a result, materials and facilities for making or securing models and sketches essential in patenting inventions are not accessible to women as to men." Facilities referred to "the materials, the tools, and the makers of sketches and models"—the vehicles of technological communication and knowledge.[118] Men, even those outside of industry, noted the report, came into contact with or understood how to hire patent attorneys, model makers, and draftsmen. Women by contrast, did not have access to the same technical and social network that facilitated patenting.[119]

Letters to the Ford Motor Company from women revealed their lack of resources to patent, much less manufacture the products they devised. In 1923, Addie Pickard wrote to Henry Ford hoping he would buy her unpatented ideas for improving the Model T. For women amateurs like Pickard, the sales letter offered an inexpensive way of pursuing a market for their ideas. Pickard, who had driven "a Henry" for eight years, wrote that she had "worked out two or three little improvements" but did not wish to "go to the expense of patenting." Without disclosing the nature of the improvements, she asked Ford to suggest a plan and noted that she was sure they would be of use to Ford and the "expense to you of adding them would be practically nothing."[120] Bertha P'Diamond also wrote to the company saying that she had "designed and developed in new materials a set of clear . . . side curtains for open touring cars and trucks." These, she wrote were practical, serviceable, and "of splendid appearance." However, like many women inventors, she did not have the financial resources to patent or manufacture. Diamond continued: "As I have not the capital to either patent or market same, would be willing to submit my design for your approval. If you would not care to purchase, would you guarantee not to use or reveal to others my idea?" She added, "you are the only manufacturer whom I would care to submit an unpatented design."[121]

However, women were not the only amateurs who lacked the money to patent, build, or advertise their ideas in a competitive way by the 1920s. The Women's Bureau concluded that average inventors lacked the finances to patent or to develop their patent to the point where they could sell the items themselves or market them to manufacturers. The report concluded, "These circumstances have wrecked the dreams of wealth of thousands of inventors, both men and women."[122] Many male inventors recognized that they could not compete with large manufacturers and corporations. Joseph A. Conroy admitted in his letter to Ford Motor Company that he lacked the resources to develop his swinging light for the automobile and hoped the company would test it for him. "I know that you have skilled engineers and experts who could work out this thing to a better advantage than I could," noted Conroy in 1923. "If I had the money I would go at this thing myself and see it through, but as I am unable, I am sending this sketch and letter to you and if you see fit that it is worth to give it a trial." He also expected Ford to pay him if the idea worked, and wrote, "You being a big broad-minded man I know will not forget me if it be a success."[123] Other letter writers reiterated this request. One asked if Ford could test his device, an electric vaporizer, and then give him advice on how to market it. "You have trained electrical engineers with adequate facilities for determining the facts and I should like to have the merits of the device passed upon by technicians competent to judge."[124] This potential inventor believed he had a good idea worth a patent, but knew he could not compete with Ford.

Even trained mechanics confessed that they could not develop their inventions without the help of a manufacturer. A mechanic at the Punta Alegra Sugar Company in San Juan, Cuba wrote to Ford Motor Company hoping that the engineers at Ford would help him work out his invention. He acknowledged, "your engineers are better posted on cars than I," and he sent sketches for his improved, inexpensive auto to the company asking for advice on its development.[125] Others wrote that they had skill but no money. William Bassett concluded his offer of an un-named improvement with the statement that he was "just an old New England body maker with more skill than money," and inquired if Edsel Ford would help him develop the idea because "everyone knows your company is doing what is right by one and all."[126]

Large manufacturers like Ford offered little help to amateur inventors. Ford engineers promptly and politely rejected the majority of outside accessory designs, whether patented or not. In the early 1920s, staff in the Experimental Engineering Department wrote individual responses to each letter. Some of these letters offered a modicum of encouragement to amateur inventors. For instance, Rudolph Weirup, who declared himself an inventor, received a response from Ford Motor Company asking him to "voluntarily submit drawings and specifications" for his unnamed accessory.[127] The letter informed Weirup, that the company would take all ideas into consideration. Another inventor and Edison phonograph salesman wrote to sell his specialty platform for Ford Coupes that carried Edison phonographs and anything weighing less than 500 pounds. The salesman thought Mr. Ford might be interested in his device since Ford and Edison were "closely connected as friends." He received a reply from the editor of *Ford News*, the company newspaper. *Ford News* would publish his photos and this might lead to some inquiries or sales prospects.[128]

The great majority of accessory ideas, however, were rejected by W. T. Fishleigh, engineer at Ford, and the staff at Experimental Engineering. Replies often stated that Ford's policy was to "leave to the individual car owner the selection of all special equipment."[129] The engineers commented that many of these ideas were not new to them and that if they were to incorporate such accessories, like trunks, beds, or signals, as standard equipment, they would use designs of their own.[130] Responses from the engineering department evolved over time into a didactic summary of why the Ford Motor Company considered some "conveniences" to be after-market accessories and therefore inappropriate for standard production. Responding to a Mrs. H. A. Stalker, who suggested that it would be a "fine thing if an electric percolator" and hot-plate could be attached to the battery of Ford cars, C. H. Foster explained that most "automobiles now in common use are not of sufficient capacity to operate a percolator and hot plate, and a generator of sufficient capacity for this work would not be practical for automobile equipment, although we quite agree with you that it would be a great convenience from the tourist's standpoint."[131] In 1923, Fishleigh replied to a letter from Einar Lund, noting that Lund's idea for a front seat that would convert into a bed was "not new to us. However, we would not be interested in consideration of the same as the demand for a body of this type would not be sufficient to warrant its manufacture in Ford production quantities."[132] Ford Motor Company would leave beds to the aftermarket specialty companies or to the few small auto manufacturers who incorporated convertible seats in their touring cars.

By 1928, after the Model T had gone out of production, the engineering department developed a more standardized response to grass-roots improvements. These letters emphasized the Fordist principles of mass production; to maintain efficiency and low prices, the company could not incorporate "special designs or equipment." The reply instructed, "It is only by standardization upon certain well-tried and generally approved features that the Ford Motor Company is able to give such great value per dollar in its various products."[133] With these considerations in mind, the engineering staff reasoned that they would determine which designs were the most efficient, thus effectively shutting out amateur inventors who might understand the design of the automobile body based on experience, but could not understand the relationship between design and the process of mass-production.

Some amateur inventors did not accept rejection easily. With the encouragement of advice experts, amateurs sometimes wrote a second or third letter challenging the engineering staff's rejections. In a particularly lengthy rebuttal, Norman Wood, a feisty inventor from Miami, wrote to Fishleigh in 1928 after Ford Motor Company rejected his turn signal. Wood felt the company had turned down his "proposition with undue haste in that you have not given it enough consideration." He continued: "You do not even know what it is as yet but regret to advise that it is not interesting. Now, if I did not know that it is interesting, I most assuredly would not have put it up [to] the largest manufacturers in the world." He assured Fishleigh that the signal would it be "required on all cars by law" shortly. He refused to describe its revolutionary aspects fully, however. This was a matter of "self-protection," said Wood; "you are an ingineer [sic] and in lots of instances it only takes a hint to get you started toward perfecting ideas."[134] Wood concluded that he would not bother the company further but advised them that they should take "a hard-headed" look at his idea because it could earn Ford millions of dollars.

Advice literature addressed the trend toward corporate control of invention and innovation, but continued to champion amateurs' creativity and experiential knowledge. As early as 1911, patent attorney Labofish lectured his readers not to despair if they received rejection letters from manufacturers when trying to market their ideas. "Every manufacturer," he wrote, "thinks his product is as good as it can be made and has a lively disdain for improvements made by anyone but his own factory experts. Experience shows that outsiders make the best improvements, and the manufacturer knows it."[135] Writers for *Popular Mechanics* and *Scientific American* insisted that the best, most creative ideas originated outside of the corporate research lab.[136] A 1929 article in *Scientific American* stressed that corporations simply did not know what consumers wanted; only users could offer valuable improvements. Therefore, the writer noted, corporations should cooperate with outside inventors.[137]

Advice experts repeatedly advocated for the firsthand knowledge and ingenuity of "outside" inventors over the specialized training of engineers in part because they made their living from amateur inventions. Attorney Raymond Francis Yates assured grass-roots inventors in 1934 that they still had a vital role to play in the development of consumer technologies: "The men in the research department and engineering offices are usually men of wide experience and can give very sound technical advice but unfortunately they are not imaginative." Unlike the amateur inventor, noted Yates, engineers "cannot dream dreams. They cannot understand anything beyond cold facts and still colder figures. Their opinion, in general, of a market for a new article would be pathetic because it would be arrived at by more or less scientific means."[138] This advice may have boosted the spirits of grass-roots inventors, but it seemed to have little effect on improving the commercial opportunities of inventors who were seen as "outsiders" by industry.

Like Ford, General Motors refused the great majority, if not all, of the outside inventions sent to the New Devices Committee, which became the butt of internal company jokes about the number of useless ideas sent in by users. In a vaudeville act at the General Motor Executive Convention in 1934, a two-man comedy team noted that the New Devices Committee should be renamed "The We Thought of That a Long Time Ago Committee." This comment incited banter over the unbelievably large number of ideas that were discarded. One actor commented, "We made a thorough investigation of 18,946,802 ideas last year." His partner asked, "How many ideas DID you accept?" The reply: "Two."[139] Even Charles Kettering complained of the overwhelming numbers of untested and simply bad ideas sent to the committee. Kettering confirmed that only about one out of every five thousand ideas sent in by individuals was practicable and potentially profitable. "What would companies do if they depended entirely on outside ideas for progress?" asked Kettering. "Progress would be slow, products less desirable, and profits small." Both Kettering and head of the committee, Harry Dumville, maintained that even if an amateur had a good idea, he could not compete with research labs. "When an inventor presents an idea, the manufacturer knows, unless it is already on the market, that it is in all probability as far from being a commercially practicable device as New York is from Los Angeles," wrote Boss Kettering.[140]

*   *   *

Advice literature and a wide discourse on ingenuity encouraged tinkerers to engage in a more formalized process of invention by patenting and marketing their improvements to the automobile. Advice experts promoted the idea that consumers could become grass-roots inventors through a process of hard work and keen observation, drawing on their own experiences as users and the expertise of patent lawyers. Although Americans who became amateur inventors gained patents for automobile accessories, they met stiff resistance from the automotive industry in trying to sell their ideas for standard production and were limited to marketing their ideas through aftermarket manufacturers or placing their own ads in magazines and local news sources. To enter the market-place of accessories they had to rely on their own limited resources.

In the 1930s, patents for automobile accessories declined and grass-roots inventors faced an even more difficult path in patenting and pro-moting their ideas due to the Depression, incorporation of more acces-sories into the standard equipment of the automobile, and shifting authority over design that privileged corporate engineers and designers as leaders of innovation. The landscape of invention and innovation changed during the interwar period, and amateurs found themselves at a disadvantage in competition with engineers and trained designers.[141] As Waldemar Kaempffert observed, "The hired inventors and research engineers have at their command resources of which the outsider is hardly cognizant, the splendidly equipped libraries, experimental appa-ratus, patent lawyers to guide them, time and money." He lamented, "Compelled to compete with organized research . . . the outside 'heroic' inventor who worked picturesquely and alone in a garret is disap-pearing."[142]

One grass-roots inventor, Earl S. Tupper, might deserve the label "heroic" for his eight-year effort to patent and sell an automotive acces-sory during the Great Depression. Tupper embraced the technological enthusiasm of the early twentieth century and followed the advice of cul-tural mediators, hoping to earn a fortune by improving the automobile. Beginning as a self-educated tinkerer and eventually becoming an indus-trial designer, Tupper's early work in the 1930s bridged the nineteenth-century idea of the democratic invention and the modern necessity of working within the corporate structure.

Chapter 4

A Tinkerer's Story

Earl Silas Tupper represents one grass-roots inventor who embraced the prolific advice literature on the importance of individual inventors and the profitability of patents during the Great Depression.[1] Tupper, creator of the famous plastic containers that bear his name, was an avid tinkerer who began his inventive career by patenting and promoting an automobile accessory. In the 1930s, a young Earl Tupper tinkered with the design of numerous consumer novelties ranging from hairpins and permanently creased dress pants to a streamlined sled.[2] While many of these were fleeting ideas, he promoted some quite vigorously. Tupper kept detailed diaries and notes of his daily activities between 1933 and 1937, and these documents reveal the intense efforts of one consumer-turned-amateur inventor to heed popular advice on invention, to emulate an older generation of independent inventors, and to successfully market his automotive improvements for profit.

Even as the design of the automobile became more complete in the 1930s and university-trained engineers and designers took greater control of technological innovations in the car, Tupper proved that tinkerers still saw the automobile as a fertile field for improvement. Tupper focused his efforts on patenting and marketing a collapsible top for rumble seats, which he dubbed the Clipper Rumble-Top. The rumble-seat top embodied Tupper's hopes for gaining fame and fortune from invention. His writings reflect the widely held belief in the democratic nature of invention. Like many inventors, he hoped his patents would provide the capital on which to build personal financial security.

For Tupper, invention provided the key to individual success. Although Tupper wrote about the humanitarian benefits of invention, the bulk of his diary entries reflected his more immediate worries about money and his goal of improving his own material circumstances through patenting and selling his ideas. Popular advice encouraged tinkerers like Tupper to model themselves on inventor-heroes of previous generations and to use their own experience to redesign existing machines. A devoted student of popular magazine stories about invention, Tupper embodied what historian Brooke Hindle has called the process of emulation, an empirical approach to invention in the nineteenth century that relied on "fingertip knowledge," creativity, and a desire to "equal and surpass the work of other [inventors]."[3] Advice experts and committed grass-roots inventors like Tupper continued the process of emulation into the twentieth century, sustaining the efforts of those who invented outside a growing system of corporate research and development laboratories.

Earl Tupper's coming of age in New England fit the genre of inventor biographies circulating in the popular literature of the early twentieth century.[4] Born on a New Hampshire farm to a family of modest means, Tupper "developed a love of invention" and "showed an enterprising and entrepreneurial spirit" by the age of ten.[5] Tupper worked at odd jobs and, through study and persistence, achieved success by inventing a simple plastic container. This simplified story, however, obscures the haphazard and difficult path Tupper followed prior to his success. Tupper had a complex relationship to automobility and to invention. His diaries speak not only to the economic hardships faced by many Americans during the Great Depression but also the hopes and difficulties of patent management for grass-roots inventors. Tupper's experiences serve as a bridge between nineteenth-century ideas of invention as democratic and accessible and a modern corporate structure that placed invention and innovation in the hands of trained scientists and engineers who worked for large corporations.[6]

The Persistence of the Self-Educated Inventor

In a 1934 memo to his patent attorney, Earl Tupper stated, "My hobby has always been inventing."[7] Written to establish his claim as the first inventor of the auto rumble-seat cover, the letter expressed a deeper truth about Tupper and how he thought about tinkering. Hobbies, which became socially acceptable leisure after World War I, and a veritable craze in the 1930s, reproduced the core values of corporate capitalism. As a conservative form of leisure, hobbies provided relief from work but at the same time reinforced a traditional work ethic; they developed specialized skills, rewarded perseverance, and occasionally provided paid employment.[8]

Claiming invention as his hobby, Tupper echoed the language of magazines such as *Popular Mechanics* that encouraged modern men and boys to combine new values of consumption, physical vitality, and personality with older ideals of character and industriousness. Cultural historians have noted that the growth of advertising and a host of popular magazines constructed a new male identity in the interwar period "based around consumerism, the cult of personality, and self-improvement."[9] A mastery of technology formed one of the "central dilemmas facing men of this era," as historian Tom Pendergast has written in his work on masculinity and magazine culture. "Faced with a world grown suddenly complex, filled with giant machines and complicated technology," magazine writers and editors instructed modern men to "tap into their innate knowledge of how things work[ed]" and to master the technology around them as part of the complex recipe for success.[10] Magazines like *Popular Mechanics* and *Scientific American* portrayed famous inventors such as Alexander Graham Bell as role models and as hobbyists who got lucky.[11] These stories informed Tupper's experience; he devoted a good deal of his leisure time to reading magazines as well as tinkering.

Invention was more than a hobby for Tupper, however; it was his hope for financial success. Between 1933 and 1937, Tupper ran first his parents' plant nursery and then his own successful landscaping and tree trimming business, Tupper Tree Doctors. Although the landscaping business was moderately successful after 1933, providing an income to support his wife, Marie, and his two sons, Tupper focused his hopes for more substantial gains on selling his inventions. In the fall of 1934, he confided in his diary: "I've just got to put some of my inventions onto the market. If I can get a little money ahead . . . I can take my nose from the tree business for a day."[12] He saw himself as a potential inventor first; all other jobs served to finance the hope of creating a successful invention.

Tupper came of age in a culture that revered inventors. As a young man he absorbed a national enthusiasm for technology and wholeheartedly subscribed to a national ideology that placed inventors at the center of social progress.[13] He also identified closely with famous innovators, hoping to emulate their characteristics and their success. In his early notebooks, he saved stories of Thomas Edison and Thomas Jefferson as inventors who contributed to the progress of the nation. Under a drawing of Thomas Jefferson entitled "The American Leonardo Da Vinci," Tupper wrote, "Da Vinci and Jefferson, Edison and a host of others are proof that an inventive, . . . enthusiastic and trained mind continues to experiment, study, . . . and develop along the entire line of human endeavor."[14] To this end, Tupper embraced literature on self-improvement and invention circulating in the interwar period, and combined them into a rigorous program of hard work, physical exercise, and self-education.

In the January 1 entry in his diary in 1933, Tupper listed his New Year's resolutions to work harder, to develop mentally and physically, and to read more. Tupper completed high school in 1925 but did not go to college and regretted later that he had not furthered his education. High school and college enrollment skyrocketed between 1900 and

1930, with high school attendance increasing 650 percent between 1900 and 1920 alone.[15] With his family responsibilities and lack of money in 1933, Tupper could not pursue college courses, although he was sure he could complete four years of college in eighteen months. He confided in his diary, "Lately I have developed a ravenous appetite for knowledge," and, he wondered, "Why couldn't I have realized my real future desires while in school?"[16] Part of a middle-class culture that recognized the value of higher education and tied class mobility to specialized knowledge, Tupper embarked on a rigorous program of self-improvement after graduating from high school. He also adopted new masculine standards of physical fitness and flirted with body-building, recording his chest measurements in his diary.[17]

Tupper was much more invested in training his mind than his body. Early in January 1933, he wrote that he had outlined a program of study to improve his English and his understanding of business and marketing. "I'll be a super being if I successfully complete it," he joked.[18] A week later he enthused, "I am ever impressed by the vast amount of interesting—fascinating—and elevating knowledge to be had by the ambitious in this world. It is impossible to live long enough to acquire it all."[19] Reading and correspondence courses provided the core of his program for acquiring the knowledge to advance in a modern, white-collar profession.

Reading formed an important component of the middlebrow culture in the interwar years. Publishers produced books for middle-class audiences, and for those who aspired to white-collar and professional jobs, who wanted to further their education or acquire a greater understanding of the various specialized categories of knowledge appearing in the early twentieth century. Janice Radway argued that reading held out the promise of self-improvement to the aspiring middle-classes.[20] Books and magazines became totems of class status, and underscored the importance of technical and highly specialized knowledge.[21]

Tupper embraced reading for just these reasons, digesting the information in magazines like *American Mercury, Popular Mechanics, Printer's Ink,* and *Scientific American.* He made frequent trips to the library to study subjects that informed his inventions, taking notes on ideas and phrases that expressed his own ambitious desire to get ahead.[22] Under the heading "Value of Good Book Reading," he wrote in his notebook that "a $5 book may supply an idea . . . [that] may be worth a fortune if grasped and utilized. A well-qualified author perhaps supplies in a single book the principal ideas that have made . . . him a successful man. Surely you should be able to . . . use them profitably."[23]

Bent over volumes of advice literature at the library, Tupper schooled himself in patent law and the rules of invention. Tupper recorded advice on how to become a successful inventor in his invention notebooks. These notes blended specific advice with platitudes about the social worth of invention and the importance of inventors. Under the heading "How to Invent," Tupper noted advice from *Popular Mechanics* that inventors should focus their efforts on problems rather devices. He credited himself with the idea that one should take a "substance and see how many present things can be made with it. Many improvements will develop that way."[24] He listed the procedures for establishing the date of conception, how to protect an invention from infringement, and how to realize profits. The list of advice on profiting from invention included finding the right manufacturer and doing market research. Tupper ended the list with a word of encouragement: to "believe and think constantly about that which I have to sell."[25] He practiced this last piece of advice on a daily basis.

Beyond useful knowledge, popular literature reinforced a belief in individual autonomy and technological progress. Such reading matter assuaged middle-class worries about the pace and fragmentation of American society in the first decades of the twentieth century. Radway argued that middlebrow reading answered serious social problems most often by reinforcing the "moral, ethical, and spiritual rehabilitation of the individual" rather than society.[26] In order to achieve this, books and magazine articles fostered what she terms "personalism," or a deep empathy with the individual subject, whether fictional or historical.[27] Tupper read with this same sense of total immersion, identifying with individual characters such as Thomas Edison and Leonardo da Vinci. He also rejected strains of anti-modernism in highbrow literature. When he read Balzac's *The Peasantry*, Tupper wrote, "No matter how poets and song writers play up pagan existence and Midevial [*sic*] civilizations, I'll still take modern civilization . . . and ultra modern civilization—the more advanced the better I'm for it."[28]

Correspondence courses in business and advertising underscored Tupper's desire to become a full participant in modern society—to be not just a consumer but also a producer. These courses instilled in him the idea that the key to success in invention rested as much on marketing as on the strength of the idea or the patent claims. Correspondence courses fit Tupper's need for "spare-time study" and his hope that postsecondary school training would enable him to move into a white-collar profession. Interestingly, Tupper, the aspiring inventor, did not take courses in mechanics, drafting, or engineering. Rather he focused his attention on business management, effective English, and advertising. Tupper took an introduction to advertising from the International Correspondence Schools of Scranton, Pennsylvania, in 1932, and the language and philosophy of advertising he learned there infused his writing and informed his approach to patent management. The head of the advertising school instructed his pupils that advertising built modern America. It raised living standards, informed the public of vital improvements in consumer goods, and gave students of the art "the fascinating power to get others to do your bidding."[29] Tupper wrote in one of his advertising papers that "new inventions . . . would remain forever the knowledge of a very few people were it not for the use of the various advertising mediums to extol their desire abilities to the buying public." Indeed, Tupper noted, "Progress is made up of . . . improvements most of which must be commercialized in order to be self-sustaining."[30] Working on his own early inventions, he spent more time writing advertising copy than working out the thorny problems of manufacturing.

Several years later Tupper declared that his purpose in life was to become a "super-coordinator," or an inventor who could look down and "see the blind classes" and "coordinate and improve" the products they used.[31] Tupper believed deeply that inventors were superior beings who recognized what consumers needed long before consumers themselves did. Initiating a patent application for an automobile accessory, Tupper crossed the line between consumer and inventor. As an aspiring inventor, he saw himself as occupying what one cultural mediator called the "top round of the ladder of human achievement."[32] His copious notes on the advice literature recorded the larger rhetoric that placed inventors in a privileged social position. For instance, *Popular Mechanics* declared in 1930 that independent inventors were essential to the health and wealth of the nation. The magazine confirmed that receipt of a patent admitted average men into the company of "Marconi and Bell, Morse and Berliner, Edison and Goodyear."[33] Tupper's diary revealed his identification with famous inventors, such as Leonardo da Vinci. When he compared himself to da Vinci, he focused on shared hardship rather than on shared success. Tupper wrote, "I too am strapped for money and have notebooks full of sketches and a house of models of inventions awaiting completion and business."[34] Not only did Tupper identify with the struggle of most inventors to see their ideas realized, but his problems were compounded by the circumstances of the 1930s.

The Great Depression and Obstacles to Success

Earl Tupper had a long list of potential inventions in the early 1930s and faced many hardships in his efforts to sell them. Unfortunately, he had no money to patent, manufacture, or market his ideas. The Depression and his personal financial struggles dominated Tupper's thoughts in 1933. In January of that year, Tupper wrote, "If I can get a little money ahead, I'll show the world some real inventions."[35] Tupper's experiences as a young husband and father and as an amateur inventor were deeply embedded in the Depression. The son of a farmer and small business owner, Tupper worked for two years at his parents' nursery and then at a range of jobs elsewhere. In 1931, he married Marie Whitcomb and determined to make his living by invention. However, by 1933, he and his wife and young son, Ronnie, were forced to leave their apartment in Shirley, Massachusetts, and move in with his parents. Lacking a steady income, the young Tuppers' financial insecurity resembled the situation of millions of Americans. The winter of 1932–1933 was the "most desperate" of the Depression with one-fourth of the nation's work force unemployed.[36] Similar to the majority of middle-class Americans, Earl and Marie cut back on spending. Earl, who had purchased a used Ford roadster in 1930, sold his car to his brother.[37]

Between January and July 1933, Tupper commented daily on his lack of money and the dire economic situation of the nation. Like many Americans, Tupper was prepared to "believe the worst" about his government: that corruption distracted politicians from meeting the needs of citizens.[38] Listening to the news on the radio late one February night, Tupper wrote, "it certainly is amazing what a rotten grafting game our politicians can get away with—even when the facts are broadcast to the people. If this old depression could continue for five more years, I think it would do much to awaken the masses to activity toward wiping out corruption."[39] Tupper had received a copy of the *Daily Worker* a few weeks earlier and commented that the Communists "had a lot of good ideas," even if their "goal was futile."[40] His sympathy with the writers of the *Daily Worker* reflected a more general turn to the left among many Americans in the early years of the Depression as the American dream of hard work and individual advancement seemed to deteriorate.[41] Ultimately, Tupper rejected socialism and would later complain bitterly about the first social security deduction from his pay at the Doyle Works in 1937.[42] Yet in the dark days of 1933 he heartily supported relief for the workingman and for the "good works" of both Roosevelt and Father Coughlin.[43]

Tupper worked only sporadically in 1933. On inauguration day in March he observed, "This noon we heard . . . President Roosevelt sworn into office. . . . Mr. Roosevelt said a lot of nice things if he can and will see them through. I hope this old depression either grows much worse, or leaves us entirely—and very soon. Boy! I feel more stranded than Robinson Coruso [*sic*] even could have felt. . . . It's certain things can get no worse for me—financially."[44] Although he started his own landscaping business during that year, he felt the painful scarcity of money. By September, Tupper, now twenty-six years old, wrote, "I have just $19 left to my name, no car, and apparently nothing else. With those business assets, I must take care of a fine little wife and a darling child." He mused, "I could always live, but to carry on and keep life for them worth living is a problem—it has been for a year."[45] For Tupper, a life worth living included the material comforts of the middle-class home. He and Marie went window-shopping and shared their daydreams about better furniture, a new car, and a host of other goods. Ruminating on his lack of money, Tupper noted, "I let my imagination play to-day . . . on what I would buy if I had only . . . $10,000 to spend. (Boy!—it was tough getting back to the depression)."[46] More often than not, Tupper's consumer desires were focused on a new car.

The lack of a car was a particularly vexing problem for Tupper. The automobile, in many ways, was the one material object that could help him maintain the middle-class life he envisioned for his family. By the early 1930s, the automobile had become a necessity for many Americans, especially those living in small towns and automobile suburbs. Auto sales in rural America grew in the 1910s, fueled in part by the Ford Motor Company's aggressive campaign to sell the Model T to farmers. The consolidation of population, schools, shopping and services into larger towns between 1920 and 1930 changed the automobile from a convenience into a farm necessity for most Americans.[47] At the same time, growing suburbanization made the car a necessity for many more Americans who needed the automobile to commute to cities for work and to access services. Despite the Depression, Americans still spent money on automobiles because they had become essential to everyday life.

For Tupper, the car was both a necessity and a symbol of middle-class comforts he had lost with the economic downturn. Tupper had owned several different cars in the 1920s and early 1930s. Even after the economic crash he was able to afford a new car in 1931, but had to sell it when the expenses of family life became too much. Afterward, however, a new auto assumed center stage in Tupper's consumer fantasies. At the beginning of 1933, after reading about the new models at the auto shows, he exclaimed, "How I crave a new auto now!"[48] He used his diary to record statistics on new cars, noting new features, mileage, and horsepower. In February, after he and Marie saw the newest Ford V-8 on the streets of Fitchburg, Massachusetts, Tupper noted in his diary that he had to gather "sufficient funds to get a new car this spring. And that's a big order too, in view of all the things I need so greatly."[49] Tupper also needed money to help pay for the expenses of patenting his automotive accessory, the Clipper Rumble Top, to manufacture samples, and to place ads in trade journals. Car ownership became a necessity for earning money from his tree business and sustaining a network of potential manufacturers and buyers for his patent.

Tupper's business contacts stretched from the manufacturing towns in northwestern Massachusetts to Boston. When Tupper started his tree trimming business he confronted the problem of not owning a car. In order to build a large enough list of clients to have steady work, Tupper had to cover considerable distances between towns. He relied on his brother Loren to drive him to work, but that proved unreliable and frustrating to the point that Tupper eventually made a deal with his brother to rent his own car back for a fee of $1 per day plus the cost of oil and gas. "I am more firmly then ever convinced that I must have a car if at all possible. To depend upon a brother . . . to do as it agrees is as uncertain as New England weather," wrote Tupper in June 1933.[50]

Tupper's efforts as an inventor and entrepreneur were tied directly to automobility. He needed a car to commute into Boston to meet with his patent attorney and with various manufacturers and dealers who he hoped would buy his accessory patent. In mid-August of 1933, Tupper, weighed down by the multiple domestic and business obligations that he could not meet, noted that the car would solve most of his problems: "If I had a car, I could take care of myself."[51] His business prospects improved over the course of the year, and by December, Tupper was hopeful that he could afford a new car. In less than a year, as the tree business earned a steady income and when he believed he'd found a manufacturer for his auto accessory, he bought first a used car and then, six months later a new Ford V-8 Standard Tudor Sedan.[52]

Tinkering: Tupper's Empirical Approach to Redesigning the Auto

Like many consumers-turned-amateur inventors, Tupper focused his early inventive efforts on the automobile. He tinkered with various accessories and by 1935 his list of marketable inventions included an auto bumper, mud flaps, trailer brake, child auto seat, turn signal, and a hood ornament shaped like an airplane that simulated flight by rising gently from the hood with the forward motion of the car.[53] Although he sketched designs for some of the ideas in his invention notebook and even wrote advertising copy for others, none were as fully developed as the rumble-seat top. Tupper wrote that he first conceived of the rumble top in 1928 as part of a larger combination of accessories that included a windshield, top, side curtains and rumble-seat top. His efforts paralleled Ford's introduction of the Model A, which included a rumble seat on the roadster coupe, and represented a more complete car that included a top, windshield, and other accessories as standard equipment.[54]

Tupper finally settled on developing just the rumble-seat top, because, he acknowledged, the trend in the automobile industry was toward a completely enclosed car. The rumble seat was a new addition to roadsters built from 1917 until the end of the 1930s.[55] Some auto enthusiasts have claimed that the name "rumble" derived from a nineteenth-century British carriage maker, Sir Hubert Rhumble, but rumble also accurately described the sensation of riding in a seat positioned over the rear wheels of the car. The seat was also popularly known as the mother-in-law seat, suggesting one of its varied services.[56] Whatever its origins, the fold-out seat provided extra space for packages, luggage, and passengers on the smaller cars that gained in popularity after World War I. Observing the growing popularity of roadsters in the late 1920s, and realizing that the passengers who rode in the rumble seat went unprotected from weather, Tupper determined that the rumble seat offered potential for patented improvements.

Tupper's work on automobile accessories and other novelties illustrated the prescriptive advice that amateur inventors should focus their efforts on consumer goods. Those giving the advice appealed to a democratic sense of ingenuity among Americans, encouraging them not to focus on big inventions, but on modifying the small commodities. They told folks like Tupper that "little things counted," and that there was always room for improvement in existing products.[57] In one of his lists on how to invent, Tupper noted that inventors "should not be afraid to look far, far into the future and visualize things that might be."[58] Yet, Tupper, in his daily practice of invention, did not visualize the future so much as tinker with mass-produced products. The automobile body, like the household novelties Tupper also worked on, presented Tupper with a potential field for improvement. As did many Americans who grew up with the automobile, he understood the requirements of comfort and safety from the vantage point of the user.

Although Tupper was not trained as a mechanic, machinist, or engineer, he did have the distinct advantage of living and working in New England factory towns. The center of the carriage, bicycle, and machine tool industries, New England became the home of early automotive inventors like George B. Selden, creator of the gasoline engine, and a large portion of the automotive industry outside of the Midwest.[59] The towns of Fitchburg and Groton, Massachusetts, were home to manufacturers of textiles, leather goods, machine tools, bicycles, and luggage.[60] Massachusetts reported more than 52,000 workers employed in automotive related industries in 1932–1933, the state with the third largest investment in automobile industry on the East Coast after New York and Pennsylvania. The National Automobile Chamber of Commerce identified the state as one of the largest manufacturers of textiles for cars.[61] These industries provided Tupper with a base of expertise from which to manufacture samples of his rumble top and a host of business prospects that he could interest in licensing or buying his patent.

Tupper perfected the design for the top through a combination of observation and experimentation, supplemented by the decisive and mythical mental flash. His earliest designs drew on other kinds of covers, namely the collapsible umbrella, the "box-like cover" for typewriters, and conventional auto tops. He wrote that because "the composite appearance of this top is very similar to the most popular of the conventional tops of the day, it should find more ready acceptance with the public as folks are pretty well sold on the idea of what constitutes the proper requisites for an auto top."[62] Here Tupper drew upon familiar designs and tinkered with their shape slightly to fit a new application. The earliest sketch of the top resembled a hybrid of conventional auto top and an umbrella, with a central post with spokes and a square frame for the fabric cover.[63] This design evolved over several years into the patented top that retained the box-like shape but replaced the umbrella frame with a rectangular, aluminum alloy struts.[64]

Tupper employed an intuitive and hands-on approach to invention, replicating the empirical practices of earlier independent inventors, like Edison and Bell.[65] His method for improving the design relied on building numerous models and fitting them to automobiles. He bought two different cars in 1930 to further his experiments and adapted the top to the latest Fords. Tupper designed his tops to fit Ford cars but was hampered by the yearly model changes; he couldn't build a universal top to meet each model. These models, he remarked, "worked swell," but he speculated later that the "present owner of that 1930s Ford car of mine [probably] wonders why a part of the rear deck of the car is cut to hinge open." Searching for a collapsible top that would disappear into the body of the car was inspired both by the general advice that equated the collapsible with convenience. He also copied the disappearing top on the 1932 Hudson.[66] Without a car of his own between 1933 and 1934, Tupper scrutinized new cars in parking lots and at automobile dealerships, observing their various features and taking measurements. He also took inspiration from designs seen in movies and in popular magazines. While perfecting his design, Tupper kept in mind the advice that improvements should be simple. He was convinced that his top met the requirements of good invention as articulated in the advice literature. The top featured "simplicity of construction and operation, low cost, low selling price and classy appearance, easy, quick and desirable to use."[70] He noted that the solution to the top's key problem—how to render the deployment of the top quicker and easier—came to him in a mental leap. Tupper, worried someone might steal his idea, decided to

May 28, 1935.   E. S. TUPPER   2,002,514

REMOVABLE RUMBLE SEAT TOP

Original Filed Aug. 8, 1932   2 Sheets–Sheet 1

Fig.1

Fig.2

Figure 17. Patent Record, Earl S. Tupper, Rumble Top, 28 May 1935, Earl S. Tupper Papers, Archives Center, National Museum of American History, Behring Center, Smithsonian Institution, Washington, D.C.

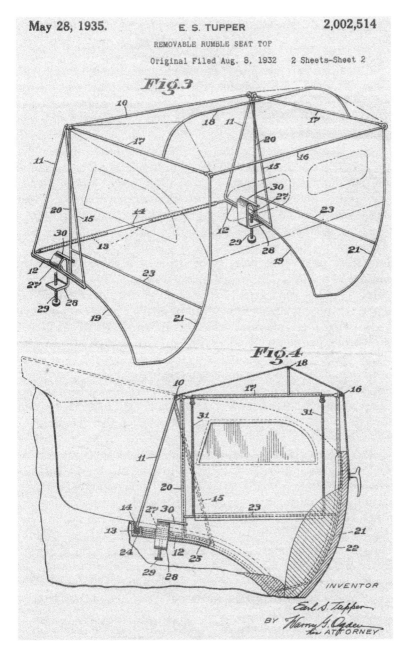

Figure 18. Patent Record, Earl S. Tupper, Rumble Top, 28 May 1935, Earl S. Tupper Papers, Archives Center, National Museum of American History, Behring Center, Smithsonian Institution, Washington, D.C.

spend time and money patenting and then promoting the rumble top because he was "sure it was far ahead of anything on the market."[67]

Tupper's rumble top, although useful, was not wholly new or "non-obvious."[68] Rather it represented only a slight change to the automobile. The idea of adding a top to rumble seat occurred to other motorists, as well. As soon as Ford Motor Company introduced a rumble seat on its two-seater sport models in 1928, the company began receiving letters suggesting it provide a top or a cover for the uncomfortable rumble seat.[69] One alert consumer in Toledo, Ohio, warned the company that "many people are hesitating to buy cars with rumble seats for the simple reason that there is no protection . . . against unfavorable weather."[70] Several others offered to sell the company their patented and unpatented designs. All of the designs, though each was slightly different from the next, echoed the saleable if not the patentable features of Tupper's top: collapsibility, invisible storage, and quick and easy deployment.

The staff at the Ford engineering department, however, rejected the suggestions as not new. The engineers explained that the "rumble seat is intended only for emergency use by those who ordinarily would not need a larger automobile, and the need of such a cover would not warrant furnishing the same as standard equipment."[71] W. T. Fishleigh, head of the Experimental Engineering at Ford, replied to self-styled inventors hawking covers for rumble seats that the "idea . . . is not new to us, and should we ever wish to furnish this equipment, we shall doubtless use one of our own design."[72] Even if the engineers at Ford did not feel there was a market for this accessory, letters indicated that consumers used the rumble seat regularly and were ready to alter the design to better fit their needs.

Popular Mechanics also published several rumble-seat covers as aftermarket accessories in the early 1930s, confirming that even if the idea was not new, consumers might find it useful.[73] Photographs of the covers revealed their problematic designs and countered the positive descriptions that claimed they would protect passengers from the weather and render the exposed seat more comfortable. Drawing on the ordinary rain slicker and the summer awning as models, neither cover effectively protected passengers from rain. Nevertheless, they demonstrated the determination of grass-roots inventors to continue to tinker with the design of the automobile, even if Ford and other large manufacturers would not buy their ideas.

Advertisements like these may have convinced Tupper that his rumble seat top would find a ready market, producing a profit and maybe even a fortune. Tupper tinkered with the clear goal of making money, and he hoped his auto top would reap a large profit and finance other inventions. On the eve of meeting with his patent attorney in Boston, Tupper wrote confidently, "That rumble top certainly looks like somebody's Million Dollars."[74] Tupper also showed a sample of the top to anyone who expressed the least interest, and many others who did not. He even fantasized about demonstrating the invention for Mrs. Roosevelt, hoping for a presidential endorsement.[75] In these demonstrations, the top became a tangible signifier of Tupper's goal of becoming a successful and profitable inventor. In August 1933, he showed the top to a client from whom he intended to buy greenhouses. The greenhouses proved unusable and the deal collapsed, but Tupper showed their owner his auto top as proof that he did not need a career as a nurseryman. "I showed [Mrs. Naylor] my rumble top and told her that I hoped to make and sell those, and make a fortune at it—starting small. I said that the prospects with the top were so good that I didn't feel too badly because I couldn't get the greenhouse," wrote Tupper later that night. Invention provided reassurance for Tupper against the many trials and disappointments of earning money and providing for a family during the Depression. If he failed at running his own business or had to string together multiple odd jobs to meet his responsibilities, he always had the belief that his real career lay in invention.

The advice literature on invention in the 1930s no doubt fed Tupper's hopes for success.[76] Beginning in the late nineteenth century, invention manuals had addressed selling inventions. However, during the Great Depression this advice took on a more urgent tone and a harder sales pitch. For instance, George Roesch, author of *Your Invention: What to Do with It*, published in 1934, began with a chapter entitled "How Can Inventions Be Made to Pay?" Roesch addressed such timely questions as "What does a fellow do when he is broke?" His answer was to persist; to develop the invention, find the money to patent it, and not sell or assign any of the rights until the terms were satisfactory. He also reminded his readers that although most inventors failed, it was because they didn't work hard enough. Roesch stressed that "would-be inventors" could succeed if they followed the regime of "Work—Sacrifice—Study—More Work—and Caution."[77] Tupper followed these rules religiously. Unable to pay for a patent or to manufacture his accessory, he spent days and weeks writing advertising copy, researching the market, and cultivating business prospects.

Methods of Modern Patent Management

Drawing on his correspondence courses in advertising, Tupper planned the marketing campaign for the rumble top before he had finalized the design, found a suitable manufacturer, or secured a patent. Aware that a memorable brand name and trademark could aid in the sale of his accessory, distinguishing it from similar products, Tupper devised several names for the rumble top. He called the first version the "Raker" for its rakish appearance and "high-class" profile, using an established advertising strategy that appealed to consumers' desire for class mobility through consumption.[78] Tupper claimed that the top represented futuristic technology. In his words, the top was "magic snatched from the future—such simplicity and perfection at once, is truly Aladdin-like."[79] Addressing motorists' desire for collapsible accessories that were easy to use and store, Tupper assured purchasers that they would not need to bother with buttons, bolts, screws, or fasteners. He also claimed that attaching the top would not mar the finish of the car in any way. In the earliest copy, Tupper promised universality and flexibility of design—that the top would fit all makes and models of automobiles. He changed this promise later when he revised his patent claims to give him a monopoly how the top attached to the car, and it was easier to make tops for Ford cars exclusively. While these promises remained the same, the name changed several times while Tupper honed his sales pitch and his trademark. He produced his own sketch of a trademark for the Clipper Rumble Top, using ship imagery again to establish the connection between the rumble top and upper-class modes of transportation, such as yachts, and perhaps to evoke the impression of smooth sailing. Finally, though, Tupper settled on his own name as the brand, with the Tupper Rumble Top. These slogans and his trademark reiterated Tupper's belief that his ideas were superior to anything else on the market, and that perhaps he was a "super coordinator," combining and improving on existing designs to create a superior product.

Tupper planned a number of sales strategies. These ranged from licensing his top on a royalty basis to a manufacturer with an established distribution network to selling the patent outright. After his self-schooling in the local library, Tupper understood the rules and advantages of licensing a product on a royalty basis. Writing to his patent attorney and financial backer, Tupper stipulated that if he entered a royalty arrangement that he would demand a "minimum production" of the tops and a "minimum of selling effort." He wanted to protect himself "so that no one will 'bottle up' the invention while exploiting something else in its stead."[80] One lesson Tupper learned well from advice literature was that he should proceed cautiously and seize every opportunity to protect his product in the hands of outside manufacturers.

Tupper also considered making the tops himself and selling them through car dealers, traveling salesmen, and classified ads. He reported to his business mentor, Michael Sheedy, that he could sell at least two thousand tops in New England alone, "at more profit than we could ever realize from any of the procrastinators whom we have been trying to get

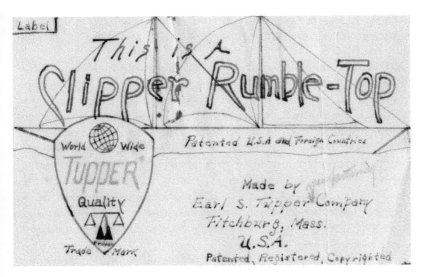

Figure 19. Influenced by the growth of advertising as an industry, Tupper spent many hours crafting a catchy advertising campaign and sketching logos for his invention. Earl Tupper "This Is a Clipper Rumble-Top," c. 1933, Earl S. Tupper Papers, Archives Center, National Museum of American History, Behring Center, Smithsonian Institution, Washington, D.C.

to take the thing over." The "procrastinators" referred to the manufacturers and automobile dealers who were reluctant to buy or invest in the accessory because of its small market. Tupper, however, was adamant that he knew "fellows with automobiles" who were experienced salesmen and who would buy the tops and then sell them directly to the public at "race tracks, air ports and beaches," anyplace where a sporting crowd with sport cars gathered.[81] He also planned to contact car dealers for lists of consumers who bought cars with rumble seats, and then his salesmen would contact these people directly.

Finally, Tupper set a high price of $20 per top, with a profit of more than 50 percent going to himself as the inventor. He clearly rejected advice that instructed amateur inventors to make their inventions affordable. Indeed *Popular Mechanics* reported years earlier that patent holders could not fix the retail price of their inventions, they were only entitled to compensation from the manufacturer or jobber who bought or licensed the product.[82] Because Tupper considered manufacturing and selling the top himself, he estimated the final price for his potential investors. He argued that the final price of $20 was high but it represented a quality product, and one that most new car buyers could afford.[83] The new car Tupper most admired, the Ford V-8, was introduced in 1932 at a cost of between $450 and $650. However, many Americans could not afford this price and bought used cars for significantly less.[84]

Although he solicited least two bids on the cost of making parts for the tops, there was little evidence that he did all the research necessary to estimate the full cost of production, nor did he weigh the cost of production against the real market possibilities. Tupper also ignored the negative responses from manufacturers. Milton Wright, editor for the Commercial Property News section of *Scientific American,* wrote that one of the fatal mistakes of individual inventors was that they thought first of how they might make money from their ideas but did not consider the cost of manufacturing or whether the invention might appeal to established manufacturers.[85] Despite his sales strategies, manufacturers and automobile dealers remained skeptical about the market potential of Tupper's auto accessory.

If the design of the accessory came fairly easily to Tupper, managing the patent to make a profit posed a more difficult set of challenges. In her work on the patents and the social construction of invention, Carolyn Cooper has noted that with the granting of a patent, "recognition did not come automatically, nor did reward."[86] Inventors could use patents to define what was new and useful, and effectively use the rights granted by the patent to monopolize an idea, process, design, or mechanism and charge manufacturers for the rights to use their ideas. They could do this by manufacturing the item, assigning the patent rights, licensing the patent rights on a royalty basis, or selling the patent outright. Even before obtaining a patent, Tupper considered all of the above as potential avenues for profiting from his idea.

Tupper acknowledged that securing a patent was key to turning his idea into a commodity he could sell. Tupper was convinced that a patent would give him control over the market for rumble-seat tops. Tupper followed the advice of mediators like George Roesch, who sternly advised "self-styled" inventors to patent their ideas before trying to sell them.[87] Tupper noted that he had done a "number of [patent] record searches" on his inventions to determine if he should apply for a patent or not. Sometimes the results were discouraging, but in the case of the auto rumble top, Tupper believed he had a "patentable and valuable" idea. A patent was particularly important to Tupper because without the money to manufacture and sell the finished tops, he could still sell the rights to the patent. However, finding the money to pay the legal and filing fees to get his idea patented was difficult: "When it came to getting the money for patenting them I was always up against it because what money I could earn barely kept me ahead of my fixed expenses."[88] Filing a patent with the help of an attorney could cost as much as $125 in the late 1920s.[89] In the case of the rumble top, Tupper determined a patent was valid and necessary because "to sell an unpatented idea is just about impossible—I have tried that many times."[90] Therefore, he invested a lot of time in acquiring a patent on the rumble top.

To raise the money for the patent fees, Tupper showed his idea to several of his tree clients in hopes of finding a financier. As patent attorney Adam Fisher instructed his readers in *Plain Talk*, potential inventors needed to meet local businessmen and search for a patron or partner to help finance their patents.[91] Tupper found such a patron and a mentor in Michael Sheedy, Jr., treasurer of the Groton Leatherboard Company. Leatherboard made luggage and leather accessories, and Tupper showed Sheedy his drawings for the auto top and asked his opinion on finding a good dependable patent attorney. Sheedy helped Tupper throughout the patent and marketing process, sending him to a patent attorney in Boston, Warren Ogden, and introducing him to other accessory manufacturers in the state.[92] Very little correspondence remains between Tupper and Sheedy, but Tupper often reflected in his diary on how grateful he was to Sheedy for the informal education he provided in patent procurement and business. In fact, Tupper noted in December 1933 that it was Michael Sheedy who encouraged him to keep a diary. Tupper had found a partner to invest in his ideas and to help guide him through the process of patent management.

However, Tupper and Sheedy had a critical disagreement about approaching the management of Tupper's auto accessory that slowed progress on obtaining the patent. Tupper wanted to patent first and sell later. Sheedy, in contrast, wanted to test the market first and patent after they were sure they could sell the idea. Tupper, who had ordered record searches for the rumble top in 1932, wanted to apply for a patent as soon as possible because he feared that someone would steal the idea or beat him to the patent office.[93] Tupper applied for a patent in the fall of 1932, but Sheedy, who had agreed to pay all of the costs, defaulted on the final government fee to claim grant of the patent in the spring of 1933. Their attorney suggested that the extra time might allow them to research and refine their claims and amendments to create a stronger patent. Tupper agreed. However, after submitting the final set of claims in a new petition in the winter of 1934, he realized his worst fears— another inventor had filed a patent three weeks prior to his for a very similar rumble top, and the U.S. patent examiner had rejected a large portion of Tupper's claims as unoriginal.[94] The burden of proof of conception then fell on Tupper, which lead him to detail the facts and dates of conception for Ogden.

Sheedy remained cautious about paying the final fees. With significantly more experience in business and manufacturing than young Tupper, Sheedy remained skeptical about the sales possibilities and also wanted a manufacturing plan. He wanted Tupper to decide if he would try to manufacture the top himself or if he would license the patent to a firm that would produce the tops. Tupper had an unshakeable conviction in the sales potential of his top, but he was unsure how to manufacture the accessory. In February, Tupper noted his disappointment: "Mr. Sheedy doesn't want to spend any more money until he sees what we can do toward merchandising the top. I believe that the patent should be granted, then we would have something to sell. As it is we have nothing." He lamented, "And since Mr. Sheedy is paying the bill, I can't say much."[95] They delayed action on the patent until June while Tupper surveyed the market.

Armed with a typewriter, Tupper sent letters to various automotive concerns requesting information on rumble seats and asking them for feedback on his top idea. His contacts included national catalog retailers, automobile manufacturers, the National Automobile Chamber of Commerce, and the Chilton Company, among others. Tupper was familiar with the practice of sending letters to manufacturers; he had by his own admission written to General Motors and to Henry Ford multiple times trying to interest Ford Motor Company in his auto accessory. However, he found that trying to sell directly to a large auto manufacturer was a dead end. "When it came to contacting Mr. Ford—that was impossible," wrote Tupper. "I wrote to him at Sudbury, at Dearborn, and at his factory, I even wrote his wife, . . . vaguely hoping that by some chance it might strike someone who would help me." Tupper stopped trying to contact Ford because "Mr. Ford . . . stole every idea he could."[96] Tupper had equally poor luck at trying to sell the idea to large retailers like Montgomery Ward, which politely turned him down in 1932.[97]

Automobile manufacturers told Tupper that the market for rumble seat tops was small and uncertain. A Chrysler representative replied to Tupper that the company had manufactured more than 36,000 cars with rumble seats in 1931, but they had decreased their numbers the following year.[98] The National Automobile Chamber of Commerce replied to Tupper's inquiry that it did not keep statistics on the number of cars with rumble seats, but advised Tupper, "it would be difficult to anticipate how the trend toward streamlining will affect the status of the rumble seat." The NACC representative cautioned Tupper that "many automobile engineers . . . are of the opinion that the stream line car of the future will be a closed car."[99] The year before, the NACC's publication *Facts and Figures of the Automobile Industry* recorded the significant growth in closed cars. By 1933 more than half the cars manufactured in the United States were completely enclosed, and NACC predicted the trend would continue, meaning that there would be little demand for aftermarket tops in the near future.[100]

Tupper received encouragement from family and friends, who thought the idea useful, and from LaSalle Extension University, which offered specific instructions on marketing. Tupper wrote to LaSalle while he was taking correspondence courses, asking for advice on marketing his auto top. N. P. Madsen, a member of the business management staff at LaSalle, suggested that Tupper could dispose of the patent in several ways. For instance, Madsen told Tupper to contact retailers who sold auto accessories, mentioning Montgomery Ward and Sears, Roebuck by name. (Tupper had already sent letters to both about the auto accessory and other inventions.) Madsen also included a list of firms that manufactured auto accessories compiled from *Thomas's Register of American Manufacturers*, citing that there were "50 or 60 or more firms" making auto tops, many of them located in Massachusetts.[101] He encouraged Tupper to make appointments with them to demonstrate his top.

Ahead of Madsen's advice, Tupper had already begun the process of cultivating local prospects for the auto top. With national auto manufacturers and retailers uninterested in the idea, Tupper pitched his idea to area manufacturers who had an interest in the after-market accessories trade, hoping to find a buyer or a manufacturer. According to Tupper's notes, he had production samples made to fit the 1932 Ford Roadster from Washburn Wireworks in Worcester and another set of samples to fit first the 1934 roadster from Back Bay Auto Top Company in Boston.[102] Finding someone to fabricate samples was not difficult, given the density of machinists and auto body accessory manufacturers in New England. However, securing a manufacturer who would buy the patent or produce the top on a royalty basis was much more difficult. Even with Michael Sheedy's contacts, Tupper struggled to find a manufacturer. He spent more than two years, in 1933 and 1934, meeting on a regular basis with business prospects in Massachusetts, most on the recommendation of Sheedy. Among the more productive were with Travelware, a company that made luggage and auto trunks located in Fitchburg, Anderson Car Company in Cambridge, and Back Bay Auto in Boston. All of the firms showed an initial interest in the top but questioned its market possibilities.

Tupper approached all the prospects with a mixture of hope, enthusiasm, and unshakeable confidence in his invention. After his initial meeting with the head of Travelware, Tupper wrote in his diary, "They look like business," and took them some sample frames and material so they could estimate the costs of manufacture. Yet, the firm moved too slowly on the project for Tupper. In the month that it took for a Mr. Von Dattan, head of Travelware, to research the cost of production, Tupper grew frustrated. "Gosh this standing around with nothing to do, is driving me crazy. I'm going to start making tops if nothing else."[103] Tupper contemplated setting up his own factory and manufacturing the tops himself. But he needed Sheedy to fund the venture, and Sheedy would not take the risk. Eight weeks after they took the top under consideration, Travelware notified Tupper that they would not buy the rights. Their research showed that Sears, Roebuck built two similar tops, "advertised them widely," and had no sales. Travelware advised Tupper that the accessory had "absolutely no market and any money put into it will be absolutely wasted."[104] Stung by the rejection, Tupper remarked, "Those birds don't mind saying mean things to a poor little inventor. Just the same, I still believe that I can make money making and selling those tops."[105]

To confirm his belief in the profitability of the tops, Tupper solicited the opinion of George Malcolm, one of his wealthy landscaping clients. Malcolm, who owned a large carbon ribbon firm in Boston, sympathized with Tupper and told him that invention was a "heartbreaking job" and that one needed a lot of experience in business to overcome all the obstacles. Malcolm obligingly put him in touch with Joe Carter a Ford dealer in the area. This seemed like a good idea to Tupper, who thought he might distribute the tops through dealers. Carter seemed uninterested, and Tupper quickly pronounced him a "dud."[106] But, in Tupper's experience, one contact led to another in an elaborate network of business prospects. Carter recommended Tupper take his top to Al Shapiro, owner of the Back Bay Auto Company.

According to Tupper, Back Bay Auto specialized in after-market automotive accessories and, specifically, auto tops. This seemed like the perfect match for Tupper because Back Bay Auto had the means and expertise to manufacture the tops and an established relationship with distributors. Back Bay would work with another company, Eastern Body, to demonstrate samples at New England Ford dealers, who could then place orders for the tops. After several meetings with Al Shapiro, Tupper was excited about the possibilities. In March 1934, Shapiro agreed to cover some sample frames and test the market. However, he said that Tupper should make the frames because Eastern Body did not have the resources to retool and manufacture metal top frames for an accessory without a proven market. Tupper, in his enthusiasm, agreed to make twenty-five to one hundred sample frames. Shapiro suggested that they build one universal frame that could fit all current models, but Tupper insisted that they produce only frames that would fit 1933 and 1934 Fords, perhaps because his patent designs were specifically adapted to Fords. This was a mistake, narrowing the market for the accessory and discouraging Shapiro from participating in the project. But in March

1934, Tupper wrote happily that he liked Shapiro's drive, that the firm had a "wonderful spirit," and that he was sure the deal would go through. Tupper agreed to produce some wire frames and deliver them to Shapiro. "Then Shapiro will cover them and feel out the market. If it looks good enough, we will make some tops," Tupper stated confidently. "I've been planning sales campaigns, moving, buying a car, and everything else. . . . I hope they sell like hot-cakes."[107] The prospect seemed so good to Tupper that he bought a used car and told Sheedy to finalize the patent. After reviewing the claims, Tupper and Sheedy had their lawyer send the final paperwork, and one year later, in May 1935, the U.S. Patent Office granted Tupper a patent on a removable rumble seat cover.[108]

In the meantime, Tupper struggled to manufacture the wire frames required by Back Bay Auto. Finding someone to build a few samples was not difficult, but creating one hundred production samples proved impossible. Tupper approached a tool and die works in Leominster and a sheet metal firm in Fitchburg, with little success. He also experimented with building them himself, but realized quickly that he did not have the skill or the time to make multiple production samples alone. He also did not have the money to pay a metal fabricator to make them. The wire skeleton of the rumble top had thirty parts, four of which required precision bending to fit the curve of the open rumble seat on Ford cars. Producing them was not a task Tupper could undertake in his spare time or at home.

He wrote to Al Shapiro in April imploring him to take over the whole project. "As I told you . . . manufacturing and selling tops is out of my line and right in your line," wrote Tupper. "For that reason I think you would make much greater and more satisfactory progress if you were to undertake the entire job of getting the frames made, covering them, and selling them." As an incentive, Tupper offered Back Bay Auto the right to name the product and he would license the patent rights on a royalty basis.[109] The offer failed to persuade Shapiro to commit his resources to an untested product. He remained firm in their earlier agreement. Tupper noted in his diary: "Shapiro said he didn't want to invest in the frames until he saw what the demand would be."[110] After several more months of trying to find a way to manufacture the frames and getting little response from Back Bay Auto, Tupper noted tersely that he did not have the time or money to make frames for Shapiro to "play with."[111] After this disappointment, Tupper seemed to give up on manufacturing the top.

Undaunted, Tupper focused on selling the patent rights, but his promotional efforts lacked their earlier zeal and intensity. By 1934, with little cash left, Tupper hoped to sell his auto-top patent for $1,000.[112] In the next two years, he solicited Auburn Motor Works, an upholstery firm in Worcester, and Angel Novelty company in Leominster, but these were poor prospects compared to local accessory manufacturers like Travelware and Back Bay Auto.[113] When the Patent Office published Tupper's patent in 1935, he received several promising inquiries on the cost of the outright sale of the patent rights, including one from the National Service Corps. Tupper replied that the NSC could buy the patent for $2,000, but never received a reply. No further correspondence exists between Tupper and potential buyers.[114] With no remaining prospects, Tupper gave a copy of the patent to his brother Loren in 1937 with permission to sell it.[115] Tupper then turned to the dozens of other inventions he had in the works.

Failure and Its Lessons: From Grass-Roots Inventor to Industrial Designer

Ostensibly, Tupper's auto accessory failed for multiple reasons, including his lack of money and his lack of experience in manufacturing and patent management. Tupper's failure was also partially due to changes in automobile design. First, the rumble-top had a small market and a short life. Secondly, the market for accessories such as tops slowed in the 1930s as most new cars were enclosed with streamlined, all steel tops, and bodies that were more difficult for consumers to alter. The uncertain market possibilities discouraged accessory manufacturers from investing in Tupper's patent and made his job of managing the patent even more difficult. Every year he delayed the patent and failed to put the accessory on the market, the market for such an item narrowed. In addition, the very economic problems that fueled his desire to make money from his patent also prevented manufacturers from buying his idea.

Last and more generally, the automobile industry began to actively discourage "self-styled" inventors from improving the automobile and took firm control of design in the interwar period. Tupper's steadfast belief that amateur inventors could intervene in the design of mass-produced consumer products like the automobile illustrated the tensions between popular rhetoric on the democratic nature of invention and the reality that most automotive improvements had become the domain of trained engineers working for large corporations.

Although Tupper's auto accessory illustrated what some mediators in the 1930s called the "grim reality" of amateur inventors, Tupper learned valuable lessons.[116] These lessons contributed to his self-education in patent management—the process of designing a strong patent, and the considerations of manufacturing and selling the item. Most important, he learned that intervening in the market as an independent inventor was almost impossible. In January 1937, Tupper resolved in his diary to pursue a career as a designer, someone who would design on a contract basis. He wrote, "I can do this designing better than I can do anything else."[117] Tupper adopted the new language of corporate research laboratories that hired trained designers rather than inventors.

In the late 1930s, Tupper promoted designs for novelties including a sled, which he hoped to sell to Sears, and a waterproof watch that eventually earned him a critical job at Doyle Works, a plastics company in Leominster that did contract work for DuPont. Tupper approached the Doyle Works to interest them in some of his ideas and, in the fall of 1937 he accepted a job in their design department as a sample maker.[118] As such, Tupper used the raw materials and manufacturing expertise of the company to make samples. If he had an idea that the company thought patentable, they would finance the patent in his name, assign it to DuPont, and pay him a 2 to 5 percent royalty.[119] This was a virtually risk-free arrangement for Tupper and did not require the personal resources that held him back in patenting and promoting his auto accessory. In addition, because plastics was a relatively new field, compared to the automobile industry, DuPont was open to arrangements like the one with Tupper that reduced its costs and brought in new ideas.[120]

Tupper continued his education in manufacturing and design at Doyle Works. Indeed, he used the opportunity to learn each step of the manufacturing process of early plastics. Three days after beginning work, Tupper wrote, "I have asked questions by the book full, and gaped like a tourist and studied like an engineer about everything at Doyle Works. . . . One of the things I've learned is that most people there know only a very little and that only about his own department." Tupper predicted confidently, "I believe I'll know more about the place in a year than anyone else there."[121]

Indeed, Tupper advertised himself as industrial designer for hire in December 1937 and formed his own plastic novelty company in 1939.[122] On his new letterhead, Tupper billed himself as an "industrial inventor-designer," selecting a hybrid identity that bridged older notions of the independent inventor with the more modern career of industrial designer. For Tupper, the advantage in becoming a designer meant that he could leave the problems of manufacturing to experienced engineers and machinists.[123] Tupper informed potential customers that he had worked for DuPont, underscoring his experience as a corporate sample maker. However, in large type at the bottom of the letterhead Tupper employed the popular rhetoric of invention. He wrote "There is Fun— Progress—A Million Dollars in Your Ideas and Mine. Let's Develop Them Now!"[124] Without a formal education in industrial design or engineering, Tupper drew upon practical experience and the popular advice to launch a fledgling career as an industrial designer and inventor. Even though his early attempts at promoting an auto accessory failed, his determination, enthusiasm, and informal education ultimately paid off.

*   *   *

Tupper's early failure with the automobile was as important as his later success with plastics. His efforts to design, patent and sell his rumble-top provided him with valuable experience in the patent process and the difficulties of patent management, teaching him the value of working within the structure of a large corporation rather than as an independent inventor. Although he would struggle for the first several years as an inventor-designer, Tupper eventually worked as a semi-independent inventor under contract to Du Pont, obtained war contracts during World War II for molded plastic products, invented a new process for purifying polyethylene slag, and patented the now-famous Tupperware seal.[125]

His informal self-education and his determination may have contributed to his later success, but it was not the path most innovators followed in the mid-twentieth century. Historians of technology have recorded the rise of corporate research laboratories and the decline of independent inventors in the interwar period and particularly in the 1930s.[126] The rates of patents awarded to individuals declined significantly in the 1930s: "As late as 1921, 72 percent of patents had been awarded to individuals; by 1938, the majority went to corporations."[127] Although the popular press reported that a majority of automotive patents were granted to individuals in the 1930s, experts on the social effects of invention grew worried about the overall decline in individual patent activity.[128] It was just such minor inventions and gadgets as Tupper's rumble-top that worried critics of the U.S. Patent Office. These critics decried the declining number and quality of American patents. As one sociologist charged, "only a very small percentage—sometimes estimated as low as 1 per cent—have any practical utility."[129] The significant decline of patents awarded to individuals in the 1930s initiated investigations into the patent process and inspired debates about the ability of independent or lone inventors to compete with corporations and contribute to innovation in America.

As Tupper worked on his rumble-top, changes in automotive design and a concerted effort by the automobile industry limited the space in which individual tinkerers could intervene in the design of the automobile. By the mid-1930s, the popular authority of tinkerers and grass-roots inventors was in jeopardy as automotive design became the province of corporate engineers and industrial designers. A host of factors contributed to the decline of automotive tinkering and individual patents in this decade. As in Earl Tupper's case, the Depression discouraged amateurs with limited financial resources from applying for patents.[130] The rise of the travel trailer and motels provided travelers with many of the home-like amenities they desired.[131] At the same time, manufacturers added many after-market accessories, like the trunk, as standard equipment on the car, and the automobile had become more complex; engines took more skill to fix and new streamlined bodies left little room for user modification. And, the automotive industry actively discouraged amateur invention and characterized tinkering as useless and inefficient.[132] In the 1930s, the automotive industry moved the debates over ingenuity and progress to the public arenas of automobile shows and world's fairs. The intent of these automotive exhibits was threefold: to create goodwill and establish faith in industry leadership, to manage consumers through market surveys, and at the same time to educate users in a hierarchy of technological knowledge that privileged corporate membership over older notions of the hero-inventor and the home tinkerer.

Chapter 5

The Automotive Industry Takes the Stage

In 1933, Henry Ford's public relations staff wrote, "There are two ways to build a car. You can give the buyer only what he expects. . . . Or, you can give him . . . what we engineers know he ought to have."[1] Shortly after the introduction of the V-8, Ford's staff expressed the new voice of industry intent on asserting its professional authority over automotive design and the consumer. Coupled with material changes in the automobile, such as streamlining and the addition of accessories as standard equipment, the automotive industry solidified its control over design and innovation by presenting stories of technological progress that cast corporations rather than individuals as innovators. Cultural theorist Stuart Hall has argued that "'cultural change' is a polite euphemism for the process by which some cultural forms and practices are driven out of the center of popular life, actively marginalized."[2] In the 1930s, the automotive industry actively tried to overturn the notion that consumers could also be innovators. Building on Hall's argument, I examine the automotive industry's role in reinventing the perception of ingenuity through the medium of public exhibitions during the Great Depression. In the eyes of the industry the perfect consumer did not tinker, but rather told the manufacturer what he or she wanted and then waited to receive the benefits of the "holy trinity" of the modern age: science, industry, and progress.[3]

During the uncertain years of the early 1930s, auto manufacturers invested in public exhibitions that highlighted the corporations' role as a national leaders. Embedded in the broader message about corporate leadership and authority, the automotive industry at the same time revised ideas about ingenuity, casting the producer, rather than the user or the amateur inventor, as the catalyst behind innovation. Narratives of corporate-led progress overturned older practices of emulation and invention that focused on individuals as innovators. Automotive exhibits at the National Automobile Show in New York and at the Century of Progress World's Fair in Chicago forged a hierarchy of technological knowledge that privileged manufacturers, engineers, and professional designers over consumers and grass-roots inventors.[4] The Chicago fair in 1933–1934 coincided with some of the most difficult years of the Depression, and it was at this fair that the auto industry broke new ground in styling and consumer research.

The Great Depression: "Will Automobiles Lead the Way?"

Even as the economy slowed in the first years of the Depression, Americans still traveled by car and many participated in sleek fantasies of modern consumption and technological progress available in films, magazines, and, most dramatically, at world's fairs. In 1933, sociologist Jesse Frederick Steiner reported that the bulk of the American leisure dollar was spent on motor travel. The lure of the open road and the affordability of automobile touring still drew Americans to the automobile as a pleasure vehicle. Steiner wrote that "until better means of transportation have developed, motor touring will likely tend to increase among those who are able to afford this luxury."[5] For those with leisure time and the ability to travel, many chose to attend the great modern spectacles of the 1930s, the world's fairs. Historian Robert Rydell has noted the stark contrast between the modernism of the Depression-era exhibitions and the harsh reality of everyday life.[6] He has also argued that even while the fairs underscored the stark inequalities present in America, they also upheld the ideals of capitalism and technological progress. "The vast sums of money that went into these revelries of corporate capitalism . . . highlighted the commitment of those atop America's economic pyramid to diffusing the potentially explosive political situation that confronted them during the 1930s."[7] World's fairs alone did not stave off a social revolution, but they did give form and substance to Herbert Hoover's reassuring rhetoric that prosperity lurked just around the corner. The 1933–1934 Century of Progress World's Fair in Chicago linked prosperity to better products through advanced technology and corporate planning. The fairs were perhaps the most glamorous reiteration of progress talk, presenting Americans with a vision of technological utopianism.[8] They were "festivals of American corporate power that would put breathtaking amounts of surplus capital to work in the field of cultural production and ideological representation."[9] At the center of this vision of technological, social, and economic progress was the auto industry.

Among the chief sponsors of the fair, the auto industry formed powerful alliances with politicians, scientists, engineers, and industrial designers to present an alternative vision of American life, as one with a bright future based on corporate leadership. Howard Florence, in *Review of Reviews* in January 1933, titled an article "Will Automobiles Lead the Way [out of the Depression]?" This was almost a rhetorical question.

"What industry has a better claim to leadership?" wrote Florence. "It ranks first in value of its products, according to the last Census of Manufacturers." In addition, he argued, "declining sales have exercised no retarding influence upon automotive engineering and design." Even as the hardships of the Depression limited the ability of amateur inventors like Earl Tupper to finance and produce their designs, Florence asserted that a poor economy did not hamper innovation among the auto giants. The writer also reminded readers that it was this large industry that led the nation out of the economic depression following World War I, and proclaimed that with a combined value of more than $3 billion, automobiles could again lead the way to prosperity. Nevertheless, he observed, consumers had to do their part. "Buy that new car," he advised readers, "and you will keep the wheels turning in a score of other industries."[10]

Automakers sustained significant financial and public relations losses between 1930 and 1933. Production at Ford Motor Company dropped from 1.5 million cars in 1929 to an astonishingly low 232,000 new cars in 1932, and the privately held company lost more than $120 million between 1931 and 1933. To compensate, the company lowered wages from six dollars a day to four.[11] General Motors faired slightly better, but also cut its workforce by two-thirds. Hard times also culled many smaller, independent firms from the ranks of the automotive industry. By mid-decade, manufacturers of cars had consolidated into six large companies with General Motors the largest and Chrysler the top seller.[12] Ford Motor Company had slipped to number three by the end of the decade.[13] Several factors worked against Ford: the company was still firmly under the control of its founder, depended on one model (now the Model A), and sold to the lower end of the economic scale, the group hardest hit by the Depression.[14] As automakers cut wages and jobs, other problems confronted the business elite in Detroit.

The auto industry might have been the self-selected leader of progress, but its leaders had real reasons to be worried about social discontent with corporate capitalism. The Hunger March of the spring of 1932 showed the uglier side of automotive manufacturers. Organized by the Communist Party, the mass demonstration was made up of 3,000 unemployed auto workers who walked from Detroit to Ford's River Rouge plant. Although the Detroit police escorted the demonstrators through the city without problems, the Dearborn police and Ford's own security servicemen met the marchers with deadly force. Dearborn police turned fire hoses on the crowd and then fired machineguns into the crowd, killing four demonstrators. The *New York Herald Tribune* observed, "Such action must arouse resentment among the unemployed everywhere and accentuate class antagonisms so alien to our American life."[15] The event took place just weeks before the unveiling of Ford's new V-8. It left a black mark on Ford's populist image and predicted future labor unrest. Indeed, throughout the 1930s auto plants became forums for strikes and the organization of workers by industrial unions, including the formation of the United Auto Workers and the Committee for Industrial Organization in 1935. Almost one year after the hunger demonstration, in March and April 1933, Detroit banks declared an extended holiday that left what Ford biographer Robert Lacey has called a lasting scar on the city. At the center of the bank failure in Detroit stood the Guardian Group, an institution closely associated with, among other auto industry leaders, Edsel Ford. Lacey has argued that the bank collapse "permanently shattered the Motor City's bid to become the financial capital of the Midwest" and the "bank holiday made clear the narrow vulnerable economic base of the Motor City."[16]

With these events in mind, the auto industry invested in lavish representations of corporate goodwill and technological utopianism at the auto shows and the world's fairs of the 1930s. The automobile industry was no stranger to public relations, showmanship, or expensive exhibits that embedded automobiles in larger notions of progress and national prosperity. Automakers had learned about the importance of public relations and showing off new automobile designs through the venue of the National Automobile Shows. By the Depression, automakers had for thirty years put on annual automobile shows that rivaled the exhibitions at world's fairs in their planning, glitziness, and carefully crafted messages for the public.

National Automobile Show, New York

In 1935 *Automotive Industries* declared, "The auto show is to the industry what the 'first night' is to the stage." The journal observed that the New York show was the best place at which to "feel the public pulse."[17] The National Automobile Show in New York offered the automotive industry a venue in which to hone its skills at speaking to the public, displaying new models, promoting industrial research, and embarking on consumer research. In the 1930s, the New York Show became the primary venue for promoting new styles, such as streamlining, as evidence of corporate leadership and technological progress.

Begun in 1900, the New York Automobile Show became the first of many annual auto exhibitions that brought manufacturers, dealers, and the public together. Early automobile exhibits grew out of the efforts at sporting clubs who embraced the early automobile and championed its makers. However, the local gatherings evolved into a set of prominent national events by 1910, produced by professional showmen in cooperation with the National Automobile Chamber of Commerce (NACC).

These events have a long and complex history that offers a valuable window into the business history and public relations of the young auto industry that cannot be recounted here. However, the shows had an important dual purpose that informed the industry's participation in world's fairs: to bring members of the auto industry together to discuss current business strategies and address problems within the industry, and to engage the public and promote the automobile's contribution to American life. In the early years, divisions within the industry affected the public appearance of the show. Between 1906 and 1911, the New York Show divided into two camps, reflecting the rift among manufacturers involved in the Selden patent case. Manufacturers licensed to manufacture motorcars under George Selden's patent for the gasoline engine hosted one show at Madison Square Garden, and the "Independents" or the unlicensed exhibited their cars at the Grand Central Palace.[18] However, by 1911 the case had been resolved and the shows came together under one roof. Henry Ford, the most independent manufacturer and the challenger in the Selden patent suit, continued to host his own independent exhibitions at the Armory in New York even after the rift was mended.

For the public, automobile shows were exciting events where they could see the latest models and accessories and walk among the elaborate decorations. Entering an automotive exhibition hall, visitors could expect to see automobiles displayed among exotic Roman or Japanese gardens replete with statuary, drooping wisteria, fountains, electric lights, and hundreds of yards of colorful fabric. Automobile journals reviewed the decorative settings every year along with their discussion of current events and model changes.[19] *Automobile Trade Journal* noted in 1910 that the show decorations were "carefully planned to attract the feminine attention as any window trimming on Firth Avenue," because automakers understood that not only were women a growing market but they also held sway over their husbands, the largest consumers of cars.[20] Automotive publications in the 1910s and 1920s also discussed the shows as forms of public education, where middle-class consumers learned about the technology and the social meanings of the automobile.[21] Exhibits gave the public the opportunity to inspect and study the mechanisms of the automobile. The shows marked the growing affordability and popularity of the automobile prior to World War I and promoted the integral role of the automobile in the health and wealth of the nation, reiterating the ideology of the open road.[22] On the silver anniversary of the New York show, *Automobile Trade Journal* noted, "The industrial showmen of the late 1890s were quick to appreciate the possibilities of the automobile from an exhibition standpoint."[23]

Show promoters like National Automobile Show manager Samuel L.

Miles made annual shows mediums for articulating the cultural importance of the new technology. Miles owned the magazine *Motor Age* and
developed the Chicago Inter-Ocean auto exhibition. He quickly became
manager for the nation's largest auto exhibits in New York and Chicago.[24] *Automobile Trade Journal* credited Miles with refining the art of
exhibiting motorcars and using lavish decorations to pique the public's
interest. In 1924, Miles hired two hundred men and women to install
250,000 square feet of material, sixty tons of linoleum, and eighty-four
statues depicting the Goddess of Transportation for the National Automobile Show in New York.[25] Under Miles's direction the events consistently linked national prosperity to the health of the auto industry. In
the 1920s, the promotional booklet at the Grand Central Palace in New
York, where the show was held, observed, "Unlike any other advertising
medium, an exposition brings a man's prospects to him for a heart to
heart talk." The publicity staff went on to note that this personal contact
was beneficial because it gave the manufacturer an "opportunity to meet
dissatisfied buyers and straighten out their attitude."[26]

By the 1930s, the National Automobile Show had become the primary
venue in which to foster corporate goodwill among consumers and help
professional industrial designers stake their claim to authority over styling. *Motor* called the New York Show "the greatest piece of industrial
publicity in existence to-day."[27] General Motors designed its institutional
advertising to incorporate the consumer in the process of industrial capitalism.[28] The 1934 show opened with a great deal of drama that had
little to do with cars or the resiliency of capitalism. On the show floor,
the Studebaker Golden Girls, who handed out golden keys to a new car,
competed with the DeSoto puppet show that narrated four hundred
years of technological progress culminating in the automobile.[29] At the
New York show, the industry tailored its salesmanship to various groups
of consumers. For instance, the NACC hosted "society day" and "wom-
en's day," when specific segments of the car-buying public were asked
to come and view automotive offerings as a group.[30] After hours of being
crushed between cars and enthusiastic performers, theater critic Arthur
Little commented: "Having seen the 1934 performance, I'm convinced
that at an automobile show automobiles are out of place."[31]

Contrary to Little's observation, automobile bodies dominated the
shows of the 1930s; designers and manufacturers believed that changes
in body design would spur consumer confidence and economic recovery. Automotive exhibits that focused on changes in styling gave industry
the opportunity to present itself as a corporate innovator at a time when
major advances in engineering were few.[32] By 1929 the automobile had
reached its modern form in terms of major technical innovations. One
of the tasks of public relations departments of the major manufacturers,

then, was to appeal to the consumer on the level of styling and minor mechanical changes. In response to consumer demand, manufacturers claimed that many of these new "innovations" enhanced the economy and comfort of the automobile.[33] In the mid-1930s, GM introduced knee-action (independent suspension), and synchro-mesh transmission, as milestones in passenger comfort.[34] "None of these techniques . . . was 'invented' at this time," notes automotive historian John B. Rae, "although the advertising might have given this impression."[35] Practically all of these minor improvements had been invented earlier, but were not introduced on regular production models until the 1930s. Incremental introduction of minor innovations made older cars seem obsolete, thus serving the corporation by boosting sales. Planned obsolescence resulted from a "symbiotic relationship between business and consumers" and that "rather than manipulating the public, many manufacturers were trying to catch up with demands for novelty. . . . If the business sector later grew proficient in manipulating style trends, consumers in part brought the curse of planned obsolescence down on themselves."[36] Whether the incorporation of one-time accessories and minor styling changes were made in response to consumer or not, they served to put control of styling in the hands of automobile manufacturers, leaving little room for amateur inventors.

In the early decades of the twentieth century, for the average consumer, the body was the most accessible part of the machine. Reviewing the 1914 New York Auto Show, *Motor Life* commented, "To many motor car users the body is the whole thing. This they see, ride in, talk about, and enjoy."[37] As a result, the automobile body represented a contested terrain where users could claim a modicum of control and knowledge about the design of cars based on personal experience. In the late 1920s and 1930s, the automotive industry equated changes in styling with industrial progress. Streamlining and other slight improvements in styling conflated style with notions of improved engineering. With the introduction of the Chrysler Airflow at the 1934 National Auto Show, streamlining became the most talked about style change of the interwar period.[38] Automotive engineers debated whether the teardrop shapes actually reduced fuel consumption or improved speed.[39] Corporate heads and advertisers believed that the radically different and seemingly advanced shapes would improve sales. *Sales Management* reported: "Streamlining, air-flow, or whatever you are to term it, was on everyone's lips" at the New York Auto Show, and the reporter speculated that the new design would "force obsolescence and thus lend further impetus to the industry in its valiant effort to lead the country out of the depression."[40] Streamlining not only aided obsolescence but also enhanced corporate identity, tying industrial research to notions of progress, power, and innovation.

Streamlined designs unified the various elements of the automobile body and, in doing so, discouraged tinkering by consumers and grassroots inventors. After strolling through the 1934 New York show, a reporter for the *New York Times* wrote, "For one thing, the automobile of today is a unit. Not long ago the body of a car looked as if it had been added to the chassis as an afterthought. . . . [Now] they are parts of a complete vehicle."[41] The automobile of twenty years before looked like a compilation of aftermarket parts and accessories, fenders, trunks, headlights jutted from the frame of the car.[42] These older designs held many advantages for users. Cars with few standard accessories, like the Model T, were less expensive and more open to tinkering by users. Repair costs were also lower. In the event of an accident, owners could replace damaged parts cheaply and quickly. By 1933, however, industrial designers had submerged protruding headlights and incorporated fenders, bumpers, lights and trunks into the molded exterior of the body.

As a design philosophy, unity reinforced the authority of the professional designer. According to Walter Dorwin Teague, a prominent industrial designer, the days of aftermarket accessories and tinkering ended with the rise of professionals in the 1920s.[43] In order to "redesign" a product, Teague argued, one had to understand the "universal principles of good design." In 1934, Teague asserted that good automotive design constituted a principle of "fitness" that expressed the "perfect adaptation of means to an end." The laws of fitness were "unchangeable and invariable"—principles to be studied and learned. Understanding these ideas distinguished professionals from amateurs. Teague wrote, "Any organism must be conceived as a unity, one theme, one purpose, must dominate it; all its elements must be integrated as closely as possible, so that it looks as if it had been poured in a single mold."[44] Good design excluded the multifunctional, aftermarket modifications of tinkerers. Accessories added by the motorist might improve the fit between the product and the user but, under Teague's definition, such tinkering destroyed unity.[45]

The unified shape of the streamlined automobile proved largely tinker-resistant, especially after the development of the all-steel bodies in the mid-1920s. Unlike the earlier and more pliable metal-covered wooden bodies, steel bodies were virtually impervious to the average car owner's tools.[46] In addition, smooth surfaces and curved shapes made even temporary additions such as home-built luggage racks difficult to attach to the car. As one travel expert commented in 1935, "On older cars it was possible to build a flat box on the running board over which the car doors would open." But, he continued, "there is practically no room on these new, low, streamlined cars for storage . . . one must turn to the trunk rack on the back."[47] As a grass-roots inventor, Earl Tupper also confronted the new challenges of the streamlined all-steel body when designing and marketing his rumble seat cover. One of Tupper's chief problems in designing a removable top was how to attach the top to the rear of the automobile without screwing the frame into the body of the car. Additionally, he faced the criticism when marketing the top that it destroyed the integrity or streamlined unity of the automobile.

By the 1934 National Auto Show, most automobile manufacturers had incorporated consumer modifications, like the trunk, into the body of the automobile and eliminated the need for drivers to build accessories. After twenty years of home-built storage boxes, patented luggage carriers, and various aftermarket accessories that promised to "solve the baggage problem," General Motors announced the introduction of the "integrated" trunk as a standard feature on mid-priced cars in 1933.[48] Despite numerous consumer experiments with trunks in the 1910s and 1920s, manufacturers and designers claimed that interior trunks were solely the product of modern engineering and unified styling. General Motors claimed that such innovations as the trunk, "if adopted individually would have done little to improve the appearance of the automobile. . . . When molded together according to a plan conceived in the imaginative minds of the Stylists, however, these features completed the evolution of the body from a coach to an automobile."[49] GM promoted the addition of the trunk as its own innovation.

The automotive industry declared that styling improved the automobile and illustrated the monumental contribution of the automotive industry to the prosperity of the United States.[50] The President of Nash, for instance, told the *New York Times*: "this colorful exposition is more than just a view of the latest American merchandise on parade. It's a cross-section of transportation progress, a proud expression of national confidence."[51] Alvan Macauley, president of the NACC, declared that the auto had become "the most important necessity of American life," and therefore the National Automobile Show took on an "economic and social significance far exceeding in importance that of any ordinary merchandise."[52]

Century of Progress World's Fair, Chicago, 1933–1934

Chicago's Century of Progress World's Fair gave the automobile industry an opportunity to change more than just the shape of automobiles. Exhibitions at the world's fair, like automobile shows, offered manufacturers the best place to reach a wide audience and to shift perceptions of progress. At dynamic exhibits, the automobile industry defined progress as the product of corporate planning and control and revised popular narratives created by magazines, serial fiction, and travel narratives that portrayed users and grass-roots inventors as agents of change. Indeed the world's fairs taught the public "the prominence of machines as instruments of distinctly American progress."[53] At the fair, car companies placed themselves at the helm of American progress through technological pageantry.[54]

Pageants of technological progress had a long history. Beginning in the late nineteenth century, civic officials and manufacturers had used pageantry to draw together the disparate elements of society and rationalize a social and technological hierarchy.[55] Early industrial pageants promoted industrial growth as the catalyst of human progress, and became a "powerful advertisement" for technology and "those whose interests it served"—namely, manufacturers.[56] The industrial elite used the Chicago fair to delineate who contributed to technological progress and in what order. This was illustrated by the slogan of the fair: "Science discovers, genius invents, industry applies, and man adapts himself to, or is molded by, new things."[57] The official program explained the purpose of the exposition: to "help the American people to understand themselves, and to make clear to the coming generation the forces which have built this nation."[58] In particular, exhibits sponsored by Ford and General Motors cast the automotive industry as the most important force in building modern America.

The industry's investment in the fair went beyond boosting public faith in pure science.[59] Ford, General Motors, and Chrysler had cars to sell, and they, as well as smaller automotive manufacturers, used the fair to promote both their economic leadership and their products. Although automobile sales had dropped to a quarter of their pre-Depression numbers in 1929, the press believed the automobile industry was an economic leader that would end the Depression through increased production and consumption.[60] A journalist for the *Economist* and *Business Week* reported that the automobile industry "has been the liveliest and most alert industry in the country when all else was gloom." He claimed that through "improvement of models, lower prices, sounder merchandising methods," automobile corporations had provided a viable model for economic recovery "making more goods and creating more wants."[61]

The industry embraced public relations as a way to improve its image and its sales during the Depression. In the past, Henry Ford had often slowed the company's public relations efforts by arguing that the quality of the product would speak for itself and generate sales.[62] But after the negative events of 1932 and 1933, the Ford Motor Company reassessed its approach. Also in a bid to compete with popular exhibits of Chrysler and General Motors, Ford opened a lavish exhibition hall and park at Century of Progress World's Fair in 1934.[63] Sales specialists at Ford noted, "In the main there are two kinds of advertising—informative, and good-will building, and Ford uses them both." Along with participation in the fair, Ford sponsored radio broadcasts of symphony programs and the World Series in 1934. Ford's public relations staff admitted, "such advertising is rather difficult to justify on the basis of immediate sales returns, but nevertheless has its place and value." The company noted that radio sponsorship, "like our Exposition at Chicago, . . . [has] a carry-over of institutional value that builds reputation for the organization and creates good-will."[64] Reviews of car sales by leading business magazines showed that Ford's advertising scheme might have worked; after three years of losses the company doubled its sales in 1934 and ended the year with a profit. Ford cars accounted for the highest number of new car registrations in 1934.[65]

General Motors, in contrast, had been an aggressive corporate advertiser since the mid-1920s.[66] Events like the Chicago fair illustrated attempts by General Motors to construct a public image as a leader in engineering research. In the 1930s, Charles Kettering became GM's public persona in that arena.[67] In conjunction with the opening of the National Automobile Show in January 1933, *Time* featured Kettering on its cover.[68] "Boss" Kettering rivaled Henry Ford as a figure who was accessible to the majority of middle-class American drivers. Like Ford, Kettering had left the farm for the opportunities of industrialization but remained full of folksy advice.[69] Kettering invented his way to financial success by creating one of the first successful electric starters for automobiles. Before joining General Motors in early 1919, Kettering headed the Dayton Engineering Laboratories Company (Delco), an industrial research laboratory and automotive accessories firm that became part of GM.[70]

"Boss" Kettering was arguably as savvy about public relations as General Motors president, Alfred E. Sloan. In the 1920s, Kettering opened the GM research laboratory to tours. Sloan took a "dim view" of showing the local chamber of commerce through the lab because of the security risk. Kettering eventually set up a special lab just for tourists where white-coated engineers performed trivial experiments.[71] Through numerous public speeches and through his work in setting up GM's exhibit at the 1933–34 Chicago fair, Kettering became the public face of General Motors. R. K. Evans, vice president in charge of diesel engines, recalled, "I always had the feeling that General Motors lost a great deal in its competition with Ford, because it was a headless corporation insofar as the public was concerned." Evans recalled that none of the divisional heads of General Motors measured up to Ford for public recognition, except for Kettering. "Ket's activities from the very early days were of real value in at least having one individual appearing before the public in various ways and establishing some record of contribution of the Corporation . . . to the progress of the country."[72] Kenneth Meade, head of the Education Relations Section at GM, praised the Boss's interest in turning all public appearances into educational experiences. These included commissioning Meade to bring school groups through the Chicago exhibits and using the dioramas and the assembly line "to tell the story of research."[73] Allen Orth, a fellow engineer and architect of the General Motors exhibit at Chicago who later became a public relations man, remembered that Kettering was "quick to take advantage of all media available to reach people and even conceived of some novel means of his own."[74]

In 1934, General Motors hosted a "Previews of Progress" dinner at the fair as an organized show of confidence in corporate capitalism.[75] General Motors invited corporate presidents, research engineers, historians, and journalists to articulate the alliance among science and industry and progress.[76] One journalist praised Alfred Sloan for facilitating an event where the "calm and unshaken confidence in the future was presented by men of knowledge and imagination."[77] A positive but illusive value, progress for these men encompassed both scientific and social change and was most easily measured through the production of new goods. L. W. Chubb, director of the Westinghouse Research Laboratories, told his colleagues, "Science, invention and engineering progress have been the greatest contributors to world progress and a high standard of living for years."[78] Chubb pinned his hopes for economic recovery and continued innovation not on the individual citizen, lone inventor, or even experienced political leader, but on corporations that employed trained scientists and engineers.

Yet the industry did not lose sight of the consumer as an integral player in the economic forces of recovery. One of Kettering's favorite arguments was that industry could spur economic recovery only if manufacturers produced things people wanted to buy. He told the Advertising Federation of America, "if one-tenth of the energy was spent getting products that people wanted . . . instead of stirring up the mud, we would get along a lot better."[79]

Although the newly-elected Franklin Roosevelt supported the Century of Progress fair and cooperation between business and government, the Previews of Progress speeches disapproved of regulation that limited production and advocated consumer protection.[80] Richard Harte, President of Ames Baldwin Wyoming Company, characterized Roosevelt's National Industrial Recovery Act as "illusory and false and political quackery."[81] According to Kettering who, in many ways, became the face of General Motors in the 1930s, increased production and consumption rather than economic or political reform provided way out of the Depression.

Auto manufacturers were aided in their mission to both impress the public and shift the discourse of ingenuity in their favor by a new breed of experts—professional industrial designers. Henry Dreyfuss, Walter Dorwin Teague, and Norman Bel Geddes infused the automotive exhibits of the 1930s with a new philosophy on design that articulated the agendas of their corporate sponsors.[82] Designers such as Teague, who contributed to Ford's pavilion, intended their exhibits to impress the general public with the superiority of professional design. Teague predicted that the "American public will receive a new revelation. . . . The throngs who wander through this strange city will never again think of design in quite the same way. They cannot help being awed; they cannot refuse to accept these new forms as practical and sound, and if their hostility survives it will at least be shaken and on the defensive."[83] The automotive industry and their attendant designers wanted visitors to see the material elements of their everyday lives refashioned, updated, and improved by industry.

In sharp contrast to the stalled economy, the automotive pavilions at the World's Fair provided a vision of the automobile industry as dynamic. The dominant theme of the exhibits, as articulated by their sponsors, was "process." This focus on movement had its roots in the auto shows that preceded the Chicago fair and was developed as yet another way to capture the attention of the public. Before the automobile show in Atlantic City in 1927, Alfred Sloan wrote to Charles Kettering on the importance of creating dynamic auto exhibits that focused on styling over technical innovations. Sloan wrote, "What we want is something that moves—something that is original and makes an impression on the minds that the Corporation is progressing. . . . Manifestly, the thing that [the visitors] see need not have anything to do with the quality of the car."[84]

During the Depression-era fairs, process-oriented exhibits underscored the idea that auto manufacturers were constantly at work to make new and improved products for the benefit of Americans. "Almost everything moves," declared James Weber Linn, chronicler of the fair, in 1933.[85] The journal of the Society of Automotive Engineers (SAE) also praised automotive exhibits for striking "a new note in animation and motion in its many displays."[86] All of the automotive displays incorporated movement into their exhibits, with varying results from superficial showmanship to lessons in mass production. The SAE described Chrysler's exhibit hall as belonging to "the modern idyllic school of architecture, the motif being one of progress and motion in motive engineering."[87] Constructed of enormous sheets of glass, the Chrysler building was also one of the largest automotive show rooms showcasing the Airflow and other modern designs. The Nash building claimed one of the most dynamic pieces of exhibit architecture at the fair: a tall glass structure surrounding a machine that resembled an automotive Ferris wheel. A cross between an elevator and a motorized parking garage, the exhibit featured a conveyor belt that moved sixteen automobiles up and down on an "endless vertical chain."[88] The glass walls drew the viewer's attention to the product and to the extraordinary mechanism that lifted tons of steel in a smooth, neverending rotation.

The power to move large machinery became an important element of automotive exhibits, which embraced sensationalism along with loftier goals of progress. Studebaker's exhibit, for example, consisted of catapulting new cars into a rock quarry. This exhibit won praise from marketing specialists because it drew large crowds, although it is difficult to say what message the crowds took away from such a destructive display. (One might interpret the exhibit as a metaphor for the economic problems facing automakers in the Depression.) Ford also flexed its corporate muscle on the fairgrounds by suspending three sedans from a standard Ford wheel rim as the centerpiece of its pavilion. Besides demonstrating the strength of Ford products and the integrity of its engineering, the sheer size of the exhibit displayed the power of the automotive industry; only a company with the resources of Ford could mount such a heavy, if pointless, experiment.

Designers denied stooping to showmanship and argued that such process-oriented demonstrations educated the public about production and durability. Exhibit designers emphasized "process rather than product," relying on motion to attract visitors and explain the principles of flexible mass production.[89] The National Research Council, which organized the exhibitions at the fair, promoted these displays as highly educational for the average American, who they said had little knowledge of science, technology, or production.[90] Yet, the more practical impression was one of America at work, or the illusion that the auto industry still had its plants running and that prosperity was indeed just around the corner. All American consumers had to do was to hold up their end of the economy by purchasing more new cars.

According to James Weber Linn, the majority of the exhibits were patterned on "what has come to be called the 'diorama' as a pictorial presentation of movement." He noted that the "innumerable dioramas show man and even nature . . . set forth at work."[91] General Motors, for instance, installed an entire Chevrolet assembly line in its exhibit hall as a moving diorama.[92] *Automotive Industries* reported that "each niche" of the Chrysler fair building, designed by Alexis de Sakhnoffsky, was "given up to demonstrations of major Chrysler car features from an engineering-design viewpoint."[93] A miniature steel plant produced alloy used in steel cars, and a "gigantic forging hammer" made steering spindles for Plymouths once every two minutes. Visitors could also witness firsthand the advantages of streamlining and new industrial testing methods by watching gale-force winds pummel the Chrysler Airflow in a wind tunnel. One of the most interactive exhibits, a "floating power platform," demonstrated the impact of flexibly mounted engines on riding comfort. Visitors were asked to stand on the platform and experience the differences in vibration caused by solidly mounted versus flexibly mounted engines.[94] Although this exhibit resembled a funhouse trick, one of the fair organizers wrote, "Here is innovation, perhaps a sign of the new order of things—industry joining hands to show the world the fundamentals of their craftsmanship . . . and spending fortunes to do it."[95] However, the automotive industry did not spend millions on fair exhibits just to entertain visitors. Manufacturers hoped to win the goodwill of the public, foster brand loyalty, and demonstrate to the consumer that modern industrial research contributed to improved automotive design and the quality of life in the United States.

Educating Consumers

The Ford Motor Company embraced the educational project of the exhibits at the Chicago fair. Henry Ford told *Commerce* in the spring of 1934 that "we want our exposition to be just as instructive as it is possible to make it. . . . Wherever possible each exhibit will be in action, producing something. We want the exposition to be a moving demonstration of the contribution made by various industries . . . to the modern automobile."[96] According to Edsel Ford, Henry's son and president of Ford Motor Company, the company had participated in world's fairs beginning with the St. Louis Exposition in 1904 solely because of their educational value.[97] The younger Ford explained, "We believe that in the crowds . . . passing through the gates . . . will be many of tomorrow's scientists, inventors, . . . engineers and technicians."[98] True to the company's populist philosophy, Ford left the door open for the average American to become an innovator. Ford Motor Company exhibits taught the values of technical training, while firmly maintaining the hegemony of large manufacturers like Ford over all aspects or design and production.[99]

In fact, Ford exhibits at the Chicago fair limited the imaginary scope of who could contribute to automotive innovation in the twentieth century. The extensive displays and historical dioramas constructed a hierarchy of innovation that obscured the contributions of not only individual inventors but people in general, focusing solely on the power of the large company. A latecomer to the fair, Henry Ford felt his building had to be larger and more impressive than any of his competitors. Designed by architect Albert Kahn, the building (900 feet long and 213 feet wide) sat on eleven acres of lakefront property.[100] The dramatic rotunda, not only rose twelve stories above the lake but projected beams of light a mile into the night sky. Off the rotunda, a streamlined concourse held exhibits by Ford and twenty-one large parts and accessories manufacturers. Responsible for the design of the exhibits within the building, Teague divided the sprawling space into "stanzas" or episodes in the great theme of Ford production and research. Within this poetic structure, stanzas included the past, represented by an "oldtime workshop" and some relics from an 1850 machine shop and old tools from Ford's Bagley Street garage where he built his first cars; the Drama of Transportation, a progression of vehicles that told the story of "wheel and road" through the ages beginning with King Tut's chariot and ending with Ford's V-8; industrial production that featured parts manufacturers and Ford's finish products; industrialized farming and homage to the soybean; and a display of the Ford Trade School as evidence of the "contribution of the industrial designer and mechanical engineer to modern machine production."[101] The last was one of the few sections of the exhibition that included people. Almost all the stanzas focused visitors' attention on the monolithic role of the company.

The public entered the Ford building through the central rotunda whose exhibits graphically illustrated the global reach of the company. "The main idea of the Ford exhibit is institutional," observed *Automotive Industries*. "From the showmanship standpoint it gives a conception of the so-called Ford Empire and is typified by a huge revolving globe, in the center of the rotunda."[102] Twenty feet in diameter, the globe mapped Ford branch plants and subsidiary industries (such as forests, mines, and factories) all over the world, showing a vast empire on which the sun never set. At the center of the map lay the River Rouge plant, the embodiment of Ford's dream of controlling the process of production from raw materials to finished products.[103] To make sure the public understood the concept of vertical integration, the central diorama explained how the Ford Motor Company gathered, organized, consolidated, and transformed the resources of the earth into automobiles. A cutaway Ford V-8 demonstrated to the public the many materials that went into the production of the car. Projecting from the body of the V-8, arrows connected the components of the car to the resources of the earth. The explanatory label read: "Man takes the basic materials from the soil and his ingenuity transforms them into fabricated products."[104]

Figure 20. Ford Motor Company exposition building presented tangible evidence of the links among modernist aesthetics, corporate power, and the discourses of innovation and progress. Ford Building at the Century of Progress World's Fair, Chicago, 1934, Warshaw Collection of Business Americana—World Expositions, Archives Center, National Museum of American History, Behring Center, Smithsonian Institution, Washington, D.C.

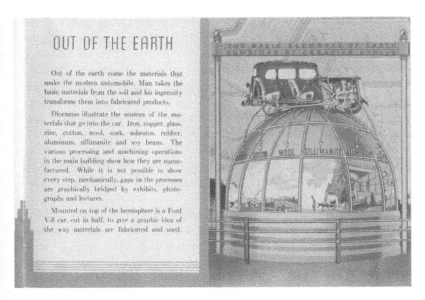

Figure 21. Exhibit in the rotunda of the Ford exposition building demonstrated the ability of the modern corporation to control the resources of the world. "Out of the Earth," Ford V-8 Exhibit, at the Century of Progress World's Fair, Chicago, 1934. From the Collections of The Henry Ford (G3792).

Despite its reference to "Man," the diorama showed no human figures and celebrated the power of the modern corporation. In the eyes of the automotive industry, the era of automobile production by small manufacturers and individual inventors, with few exceptions, had come to a graphic end.

Despite the size of the exhibit, Teague crafted a narrow vision of who could initiate in progress. The Drama of Transportation largely ignored the role of people in shaping transportation and presented a seamless, linear history of machine development that Ford exhibit designers would recycle for years to come. The rotunda exhibit was moved to Dearborn after the fair and remained open to the public until 1962.[105] The internalist history of technology embodied by the Drama of Transportation left little room for the messy stories of early tinkerers, enthusiasts, and amateur inventors who used trial and error to develop the first automobiles. Even the "oldtime machine shop" pointed to the superior facilities of the modern corporation and, in Ford's case the family-owned company, over the inadequate tools of individual mechanic or grass-roots inventor.

Despite Henry Ford's status as one of America's most successful tinkerers, the machine shop exhibit explained that lacking modern equipment "nobody, however great, even with a perfect conception of the modern automobile, could possibly have built it" using the inferior tools of 1850.[106] In the exhibit's vision, a potential inventor needed advanced equipment and a laboratory that more closely resembled Edison's Menlo Park and the training provided at the Ford Trade School. This story of innovation made Henry Ford's early work seem even more exceptional, but also firmly relegated his experiences to the past. Spatially, as well, the "oldtime machine shop" represented a detour from the main Drama of Transportation. Here, Teague drew a sharp contrast between the poorly equipped mechanic of the past and the modern professionals trained in engineering and design at the Ford Motor Company.

Automotive exhibits may have firmly dismissed the tinkerer and the grass-roots inventor to the past, but they did not want to exclude American consumers from the chain of progress. Industrial exhibits reinforced the notion that the automobile industry improved everyday life by providing new consumer goods. General Motors' Hall of Progress, for instance, situated planned obsolescence within the historical narrative of technological progress. The exhibit illustrated the difficulties and dangers of driving before the introduction of each new invention. For instance, a panel entitled "Progress and Starting" paired a line drawing of a strong man struggling to crank-start an old-fashioned motor car and a well-dressed modern woman turning the ignition key with ease. The text claimed that prior to the electric ignition the automobile could be used only by strong men and often resulted in bruised muscles and broken bones. But General Motors asserted that the auto manufacturer had ushered in a new era of comfort in which even women could drive without physical danger.[107] The exhibit neglected to mention the numerous patents for electric starters and the resistance Charles Kettering had faced when tried to sell his electric ignition to Cadillac decades earlier. In addition, newer and less significant innovations, such as knee-action suspension and no-draft ventilation, were represented as equal contributors to progress.

As part of its mission to educate the consumer, the GM Century of Progress exhibit presented automotive inventions as evidence of corporate largess. "Research at A Century of Progress," an accompanying brochure told readers, "General Motors offers . . . an exhibit of some of the tools Science has placed in the hands of Research—Research that offers assurance that General Motors is sincere in its efforts always to build better automobiles." The consumer benefited from owning cars that were indeed "more complicated," but also "infinitely more reliable" and more "easily operated" than the pioneer carriages.[108] GM's exhibits, both in its own Hall of Progress and in the Hall of Science, gave Kettering's staff a chance to perform its technical expertise in front of a live audience, unlike in print advertising. Here the staff of engineers explained the scientific and technical principals behind ordinary consumer technologies, arguing that GM understood the complexities of industrial research and that the corporation possessed technological expertise beyond that of the average driver.

Reluctant to leave the didactic venue of the world's fair behind, Kettering moved part of GM's exhibit to Detroit and in 1936 created a traveling science show entitled "Parade of Progress."[109] In a competitive move against Ford, GM scheduled the first performance in Lakeland, Florida, the same southern state where Ford had transplanted the Diorama of Progress after the Chicago fair.[110] The Parade of Progress, which began as a "Circus of Science," earned Kettering and John Reedy, a member of the public relations staff, the nicknames "Barnum and Bailey of General Motors."[111] The show fused technological expertise, corporate capitalism, and public relations into an old-fashioned traveling show. Kettering and his staff demonstrated the basic scientific principles behind the telephone, the electric light, pistons, and magnetic fields, things that would lose their drama if publicized in print or broadcast on radio. The show intended to take the average man and woman behind the scenes into research laboratories, which General Motors called "theaters of achievement," where visitors could see the "ingenious devices and methods utilized in bringing about the progress of the world we live in."[112]

Traveling in "streamlined leviathans" (experimental busses), the show carried General Motors' goodwill across the nation.[113] In the 1930s, the busses traversed the country, stopping in towns with populations between 10,000 and 100,000 and GM plant cities speaking to school groups and workers.[114] In 1937, "Previews of Progress" traveled the Northeast coast playing in small towns from Farmington, Maine, to Quincy, Massachusetts, with over 250,000 people attending the 356 shows. Following Kettering's educational vision, the show played at colleges and high schools.[115] The public relations men and staff of engineers who presented "Previews" asserted that the show inspired many "young men to continue their studies and enter the fields of research and engineering." Yet the staff also admitted that the technical and scientific information in the shows was highly simplified for a nontechnical audience.[116]

At a time of labor unrest, General Motors also hoped that Previews of Progress would build a sense of corporate loyalty among its workers. In the spring of 1938, a year after the landmark labor strike in Flint, Michigan, General Motors sent the Previews of Progress to a number of its plant cities including Pontiac, Flint, and Saginaw.[117] Paul Garrett, public relations man for GM, quoted plant managers who sponsored the show as proof of the positive public relations work done by "Previews of Progress" in plant cities. The resident manager at Grand Rapids reported: "Our employes [*sic*] reacted most favorably to each performance, and I feel assured that their interest and respect for the Corporation is at a new high."[118] Responses from the audience of workers and schoolteachers, carefully selected and quoted by Garrett in his letter to plant managers, were overwhelmingly favorable. For example, one tool and die welder allegedly remarked: "It's a treat for a fellow working on this end of the game to see what our Engineers are doing and to know that the future holds so much us." Another worker added: "Seeing a display like this . . . gives a person a lot more confidence in the future."[119] Rather than a corporation fractured by labor disputes, these quotes constructed an image of a seamless organization where every member worked together in the pursuit of progress.

Whether the Century of Progress exhibitions or "Previews of Progress" fostered a greater understanding of science and technology among audience members was not the primary concern of automotive corporations. In fact, journalists observed that crowds at both shows were not impressed by the technical demonstrations. One writer for *Sales Management* commented: "Lo, the poor manufacturer! Whenever he or engineers or scientists . . . rise to speak the consumer apparently gets a good laugh."[120] Alternatively, some audience members found a way to get only the information they needed. For instance, two young members of Kettering's audience found his detailed technical instructions of simple apparatus immediately useful. After hearing the explanation of how a telegraph worked, the boys dashed out of the auditorium. Their father approached Kettering after the show and apologized. He told Kettering that they had spent months trying to devise a way to communicate across the back yard; Kettering had given the boys the technical solution to their problem and they had gone home to build a telegraph.[121] Rather than reflecting on the larger message of General Motors' expertise, they took what was personally useful and left the show.

Programs for the general public aimed to impress consumers with the expertise of corporate engineers and scientists. Kettering and his staff offered little evidence that Previews inspired audience members to gain technical training. Previews staff characterized their audience as having only the simplest understanding of the technical demonstrations and marveled at the way Kettering, in particular, could reduce complex ideas to fit the level of the "average" audiences.[122] For Kettering and his staff, the need to simplify technical ideas proved that consumers lacked sufficient knowledge to understand the new technology or contribute to the design of the automobile on the same level as engineers.

"What Does the Public Want?"

Having assigned most Americans to the role of consumers, auto corporations nevertheless wanted to gauge the public's response to their exhibitions and their products. Participation in the Chicago World's Fair was expensive. The Ford Motor Company spent an estimated $13 million on its pavilion there.[123] Exhibits were costly, but they provided valuable information on consumers through letters, conversation, attendance numbers, and eventually market surveys. The fair brought more mail to Henry Ford, who received many letters thanking him for the Century of Progress exhibit. Still highly opinionated, Ford's correspondents also critiqued the company's policies on pricing and New Deal legislation. Although correspondents thought the price of the new Ford V-8 was too high, most writers expressed their approval of the Ford-sponsored programs at the Chicago fair and their loyalty to Ford products.[124] Letters could not accurately measure of the cost-benefit ratio of exhibiting, and the company relied on attendance records and dealer referrals acquired at the fair to measure the effectiveness of its exhibits.[125]

Visitor statistics became a point of competition among automotive manufacturers. The *New York Times*, for instance, published attendance at the annual New York Auto Show, and industry leaders consistently used the numbers as an indicator of consumer confidence, growing national prosperity, and the benefits of exhibiting.[126] Attendance at Ford exhibitions had peaked at the Chicago fair at twelve million but never again reached such heights at other fairs.[127] At the beginning of the New York World's Fair in 1939, C. W. Olmsted, who was contracted to work on the Ford exhibit, wrote to the company inquiring about the opening figures on attendance. A Ford representative responded that General Motors claimed their exhibit had attracted 100,000 people in the first few days, and then commented that this "was obviously an out and out lie and when they were called on it by the Director of Publicity of the Exposition, they pulled in their horns and since then they have refused to quote any figures on their attendance."[128]

To automobile companies invested in rational management, these methods of measuring consumer interest seemed unreliable, and they sought new ways to calculate and manage consumer desire in the 1930s. Thus consumer research was born.[129] Although the automotive industry first recognized the need to study consumers in the 1920s, the Depression saw the dawn of "consumer engineering." Consumer engineering borrowed the tenets of scientific accuracy and the ability to control not only the product but also the larger systems of production and consumption from the profession of engineering: "Using market surveys, consumer questionnaires, and behavioral psychology, consumption engineers would predict changes in buying habits and end disastrous trial-and error marketing." Automotive corporations "would truly engineer consumption by manufacturing needs that had not before existed."[130]

The automotive industry first attempted to understand buyers during the postwar economic slump of 1919–1921.[131] Manufacturing journals urged manufacturers to rethink the consumption end of automotive production. *Automotive Industries* advised manufacturers "caught unawares by the changed conditions" that they needed more direct contact with the public in order to stimulate a "mass selling system." The journal noted the manufacturer's dependency on its dealers and told manufacturers that they should take a more active hand in "creating the user demand."[132] By 1926, Leon F. Banigan, editor of *Motor World Wholesale*, told a broad audience of accessory manufacturers and large automotive companies that what they needed was more scientific control over consumption: "Over-production, over-selling and lack of selling, substitution, price-cutting, returned goods, freight bill squabbles, gypping, and most other ills . . . are natural by-products of lack of scientific control of business." Banigan suggested that the industry could save money by understanding consumer desires. He wrote that he sensed the "signs of rebellion in the ranks of consumers," who had been pressured into overstimulated buying, and advised that dealers and manufacturers, if they wanted to remain competitive, must analyze their retail customers—asking them what they bought, how much, when and why.[133] Additionally, publications such as *Machine Design* recognized that drivers could provide useful information because they were experts on use. The journal advised manufacturers, "In spite of all these precautions, the machine which you have designed will, in the customer's hands, be subjected to tests that the most fertile brain could not possibly think of in advance. . . . For the actual test of practical operation by a customer there is no substitute."[134]

General Motors, in particular, launched ambitious consumer research programs to better understand and shape what drivers wanted. Between 1933 and 1935, the question of "What Does the Public Want?" echoed through industry journals.[135] General Motors introduced one of the first consumer surveys of automotive design in 1933–34 at both the National Automobile Show in New York and at the Chicago World's Fair.[136] Although public relations people at GM claimed the company had conducted consumer research since 1921, this was the first effort that demanded its own staff to create scientific questionnaires and to analyze the responses both statistically and psychologically.

According to Henry Weaver, sales analyst, General Motors recognized that corporations had lost personal contact with the people who bought their product. Weaver reported to *American Marketing Journal* in July 1934 that GM sought to "restore something of the close personal contact and the human relations that existed between the producer and the consumer before the days of large-scale operations."[137] To this end, between 1933 and 1934 GM invited 1,500,000 "practical motorists" to "pool their practical experience with the technical skill of General Motors engineers."[138] General Motors did not seem interested in the earlier experiences and ideas sent to the New Devices Committee in the 1920s; rather, they wanted to manage the advice and expectations of consumers through carefully structured questionnaires.

General Motors devoted part of its exhibit at the Century of Progress fair to consumer research. The fair delivered large numbers of upper middle-class consumers into the hands of marketing specialists at the GM pavilion, where staff distributed "The Automobile Buyer's Guide" and "Your Car as You Would Build It."[139] The architects of the General Motors consumer survey designed its forms to show the consumer what she or he wanted rather than inviting unstructured criticism.[140] The questionnaires asked car buyers to respond to a long list of options including styling, engineering, and personal modifications. Harry Weaver advocated absolute simplicity in the questionnaires, instructing designers of similar surveys to tone down technical language even if it did not represent "the best of scientific terminology."[141] Norman Shindle also emphasized that the "Buyer's Guide" needed easy explanations of engineering features, commenting that the booklet was so simple and "pictureized" that it required no reading.[142] Simplified descriptions of features such as knee-action and rubber-mounted engines promoted and familiarized the public with these General Motors developments as opposed to offering the consumer a choice among competing technologies.[143] There was little room in the survey to offer individual or unguided opinions; only one short section at the end asked for unstructured advice on modification. Under the heading "Your Car as You Would Build It," the survey asked readers "What in your judgment should be the next important advance in automobile design?"[144] Whether General Motors incorporated any of the responses into their future design decisions is difficult to determine. When selected answers to this question appeared in the "Buyer's Guide," the research staff diplomatically dismissed them as either "tremendous trifles" or as technologically impractical. These comments were ironic coming from an industry that promoted streamlining and other minor improvements in comfort and control as progress in the 1930s. Consumer suggestions ranged from "more accessible tire valves," to "3-spoke steering wheels for better visibility of instruments"; all suggestions were lumped under the heading of gadgetry rather than advances in design or engineering.[145] Shindle called these suggestions important to sales but "minor from the standpoint of the technician."[146]

Yet styling remained a dialectical process. The text of the General Motors brochures flattered consumers by making them part of technological progress. "We have become a nation of mechanically-minded people, a people who have been around and seen things," noted the booklet entitled "Customer Research."[147] Depicting the consumer as a link in the chain of modern industry, the introduction to the questionnaire also informed the consumers of their particular position. General Motors told readers that the "average motorist is more of an expert on USE than he is on the intricacies of engineering design." Nevertheless, customer research provided "the connecting link by bringing scientific research and inventive genius into proper relation with the needs . . . of the ultimate consumer."[148] General Motors acknowledged that drivers knew something about auto design. However, the corporation's market survey cast the user as a consumer, rather than a potential innovator, who ultimately had to choose among the improvements offered by the corporation. In this way, General Motors drew a distinct line between use and innovation, the latter belonging to corporate experts alone.

Automakers regarded the consumer with almost equal measures of deference and contempt.[149] The majority of those involved in automotive production from engineering to design to sales agreed that the "consumer was King," meaning that buyers determined the success of new models and the economic health of the industry.[150] *Automotive Industries* warned automotive engineers, "Buyers remember the bugs [in automotive design] long after engineers have forgotten them." The writer conceded: "Both manufacturers and dealers well know that when the car-buying public realizes a fault exists in a new model, selling resistance is quickly created."[151] The solution to this problem: engineers should test the automobile more completely before, rather than after, production began, and change should be incremental rather than drastic. The writer acknowledged that the public, because it understood use better than some engineers, could slow production and profits by refusing to purchase poorly tested cars.[152] While the author believed that the public understood use, he did not think that consumers understood engineering well enough to make specific design suggestions.

Professional designers and engineers argued that consumers lacked technical knowledge, sophisticated taste, and even purchasing savvy. William Stout, designer and president of his own engineering laboratory, told the Society of Automotive Engineers in 1933 that the engineering department found it "impossible to design a motor car of any value by the slide rule alone, for . . . there is John Q. Public and his wife and the friends he goes with that determine what is . . . purchased."[153] Nevertheless, Stout laid out the hierarchical relationship between the public and the engineer. Not mincing words, he wrote: "John Q. Public cannot design the new vehicle; he does not know what he wants until he sees it. . . . The business of the automotive engineer therefore is to lead the purchasing public along the paths in which they should go."[154] In addition, Norman Shindle, designer of the original "Proving Ground of Public Opinion" survey, reassured engineers that their position of technological authority was safe: "The engineers know that basic motor car development lies in realms of research and technical investigation along lines which never could come within the scope of lay thinking. . . . Engineering research will not abdicate to consumer research."[155] By stripping the driver of ingenuity and technical understanding, the engineer and designer would maintain their authority over design.

The industry press reinforced the notion that consumers, though critical, were generally unknowledgeable.[156] Writing for *Sales Management,* one reporter told manufacturers that the Chicago fair was the ideal place to observe consumer behavior: "Certainly you will gain an entirely fresh impression of the domesticity and simple lack of sophistication that make up the average American purchaser of your goods."[157] A 1934 article entitled "King Customer" confirmed for manufacturers that the consumer needed help in making purchasing decisions and guidance in understanding the product, noting that simple, dramatic exhibits worked the best because "the public simply will not make the mental effort to study or interpret" symbolism. Quoting H. L. Mencken, the article advised, "'no one ever lost money underestimating the intelligence of the American public.' For very little is really self-evident to Mr. Average Citizen." In particular, they concluded that the "well-intended efforts to induce self-participation, in the Hall of Science and elsewhere" failed because "the story is too complex for most of the participants."[158] While such articles offered a critique of exhibit practice, they also underscored the belief that the average American could not be a full participant in progress.

At its most extreme, the auto industry characterized the customer as an impediment to technological progress.[159] C. B. Veal, research manager of the Society of Automotive Engineers, argued that the public retarded the development of valuable innovations. He characterized Depression-era consumers as more interested in cost than technological advancement. Veal told the *New York Times* that "as long as the public is satisfied with reasonable comfort and speed, these better and perhaps revolutionary ideas will be kept safely locked in the company's safe until such time as competition or an enlightened public demand shall cause their inclusion in new models."[160] H. J. Klingler, president of Pontiac, agreed: "Motorists themselves are the limiting factor in the development of automotive design." He argued, "engineering and inventive genius" were always "restrained by the conservative buying habits of the motoring public." Progress, therefore, was the responsibility of industry, and Klingler advised: "Progress doubtless would have been still more gradual had it not been for the educational efforts of progressive manufacturers who 'sold' the public on the advantages offered by automotive developments."[161] From the standpoint of body design, *Machine Design* commented, "Radical departures in design are not accepted readily even though they are decided improvements because . . . the designer is running years ahead of the . . . public."[162] One marketing specialist noted that indeed the consumer lacked the "means, equipment, education and socialized attitude necessary for properly evaluating merchandise," and thus business needed to accept "grave responsibility" for directing consumer behavior.[163]

Kettering summed up the changing position of users and grass-roots inventors to automotive innovation. He acknowledged that the "first automobiles constituted a virgin field for inventive genius" whose tools of invention were "necessity and observation." Kettering argued, however, that these tools had become "dulled" and amateurs, who were handicapped by an "insufficient scientific background," could not address the "new and harder problems" of automotive design. These problems were to be tackled by trained scientists working in "organized systematic research," rather than by consumers tinkering in their garages.[164] These statements created an alliance among engineers, designers, and manufacturers and promoted the professional's authority over the design of the automobile.

From the other side, users did not always agree that industrial research and design served their needs as drivers. Speaking on behalf of American motorists, E. B. White complained of the new 1933 models: "We think [streamlining] is terrible. We think motor-car designers have been gradually going crazy." Commenting on the trend toward lower chassis, introduced by designers such as Harley Earl, White observed that he had trouble getting in the car and seeing out once seated: "The whole car is built so low to the ground that it is a wonder it isn't infested with moles." He declared, "Things were, in a way, better in 1917."[165]

After viewing the new streamlined models at the New York Auto Show in 1933, critic Ashley Hewitt wrote, "I think the car manufacturers are going stark plumb crazy. All the ballyhoo and advertising in the world will not alter the fact that the present cars are utterly un-usable to quite a percentage of the population." Hewitt, standing 6 feet 2 inches tall, criticized the low-slung cars for their lack of visibility, comfort, and safety. He also advised manufacturers to cut down on the useless additions of gadgets that he noted, "can and do go wrong, which cost time, money and trouble for servicing." The author summarized the sentiments of drivers: "I think the present cars from a practical viewpoint are just a total loss. From the engineering standpoint they are very clever. But practical utility is what is being bought today, and [new cars] do not have it."[166] The popular press continued to offer consumers a voice and they used it to criticize the practicality of automotive design.

Manufacturers answered that comfort and visibility were not their only concerns, even though the loss of these features through streamlining had been criticized from within the industry, as well. "Since style is a sales factor, to which the public apparently attaches considerable weight," wrote Don Blanchard, editor of *Automotive Industries*, "designers can't just strive for comfort and let the exterior look like what it will." Subsequent models throughout the 1930s continued the low, streamlined shapes.[167] In 1938 the *Cleveland Press* hired Theodore Smith, a professor of marketing and research, to sample public opinion on new models at the Cleveland automobile show. Smith recorded numerous criticisms of comfort, safety, and repair ease that echoed those articulated by White five years earlier. Anonymous consumers complained that the steering wheels were too low, that multiple knobs above the windshield offered "just five more points of danger for injury in sudden stops," and that the rear seats of streamlined autos "must be hell on a long trip."[168]

Not limited to comfort, user observations of new, streamlined cars included criticism of higher costs and difficulty of repairing the car at home. For instance, men at the Cleveland show complained that the engines of the 1938 Ford coupe and sedans were ill placed for the home repairman. One noted: "You can't work from the side of the motor; you must either stand on your head or crawl underneath the car." On cost, one consumer looked at the 1938 Ford Phaeton, a high-end streamlined car and remarked, "Ford is crazy if he thinks he can get over $900 for this car."[169] More poignantly, Maxwell Emmer of Detroit reflected on the high price of the V-8 in 1933: "You have lost sight of one thing, Mr. Ford, and that is—people, today, cannot buy an automobile that costs . . . more than it did two, three or four years ago, no matter how much 'quality' is put into the car." Emmer, a loyal Ford customer, wrote: "I grant you that the new V-8 is a far superior automobile to the Model A I am driving. . . . But—when I purchased my Ford 'A', I could afford to pay $538.75. . . . But I cannot with today's income pay out the same amount."[170]

Emmer was not alone in his observation that manufacturers should pay more attention to cost and less to styling. Secretary of Labor Frances Perkins also criticized the automotive industry in 1934 for its promotion of annual style changes over cost. She noted that annual retooling led to market fluctuations and economic hardship for laborers. *Automotive Industries* quoted Perkins as saying, "Putting style into the automobile is one of the most absurd things the industry ever did." Advocating a return to standardization in bodies to even out prices and jagged employment and production curves, Perkins stated, "I am old fashioned enough still to admire the old Model T Ford."[171] A few years after this statement, the National Automobile Chamber of Commerce moved the New York Auto Show from January to November to reduce market fluctuations.[172] Yet they did little to reduce the price of cars. Blanchard, from his editorial desk at *Automotive Industries*, criticized Perkins for being naive. He argued the automotive industry was at the mercy of the consumer, and that planned obsolescence induced the public to buy more cars and therefore allowed the industry to employ more workers, if unevenly. Despite industry's efforts to cultivate corporate goodwill, industry spokesmen such as Blanchard sometimes found themselves on the defensive. Even if consumers tinkered less, they challenged ideas of industry-led progress and new designs featured at auto exhibits.

* * *

Through a powerful combination of design and institutional advertising, automotive corporations influenced the changing relationship between the motorist and the machine in the 1930s. At national automobile shows and worlds fairs, automakers moved the struggle over automotive design from the pages of user-oriented journals, the corporate mail room, and the patent office to a public arena where they could design the message and attempt to educate the consumer about the process of innovation. The January 1935 cover of *Automobile Trade Journal* annual auto show issue captured industry's vision of their relationship to the consumer. The colorful image depicted a goddess of Progress, an icon for auto corporations, standing far above the heads of the public who grasped at the streamlined cars she offered. Fast receding into the past were the days when automotive journals served a mixed audience of producers, sellers, and consumers and lauded the ingenuity of users.

Popular journalists recorded the change, as well. In 1936, Myron Stearns, reporter for *Harper's Monthly*, drove cross-country and noted the changes in motoring since his first transcontinental auto trip in 1915. While Stearns found the roads better and the trip generally easier than at the beginning of automobility, he also wrote that the automobile was

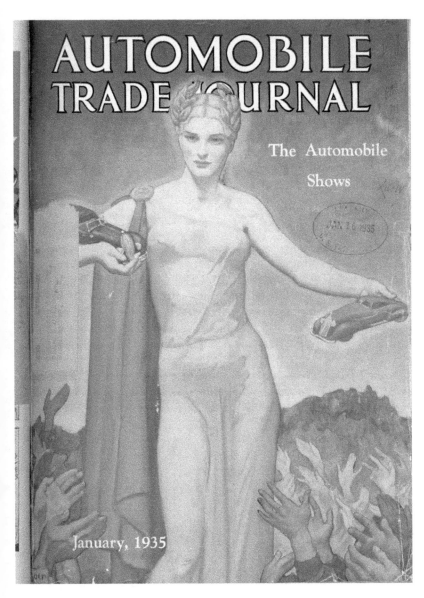

Figure 22. The cover of *Automobile Trade Journal* celebrated the annual National Automobile Show in its 16 January 1935 issue. Here an allegorical figure representing the modern automobile corporation or, perhaps automotive progress, holds streamlined cars high above the reach of the general public, symbolically removing design from the grasp of the consumer.

less accessible and more difficult to adapt to user needs in 1936. Arguing that the mechanical complexity of automobiles in the 1930s resulted in the loss of technological know-how among a new generation of drivers, Stearns wrote, "The result of these new complexities is that, like radio sets, the innards of modern automobiles are no longer to be toyed with by triflers. You keep your new model supplied with gasoline, and otherwise leave it alone. . . . It runs by Black Magic." Stearns observed that the roadside garage and the "Home Tinkerer" were following the blacksmith into oblivion. "Fifteen years ago," remembered the author, "every growing lad was an embryo mechanic. He could discuss the merits of overhead valves with professionals. . . . But that was yesterday."[173]

As an example of the mechanical incompetence of many drivers, Stearns told the story of a young man whose car had run out of gas. Stuck on the road, the motorist could not diagnose the problem and decided to look for a mechanic. Stearns happened along the road and offered help, siphoning gas into the tank and fixing the problem. The young driver "looked at me as though I were Merlin," reported Stearns. "But I was just a veteran of an earlier era of motoring."[174] Stearns marked the decline of a certain general level of ingenuity, one in which the user with relatively little mechanical knowledge and no technical training embraced the repair and modification of his own machine. Although drivers continued to tinker throughout the Depression, more complete cars, all-steel streamlined bodies, and the concerted effort of corporations to draw a line between users and innovators worked to discourage the active modification of the automobiles by average Americans.

Epilogue

Tinkering from Customizing to Car Talk

The automobile became part of the fabric of everyday life in the first decades of the twentieth century, and the central purpose of this history has been to show how cars were vehicles for cultural expression and authority among consumers in this period. Mass consumption of the automobile and the motor vacation, in particular, provided tremendous opportunities for consumers to engage in their own, grass-roots acts of production, remaking their cultural identities, challenging and sometimes inserting themselves in social hierarchies, and redesigning the automobile.

American motorists were far from passive consumers. Many who wanted more from the design of early automobiles, outfitted, altered, cut-up and tinkered with their individual cars to render them more comfortable, efficient, and versatile vehicles for long-distance travel. Tinkering held cultural as well as technological benefits. In a culture that had a deep reverence for technological expertise, tinkering allowed consumers to participate in a larger dialog on new consumer technologies and to insert themselves, as knowledgeable users, into the national discourses that praised ingenuity. Women drivers, for instance, used their mechanical skill and ingenuity to demonstrate their autonomy. Middle-class travelers of both genders actively remade the automobile to better conform to their standards of comfort and efficiency, often writing to manufacturers requesting permanent changes in design. Grass-roots inventors, on the other hand, attempted to capitalize on their ingenuity and enter the booming marketplace of automotive accessories. For each of these communities automotive skill translated into at least a modicum of cultural authority, whether in the form of admiration of other drivers or gaining the imprimatur of the U.S. Patent Office to legitimate a design.

This window of opportunity did not last, however. By the later years of the 1930s consumers found it more difficult to tinker with their automobiles, harder to communicate with manufacturers, and a struggle to gain patent rights for improvements and accessories. Changes in the standard design of automobiles and the growth of corporate-sponsored invention limited consumer access to and authority over automotive design.

Did consumers continue to tinker with their automobiles after 1939? The answer is yes, some smaller subsets of consumers continued to tinker and in fact, modification in the form of customizing cars became important means for expressing sub-cultural identity in the later half of the twentieth century. Car camping, hotrods, and customizing represent just three examples. However, I would argue that tinkering with cars was no longer the pastime of a wide cross-section of middle-class American consumers as it was when the automobile was new.[1]

The American tradition of sleeping in the car faded in the years just before World War II as the growth of two separate travel industries, motels and travel trailers, provided the comfort motor travelers sought on the road and dispensed with the need among the middle-class to remake the interiors of their cars.[2] Yet, motorists on a tight budget and those who wanted to travel outside the mainstream of consumer culture continued the tradition of sleeping inside the vehicle. The most direct descendants of technologically savvy autocampers of the 1920s were car campers who bought kits to convert cars, buses, vans, and trucks for sleeping in the 1960s and 1970s. Auto historian Roger White has documented the centrality of customizing busses and vans for youthful members of the counterculture in the late 1960s.[3]

Tinkering in the form of customization of cars also survived among several subcultures after World War II. Hot rods, drag racing, and stock car racing which grew as distinctly male subcultures in the 1950s had their roots in the era of shade-tree mechanics of earlier decades.[4] In addition, American drivers' penchant customizing and enhancing the performance of their cars contributed to the longevity of aftermarket parts and auto body industry. Customizing also became a form of community and an expression of identity. Low riders and, more recently, hip-hop fans have used cars as critical means of cultural expression and critique from the margins of American society. Low rider culture has traditionally valued two of the central ideas associated with the car, mobility and opportunity, and developed its own car clubs and publications such as *Low Rider* magazine that circulate drivers' designs and the shared aesthetics of the community. Cars as "a canvas for personal and cultural representation," have come to express cultural difference and complex narratives of "outsider aesthetics" that draw on unique, class, ethnic, and racial urban experiences.[5]

Most recently cable television has co-opted customizing cars as one of the multiple variations on reality programming. Shows like MTV's *Pimp My Ride*, a hip-hop version of customizing, and The Learning Channel's *Overhaulin*,' represent a new, male twist on the idea of the "make-over" show. They also demonstrate that, by-and-large, restyling and tinkering with automobiles now takes place in a shop under the directions of experts rather than in the home garage. Both shows require that drivers hand the car over to professional body guys, mechanics and designers. For instance, Chip Foose, one member of the "A-Team" on *Overhaulin'*, began working in a professional design shop as a child, majored in product design in college and now operates his own product design company.[6] These TV venues celebrate the expertise of professionals and the vast resources of media corporations such as MTV that lavish tens of thousands of dollars remaking cars, placing customizing out of the reach of the average car owner.

What about the wider realm drivers who are not part of these subcultures of customization? Are Americans still interested in tinkering with their cars at home? These questions certainly merit more research, and one of the current forums for consumers to discuss their cars and auto culture is National Public Radio's *Car Talk*. In the tradition of user-oriented magazines, such as *Popular Mechanics* and *Fordowner*, radio show has provided a cultural meeting ground for a wide range of drivers seeking advice since 1977. From the beginning, hosts Tom and Ray Magliozzi have diagnosed mechanical problems over the air. They noted, "The early days of *Car Talk* was [*sic*] a time when dinosaurs roamed the earth and people actually worked on their own cars."[7] They remembered, "We answered a lot of questions like, 'I'm stuck with my left arm in the transmission, how do I get it out?'"[8] New technologies, such as computerized fuel injection systems that replaced carburetors in the late 1980s and early 1990s, further cut down on the number of home mechanics. In a discussion of computers and the difficulties of fixing one's car at home, Ray Magliozzi observed, "Tinkering with cars used to be a great American pastime. Guys would spend Saturdays out in the driveway taking things apart, and then trying to put them back together before it got dark. . . . That's no longer possible."[9] New cars may be more difficult to maintain at home, requiring special equipment that average drivers do not possess, but apparently they do not preclude tinkering. Many of the respondents to a 1999 online survey entitled, "*Car Talk* Survey of Car Owners" noted that they love to tinker, either by maintaining the engine or by changing both the interior and exterior of the body.[10]

In addition to a continued interest in tinkering, many of the drivers who participate in the show use the car to talk about human relationships, and in particular the gendered nature of automotive skill. *Car Talk* provides an opportunity to think about the continuing gender hierarchies and who can claim knowledge of the car. In my survey of the show's on-line archives, women often called seeking advice on how to communicate effectively about the car with either their mechanics or

their male partners.[11] Like women in the late 1920s, these female drivers
charge that their husbands, boyfriends, or mechanics have disparaged
their mechanical knowledge. The hosts discuss the differences between
men and women and note that for men the knowledge of the car
has become tied to ideas of authority. According to the Magliozzis,
men often pretend to know what they are talking about and use a lot
of vague technical terms to describe problems even when they have no
knowledge at all. "Men feel a need to act as if they know what's
wrong," observed Ray Magliozzi to one male caller.[12] Unlike men,
women often begin by admitting they have scant knowledge of automobile mechanics.[13]

    Car Talk has consciously opened a space for the public discussion of
automobiles that includes women. Yet, one disgruntled listener wrote to
ask why the Magliozzis so frequently defend women at the expense of
men. "You guys are always downgrading men when it comes to automotive knowledge," he wrote. "You almost always publish incidents where
the woman is right and the hubby (or some other guy) is wrong. Are you
guys afraid of women?"[14] The Magliozzis answered, "We just believe it's
important to state publicly that men don't always know what they're talking about just because the subject is cars." Ray Magliozzi, added, "We
think it is incumbent upon us to tell the American public that in our
experience fixing cars, women are better at describing problems, better
at answering questions . . . and, in general, have less of their egos tied
up in pretending that they know everything." In other words, women
are better car owners because women recognize their status as amateurs.[15] Statements such as this turn the popular talk show into a political
arena where the hosts encourage the audience to rethink gender difference and consumers' relationship to the car.

    The radio show which has spawned a website and newspaper columns,
also serves as an important public space in which drivers criticize current
automotive design.[16] For instance, one woman called to say that she
thought the "digital LED readout" on her 1976 Toyota Celica was a haz-
ard and to ask if she could have it removed.[17] The hosts confirmed her
desire to get rid of the display by putting "black tape on it" or unplug-
ging it, both of which she could do herself. Surprised and happy that
the experts were on her side, the caller also suggested that pounding it
with a blunt object would be both cathartic and a comment on poor
design.[18] In more radical moments, drivers have accused the automotive
industry of a conspiracy to design cars that users could not fix or maintain themselves. One spirited listener complained of the difficulty of
performing once-simple tasks such as changing spark plugs and drain-
ing anti-freeze out of the radiator. In his opinion, automotive design
engineers make the "various car components impossible to locate,"

thereby supplying large auto repair franchises with more business. "It becomes more apparent with each journey I take under the hood of my car (any car)," he noted, "that there is a sinister conspiracy afoot . . . to wrest from the hands of the common civilian any possibility that he may perform his own basic maintenance and thereby save a bundle." He exhorted *Car Talk* listeners to "Start a revolution here. Hold the pitiable idiots who design this nonsense accountable for their transgressions against common sense and humanity."[19] Reminiscent of consumer criticism of the low-slung cars of the late 1930s, the writer acknowledged the power of professional designers to limit users' access to the machine, and he demonstrated that consumers should not quietly accept designs that did not serve their needs; they should talk back to the automotive industry.

Discussion of automotive design and use on *Car Talk*, underscores the importance of understanding the historical circumstances that have limited access to automotive design and technological knowledge. Americans still live with ideas about automotive authority forged in the early twentieth century; that men are more knowledgeable and ingenious than women and that professional designers and engineers know more about good design than consumers of either gender. Yet, creating and maintaining hegemony was hard work for the auto industry in the 1930s.[20] Auto manufacturers spent millions of dollars during the Depression to design more complete cars, to exhibit their expertise, and to cast new, less ingenious roles for users. Despite these efforts, the industry still negotiated with consumers, at some level, through the medium of market surveys. So, tinkering gave consumers a stake in the design of the automobile and the meaning of ingenuity.

The concept of tinkering is useful in scholarly terms because it acknowledges that small changes to technology were important in challenging dominant ideas about who could access and have some power over new technologies and who could cross the boundaries between consumption and invention. Tinkering was recognized as a kind of ingenuity in the early twentieth century and a process by which consumers could become grass-roots inventors. In addition, every time motorists bought aftermarket accessories and added them to their cars or supplemented cars with gadgets of their own design, they participated in acts of production. They appropriated and remade the goods available. Adopting the words of patent experts, small improvements counted. Tinkering with technology might not always contribute to the radical invention of new technologies, but it challenged manufacturers to incorporate changes from the bottom up and gave users a sense of authority to rewrite the shape, use, and meanings of new technologies like the automobile. As a form of popular culture, tinkering also allowed consumers to reinvent their identities. The political promise of popular culture is that it constitutes one of the sites where average folks can negotiate the power of social and technological hierarchies based on gender, race, class, and education, and thus serves as an important realm in which to study the reception and use of new technologies.[21] More attention to tinkering, as a form of popular culture and as a technological process can explain the ways in which consumers engaged, on their own terms, new technologies, invention, and corporate capitalism in the twentieth century.

Notes

Introduction

1. Emily Post, *By Motor to the Golden Gate* (New York: D. Appleton, 1916).
2. Edwin Post, *Truly Emily Post* (New York: Funk & Wagnalls, 1961), 183, 181–194, 240.
3. Post, *By Motor to the Golden Gate*, 249, 131, 140–141, 138–139.
4. "Ford Camp Touring," *Fordowner*, Jan. 1915, 11–13.
5. Ibid., 12.
6. "America's Automobile Increase as Shown in Registration for Six Years," *Automotive Manufacturer*, Jan. 1920, 14; "Car and Truck Price Reductions of Recent Date," *Automotive Manufacturer*, June 1921, 12. On the development of GMAC and the growth of the automobile finance corporations, see James Flink, *The Automobile Age* (Cambridge: MIT Press, 1988), 191.
7. *Facts and Figures of the Automobile Industry* (New York: National Automobile Chamber of Commerce, 1920), 13; "Ford Announces Price Reduction to Pre-War Levels on All Cars," *New York Times*, 22 Sept. 1920, 9:2; "Reductions Announced on Willys-Overland, Willys-Knight, Hudson and Essex Cars," *New York Times*, 29 Sept. 1920, 21:2; "Reductions Announced by Maxwell, Chalmers, Paige, Chandler and Cleveland Cars," *New York Times*, 30 Sept. 1920, 9:4.
8. J. C. Long, "A Nation on Wheels," *Outlook*, 19 May 1920, n.p.
9. "An Automobile Census," *Literary Digest*, 20 Nov. 1920, 29; A. L. Westgard, "Here Are the Motor Trails," *Independent*, 7 July 1919, 360; "Only One in Ten Automobiles Is Used for Recreation Alone," *Current Opinion*, Oct. 1920, 543; John Kane Mills, "Speaking of Incomes," *Motor*, Feb. 1921, 21–22, 64; James H. Collins, "The Motor Car Has Created the Spirit of Modern America," *Motor*, Jan. 1923, 186.
10. For statistics on automobile ownership, see "An Automobile Census," *Literary Digest*, 20 Nov. 1920, 29; "Ratio of Motor Vehicles to Population in the United States," and "Cities with Greatest Relative Number of Cars," *Facts and Figures* (New York: NACC, 1920), 36–37; "Where Cars Are," *Facts and Figures* (New York: NACC, 1921), 16; "Ratio of Motor Vehicles to Population," *Facts and Figures* (New York: NACC, 1922), 53.
11. *Facts and Figures* (New York: NACC, 1920), 16–17. "Women Own 5 Percent of Cars in the U.S.," *Facts and Figures* (New York: NACC, 1923), 12. See also "Only One in Ten," 543; "Consumption Expenditures of City Wage- and Clerical-Worker Families of 2 or More Persons, 1888–91 to 1960–61," in Series G 592, Automobile Purchase and Operation, Consumer Expenditure Patterns, *Historical Abstracts of the United States Colonial Times to 1970* (Washington, D.C.: U.S. Department of Commerce, Bureau of the Census), 322.
12. "How Many People Can Buy Motor Cars," *Automotive Manufacturer*, Sept. 1921, 24.

13. On popular culture as a site for political opposition, see Stuart Hall, "Notes on Deconstructing the Popular," in Ralph Samuel, ed., *People's History and Socialist Theory* (London: Routledge, 1981), 227–240; Antonio Gramsci, as excerpted in *Culture, Ideology and Social Process: A Reader*, ed. Tony Bennett et al. (London: Open University Press, 1981), 185–219; and Michael Denning, "The End of Mass Culture," in "Scholarly Controversy: Mass Culture," *International Labor and Working-Class History* 37 (Spring 1990): 2–32. For explanations of neo-Gramscian theories of hegemony and their application to the study of popular culture, see John Storey, "The Politics of the Popular," in Storey, *An Introductory Guide to Cultural Theory and Popular Culture* (Athens: University of Georgia Press, 1993), 184–186.

14. On technology and the reconfiguration of public space as an arena for cultural negotiations, see Carolyn Marvin, *When Old Technologies Were New: Thinking About Electric Communication in the Late Nineteenth Century* (New York: Oxford University Press, 1988), 4–5; and David Nye, *Narratives and Spaces: Technology and the Construction of American Culture* (New York: Columbia University, 1997). For histories that examine cultural politics of new technologies, see Carroll Pursell, *The Machine in America: A Social History of Technology* (Baltimore: Johns Hopkins University Press, 1995); Carroll Pursell, "Seeing the Invisible: New Perceptions in the History of Technology," *Icon* 1 (1995): 10–15, Susan Douglas, *Inventing American Broadcasting, 1899–1920* (Baltimore: Johns Hopkins University Press, 1987); Susan Smulyan, *Selling Radio: The Commercialization of American Broadcasting, 1920–1934* (Washington, D.C.: Smithsonian Institution Press, 1994); Joseph Corn, *Winged Gospel: America's Romance with Aviation* (New York: Oxford University Press, 1983). For work on identity politics and recent technologies, see Constance Penley and Andrew Ross, eds., *Technoculture* (Minneapolis: University of Minnesota Press, 1991).

15. Marvin, *When Old Technologies Were New*, 4–5.

16. On the importance of narrative and the interpretation of history, see Hayden White, *The Content of Form: Narrative Discourse and Historical Representation* (Baltimore: Johns Hopkins University Press, 1987), ix, x, 1–25. On narrative form, including the function of plot and narrative point of view, see Robert Scholes and Robert Kellogg, *The Nature of Narrative* (New York: Oxford University Press, 1966). For another perspective on narrative, see Jerome Bruner, "The Narrative Construal of Reality," in Bruner, *The Culture of Education* (Cambridge: Harvard University Press, 1996), 121–123, 130–149, and Jerome Bruner, *Acts of Meaning* (Cambridge: Harvard University Press, 1990). For models of using narrative production to think about the history of technology, see Nye, *Narratives and Spaces*, and John Staudenmaier, *Technology's Storytellers: Reweaving the Human Fabric* (Cambridge: MIT Press, 1985).

17. Wilbur Hall, "A Free Car and the Open Road: Auto-Vacationing in Three States Along the Pacific," *Sunset*, July 1917, 22.

18. Howard Chudacoff and Judith Smith, *The Evolution of American Urban Society* (Englewood Cliffs, N.J.: Prentice-Hall, 1988), 225–231; Paul Groth, *Living Downtown: The History of Residential Hotels in the United States* (Berkeley: University of California Press, 1994), 201–207.

19. Paul Carter, *The Twenties in America* (Arlington Heights, Ill.: Harlan Davidson, 1975), 92–105.

20. On the construction of the wilderness as a regenerative space, see Roderick Nash, *The Wilderness and the American Mind*, 3rd ed. (New Haven: Yale University Press, 1982), 142, 145. See also T. J. Jackson Lears, *No Place of Grace:*

Antimodernism and the Transformation of American Culture, 1880–1920 (New York: Pantheon Books, 1981).

21. Bruce Calvert, *Thirty Years of the Open Road with Bruce Calvert* (New York: Greenberg, 1941), 2, 64–65; "Bruce Calvert, 73, Publisher, Writer," *New York Times*, 1 June 1940, 15:2. See also Dillon Wallace, "Open Spaces on the Map," *Outing*, April 1910, 570; Lucy E. Abel, *The Open Road and Other Poems* (Boston: Gorham Press, 1916), 7; "Call of the Open Road," *Country Life*, June 1923, 112; F. G. Jopp, "Call of the Open Road," *Illustrated World*, July 1922, 742–746, August 1922, 902–905; Owen Tweedy, "The Fellowship of the Open Road," *Atlantic*, Sept. 1932, 321; Jesse Frederick Steiner, *Americans at Play: Recent Trends in Recreation and Leisure Time Activities* (New York: McGraw-Hill, 1933), 34, 60, 183.

22. Walter Prichard Eaton, "Tenting on the New Camp Ground," *Nation*, 14 Sept. 1921, 287; Lawrence Clark, "Six Weeks in a Ford," *Outing*, July 1922, 162; Jay Norwood Darling, *The Cruise of the Bouncing Betsy: A Trailer Travelogue* (New York: Frederick A. Stokes, 1937), 93.

23. H. C. Newton, *Six Weeks in a Motor Car: The Story of Two People Who Became Twentieth Century Nomads* (Syracuse, N.Y.: Franklin Automobile Company, 1911), 3.

24. Elon Jessup, *The Motor Camping Book* (New York: G. P. Putnam's Sons, 1921), 4.

25. Frank Brimmer, *Motor Campcraft* (New York: Macmillan, 1923), 2, 1.

26. For an excellent discussion of nationalism and travel in America, see Marguerite Shaffer, *See America First: Tourism and National Identity, 1880–1940* (Washington, D.C.: Smithsonian Institution Press, 2001).

27. Nina Wilcox Putnam, *West Broadway* (New York: George H. Dornan, 1921), 43–44.

28. For statistics on black migrants in Northern cities and out-migration from the South, see Carole Marks, "Social and Economic Life of Blacks," in Alferdteen Harrison, ed., *Black Exodus: The Great Migration from the American South* (Jackson: University Press of Mississippi, 1991), 46–47; James Grossman, *Land of Hope: Chicago, Black Southerners and the Great Migration* (Chicago: University of Chicago Press, 1989); Malaika Adero, ed., *Up South: Stories, Studies, and Letters of This Century's Black Migrations* (New York: New Press, 1993); Carole Marks, *Farewell—We're Good and Gone* (Bloomington: Indiana University Press, 1989), 148–149; Stewart E. Tolnay and E. M. Beck, "Rethinking the Role of Racial Violence in the Great Migration," in Harrison, ed., *Black Exodus*, 20–32.

29. Lawrence Levine, *Highbrow, Lowbrow: The Emergence of Cultural Hierarchy in America* (Cambridge: Harvard University Press, 1988), 176–177. See also John Kasson, *Rudeness and Civility: Manners in Nineteenth-Century Urban America* (New York: Hill and Wang, 1990), 70–72.

30. Robert Wiebe, *The Search for Order, 1877–1920* (New York: Hill and Wang, 1967), 111–113.

31. Levine, *Highbrow, Lowbrow*, 176.

32. Loren Baritz, *The Good Life: The Meaning of Success for the American Middle Class* (New York: Alfred Knopf, 1989), xiii.

33. Roland Marchand, *Advertising the American Dream: Making Way for Modernity, 1920–1940* (Berkeley: University of California Press, 1986), 223–227, 336–340.

34. *Being a Selection from Mr. Ford's Page in the Dearborn Independent* (Dearborn, Mich.: Dearborn Publishing, 1926), 156, 158.

35. Robert Sloss, "Camping in an Automobile," *Outing*, May 1910, 236.

36. Harry Irving Shumway, "What Do You Get out of Auto-Camping, Anyway?" *Field and Stream*, May 1922, 58.

37. "Nomads of the Automobile," *Literary Digest*, 30 April 1921, 43. See also William Frederick Dix, "A Source of Sensible Pleasure," *Outlook*, 26 May 1906, 173; "Far from the Madd'ing Crowd," *Automobile Journal*, April 1923, 14; J. C. Long, "The Week-End Wild Man," *Outlook*, 12 July 1922, 466–467.

38. "Motorists Don't Make Socialists, They Say," *New York Times*, 4 March 1906, 12.

39. Ibid.

40. "Automobiling Has Not Bred Anarchy," *American Motorist*, 1910, 500.

41. Cornelius Vanderbilt, Jr., "The Democracy of the Motor Car," *Motor*, Dec. 1921, 21–22.

42. See Shaffer, *See America First;* Warren Belsaco, *Americans on the Road: From Autocamp to Motel, 1910–1945* (Cambridge: MIT Press, 1979); John A. Jakel, *The Tourist: Travel in Twentieth-Century North America* (Lincoln: University of Nebraska Press, 1985), 101–170.

43. Elon Jessup, "The Flight of the Tin Can Tourists," *Outlook*, 25 May 1921.

44. For an overview of segregation of recreational facilities, see Forrester B. Washington, "Recreational Facilities for the Negro," *Annals of Political and Social Science* 140 (Nov. 1928): 278. See also William M. Tuttle, Jr., *Race Riot: Chicago in the Red Summer of 1919* (New York: Atheneum, 1982), 21. See also "Democracy and Jim-Crowism," *New Republic*, 3 Sept. 1919, 151 and George E. Haynes, "Race Riots in Relation to Democracy," *Survey*, 9 Aug. 1919, 697. On the history of the black professional class, see Kevin Gaines, *Uplifting the Race: Black Leadership, Politics, and Culture in the Twentieth Century* (Chapel Hill: University of North Carolina Press, 1996); Andrew Wiese, "The Other Suburbanites: African American Suburbanization in the North Before 1950," *Journal of American History*, 85, no. 4 (March 1999): 1495–1524; Bart Landry, *The New Black Middle Class* (Berkeley: University of California Press, 1987), 21. See also E. Franklin Frazier, *Black Bourgeoisie: The Rise of a New Middle Class* (New York: Free Press, 1957), 45.

45. William Pickens, "Jim Crow in Texas," *Nation*, 15 Aug. 1923, 156; George S. Schuyler, "Traveling Jim Crow," *American Mercury*, Aug. 1930, 432; Lillian Rhodes, "One of the Groups *Middletown* Left Out," *Opportunity*, March 1933, 76; "Vacation Days," *Crisis*, Aug. 1912, 186; James A. Jackson, "Where Are You Going to Stop?" in Victor Green, ed., *The Negro Motorist Green Book* (New York: Victor Green, 1948), 1.

46. Kathleen Franz, "The Open Road: Automobility and Racial Uplift in the Inter-War Years," in Bruce Sinclair, ed., *Technology and the African-American Experience: Needs and Opportunities for Study* (Cambridge: MIT Press, 2004), 131–154.

47. Alfred Edgar Smith, "Through the Windshield," *Opportunity*, May 1933, 142.

48. Putnam, *West Broadway*, 83, 84.

49. Ibid., 102.

50. For a discussion of nativism, see David M. Kennedy, *Over Here: The First World War and American Society* (New York: Oxford University Press, 1980), 67–69, and Eric Foner, *The Story of American Freedom* (New York: Norton, 1998), 168–193.

51. Frederic Van De Water, "Discovering America in a Flivver," *Ladies' Home Journal*, May 1926, 28.

52. The Machine Age is a period historians equate with the second industrial revolution (1876–1930) and art historians identify as the period after the World War I (1918–1941) when machines, technological systems, science, and indus-

trial design infiltrated everyday life. For social and cultural histories that define and explore the Machine Age, see Gilman Ostrander, *American Civilization in the First Machine Age: 1890–1940* (New York: Harper & Row, 1970), and John M. Jordon, *Machine Age Ideology: Social Engineering and American Liberalism, 1911–1939* (Chapel Hill: University of North Carolina Press, 1994). On the machine aesthetic, Richard Guy Wilson, Dianne H. Pilgrim, and Dickran Tashjian, *The Machine Age* (New York: Brooklyn Museum and Harry N. Abrams, 1986).

53. For a history of Fordist mass production, see David Hounshell, *From the American System to Mass Production, 1800–1932: The Development of Manufacturing Technology in the United States* (Baltimore: Johns Hopkins University Press, 1984). On the economic, spatial, and cultural transformations related to Fordism, see David Harvey, *The Condition of Postmodernity: An Inquiry into the Origins of Cultural Change* (Oxford: Basil Blackwell, 1990), 121–173.

54. Pursell, *Machine in America*, 203, 250.

55. John L. Wright, "Introduction: An American Tradition," in John Wright, *Possible Dreams: Enthusiasm for Technology in America* (Dearborn, Mich.: Henry Ford Museum and Greenfield Village, 1992), 14.

56. For an overview of technology in the literary cannon, see Leo Marx, "American Literary Culture and the Fatalistic View of Technology," in Marx, *The Pilot and the Passenger: Essays on Literature, Technology and Culture in the United States* (New York: Oxford University Press, 1988), 179–207. For pre-Modernist literary critiques of technology in America, see Edward Bellamy, *Looking Backward, 2000–1887* (New York: Regent Press, 1887); Mark Train, *A Connecticut Yankee in King Arthur's Court* (New York: Book League of America, 1889). For prominent examples in the 1920s, see Sinclair Lewis, *Babbitt* (1922; reprint, New York: Signet Classic, 1980); F. Scott Fitzgerald, *The Great Gatsby* (New York: C. Scribner's Sons, 1925); Elmer Rice, *The Adding Machine: A Play in Seven Scenes* (New York: S. French, 1929).

57. Lewis, *Babbitt*, 5, 8.

58. On the cult of the machine in America, see Waldo Frank, "Gods and Cults of Power," in Loren Baritz, ed., *The Culture of the Twenties* (New York: Bobbs-Merrill, 1970), 371–382.

59. Earl Swift, "The Perfect Inventor," *Invention and Technology* 6 (Fall 1990): 24–31.

60. On the mythic importance of the American ingenuity, see Thomas P. Hughes, *American Genesis: A History of the American Genius for Invention* (New York: Penguin, 1990).

61. James J. Flink, "Three Stages of American Automobile Consciousness," *American Quarterly*, 24 (Oct. 1972): 457.

62. Pursell, *Machine in America*, 239.

63. Joseph Corn, "Educating the Enthusiast," and Susan Douglas, "Audio Outlaws: Radio and Phonograph Enthusiasts," in Wright, *Possible Dreams*, 18–33.

64. "Simplified Motoring," *Outlook* 20 Feb. 1918, 99.

65. Leo Marx, *The Machine in the Garden: Technology and the Pastoral Ideal in America* (New York: Oxford University Press, 1964); John Kasson, *Amusing the Million: Coney Island at the Turn of the Century* (New York: Hill & Wang, 1978), and Kasson, *Civilizing the Machine: Technology and Republican Values in America, 1776–1900* (New York: Penguin, 1976).

66. Mary Anderson, "Women's Contributions in the Field of Invention: A Study of the Records of the United States Patent Office" (Washington, D.C.: Government Printing Office, 1923), 27.

67. Wiebe E. Bijker, Thomas P. Hughes, and Trevor Pinch, eds., *The Social Construction of Technological Systems: New Directions in the Sociology and History of Technology* (Cambridge: MIT Press, 1987). For a recent overview of the field, see John M. Staudenmaier, "Rationality, Agency, Contingency: Recent Trends in the History of Technology," *Reviews in American History* 30, no. 1 (2002), 168–181. On recent challenges to the paradigm of social construction of technology (SCOT), see Nick Clayton, "SCOT: Does It Answer?" *Technology and Culture* 43, no. 2 (2002): 351–360, and Weibe E. Bijker and Trevor Pinch, "SCOT Answers, Other Questions," *Technology and Culture* 43, no. 2 (2002): 361–369. In their study of rural automobile users, Ronald Kline and Trevor Pinch in particular offer a model of consumers as agents of technological change Ronald Kline and Trevor Pinch, "Users as Agents of Technological Change: The Social Construction of the Automobile in the Rural United States," *Technology and Culture* 38 (Jan. 1997): 763–764. See Kline's longer study, Ronald R. Kline, *Consumers in the Country: Technology and Social Change in Rural America* (Baltimore: Johns Hopkins University Press, 2000).

68. Ruth Schwartz Cowan, "The Consumption Junction: A Proposal for Research Strategies in the Sociology of Technology," in Bijker, Hughes, and Pinch, eds., *The Social Construction of Technological Systems*, 263. For a bibliographic overview of recent scholarship on consumption, see Susan Strasser, "Making Consumption Conspicuous: Transgressive Topics Go Mainstream," *Technology and Culture*, 43 (Oct. 2002): 755–770.

69. Scholars who study material culture have argued that machines are political artifacts. Sociologists of technology have asserted that both machines and technological systems embody the political agendas of their producers. If new technologies have not been designed to explicitly support the current social order, they are at least always embedded in the political relationships of that order. For scholars that support this paradigm, see Langdon Winner, "Do Artifacts Have Politics?" in Winner, *The Whale and the Reactor: A Search for Limits in an Age of High Technology* (Chicago: University of Chicago Press, 1986), 19–39; Wiebe E. Bijker, Thomas P. Hughes, and Trevor Pinch, "The Social Construction of Facts and Artifacts," in Bijker, Hughes, and Pinch, eds., *The Social Construction of Technological Systems*, 197–214; Donald MacKenzie and Judy Wajcman, *The Social Shaping of Technology: How the Refrigerator Got Its Hum* (Philadelphia: Open University Press, 1985), 1–24. However, historians such as Steven Lubar have seen machines as mediators between groups. See Steven Lubar, "Machine Politics: The Political Construction of Technological Artifacts," in Steven Lubar and W. David Kingery, eds., *History from Things* (Washington, D.C.: Smithsonian Institution Press, 1993), 207–208.

70. On the idea of tinkering as improving the fit between users and machines, see Donald Norman, *The Design of Everyday Things* (New York: Doubleday, 1998).

71. Cowan, "Consumption Junction," 263.

72. Brooke Hindle, *Emulation and Invention* (New York: Norton, 1981).

73. On various ways of understanding technology, see Eugene Ferguson, "The Mind's Eye: Nonverbal Thought in Technology," *Science* 197 (26 Aug. 1977): 827–836; Edwin Layton, "Technology as Knowledge," *Technology and Culture* 15 (Jan. 1974): 31–41. On technological know-how as a form of power, see Steven Lubar, "Representation and Power," *Technology and Culture* 36 (Supplement to April 1995): 554–558. For other historical case studies of technological knowledge, see Nina E. Lerman, "'Preparing for the Duties and Practical Busi-

ness of Life': Technological Knowledge and Social Structure in Mid-Nineteenth-Century Philadelphia," *Technology and Culture* 38 (Jan. 1997): 31–59; Virginia P. Dawson, "Knowledge Is Power: E.G. Bailey and the Invention and Marketing of the Bailey Boiler Meter," *Technology and Culture* 37 (July 1996): 493–526. On tinkering as a form of technological knowledge, see Linnda R. Caporael, E. Gabriella Panichkul, and Dennis R. Harris, "Tinkering with Gender," *Research in Philosophy and Technology* 13 (1993): 73–99.

74. Hindle, *Emulation and Invention*, 125.

75. On methodologies for placing the audience at the center of scholarly studies of mass culture, see Rosalind Brunt, "Engaging with the Popular: Audiences for Mass Culture and What to Say About Them," in Lawrence Grossberg, Cary Nelson, and Paula Treichler, eds., *Cultural Studies* (New York: Routledge, 1992), 69–80; Susan J. Douglas, "Notes Toward a History of Media Audiences," *Radical History Review* 54 (Fall 1992): 127–138; George Lipsitz, "Listening to Learn and Learning to Listen: Popular Culture, Cultural Theory, and American Studies," *American Quarterly* 42 (Dec. 1990): 614–637; and Stuart Ewen, *All Consuming Images: The Politics of Style in Contemporary Culture* (New York: Basic Books, 1988).

76. John Fiske, *Understanding Popular Culture* (Boston: Unwin Hyman, 1989), 35.

77. On consumer practice as a process of "making do," or borrowing the language and existing products circulating in the culture, see Michel de Certeau, *The Practice of Everyday Life*, trans. Steven Rendall (Berkeley: University of California Press, 1984), 29–42.

78. Fiske, *Understanding Popular Culture*, 103.

79. Ibid., 11, 20. On the recent trend in popular culture studies sometimes called cultural populism, see John Clark, "Pessimism Versus Populism: The Problematic Politics of Popular Culture," in Richard Butsch, ed., *For Fun and Profit: The Transformation of Leisure into Consumption* (Philadelphia: Temple University Press, 1990), 34–43. On the Birmingham School, see Andrea Press, *Women Watching Television: Gender, Class, and Generation in the American Television Experience* (Philadelphia: University of Pennsylvania Press, 1991).

Chapter 1. What Consumers Wanted

1. Lee Strout White [pseud.], "Farewell, My Lovely," *New Yorker*, 16 May 1936, 20–22.

2. David Gartman, *Auto Opium: A Social History of American Automobile Design* (New York: Routledge, 1994), 58. See also John Heskett, *Industrial Design* (London: Thames and Hudson, 1980), 67; Ray Batchelor, *Henry Ford: Mass Production, Modernism and Design* (Manchester: Manchester University Press, 1995).

3. Ronald Kline and Trevor Pinch, "Users as Agents of Technological Change: The Social Construction of the Automobile in the Rural United States," *Technology and Culture*, 38 (Jan. 1997): 763–764. See also Ronald R. Kline, *Consumers in the Country: Technology and Social Change in Rural America* (Baltimore: Johns Hopkins University Press, 2000), 55–86.

4. Donald A. Norman, *The Design of Everyday Things* (New York: Doubleday, 1991), 95.

5. On the consumer ethos, see Roland Marchand, *Advertising the American Dream: Making Way for Modernity, 1920–1940* (Berkeley: University of California

Press, 1985); T. J. Jackson Lears, *Fables of Abundance: A Cultural History of Advertising in America* (New York: Basic Books, 1995). On consumption as an act production in popular culture, see John Fiske, *Understanding Popular Culture* (Boston: Unwin Hyman, 1989), 35.

6. This practice is often referred to as bricolage. On the concept of bricolage as important to the formation of subcultures in a consumer society, see Dick Hebdige, *Subculture: The Meaning of Style* (London: Methuen, 1979). In its application to tinkering with the car, and especially as a hands-on knowledge of technology, see Harper, *Working Knowledge*, 74–75.

7. On consumption as class-defining, see Stuart Blumin, *The Emergence of the Middle Class: Social Experience in the American City, 1760–1900* (Cambridge: Cambridge University Press, 1989), 138–190. For an examination of consumption and the middle class in the late twentieth century, see Grant McCracken, *Culture and Consumption: New Approaches to the Symbolic Character of Consumer Goods and Activities* (Bloomington: Indiana University Press, 1988). On the notion of class awareness as culturally rather than economically defined, see Mary R. Jackman and Robert Jackman, *Class Awareness in the U.S.* (Berkeley: University of California Press, 1983), 5–10, and Paul Fussell, *Class: A Guide Through the American Status System* (New York: Summit Books, 1983), 97–127. On the cultural formation of the middle class in the 1920s, see Loren Baritz, *The Good Life: The Meaning of Success for the American Middle Class* (New York: Alfred Knopf, 1989), 57–58, 76. For an example of using material goods to smooth the landscape of travel, see Elon Jessup, *Roughing It Smoothly* (New York: G. P. Putnam's Sons, 1923).

8. For an intellectual history of reading and the development of the middle class, see Joan Shelley Rubin, *The Making of Middle Brow Culture* (Chapel Hill: University of North Carolina Press, 1992).

9. "Every Man a Modern Scientist," *Outing*, July 1919, 268.

10. Stoddard, *The Motorists' Almanac for 1917*, n.p.

11. "Take Your Hotel with You in Your Ford," *New York World*, 16 July 1916, n.p.; Clark, "Six Weeks in a Ford," 163; Long, *Motor Camping*, 23.

12. Marietta Holley, *Samantha vs. Josiah: Being the Story of a Borrowed Automobile and What Came of It* (New York: Funk & Wagnalls, 1906), 40, 41.

13. Ibid., 38–39.

14. "Individualizing Your Automobile," *Illustrated World*, Oct. 1920, 316–317.

15. Katherine Hulme, *How's the Road?* (San Francisco: privately printed, 1928), 89.

16. Elon Jessup, *The Motor Camping Book* (New York: G.P. Putnam's Sons, 1921), 10.

17. Schumway, "The Camper on Tour," *Field and Stream*, May 1922, 58–59.

18. James Flink, *America Adopts the Automobile, 1895–1910* (Cambridge: MIT Press, 1970), 8–9.

19. "We Announce Ourselves," *Fordowner*, April 1914, 1, 2; "On the Highway to Success," *Fordowner*, May 1914, 1.

20. "Ford Camp Touring," *Fordowner*, Jan. 1915, 13. "Shilling's Auto-Camp," *Field and Stream*, May 1921, 90.

21. For a sample of touring articles that featured user modification, and in particular building beds, see "The Call of Touring," *Fordowner*, June 1914, 13–14; "Tent for Ford Campers," *Fordowner*, April 1915; "Touring Equipment," *Fordowner*, April 1917; "At Home in a Ford," *Fordowner*, Aug. 1919.

22. "Announcing a Change of Name," *Fordowner*, May 1920. For a brief history of the magazine and reproductions of selected articles see also Murray Fahnestock, *The Model T FordOwner* (Arcadia, Calif.: Post Motor Books, 1968).

23. On the mergers and name changes of large automobile journals, see list in Ralph C. Epstein, *The Automobile Industry: Its Economic and Commercial Development* (Chicago: A. W. Shaw, 1928), 385.

24. On the implementation of mechanical improvements across the industry, such as electric starters, cord tires, and demountable rims, see Epstein, *Automobile Industry*, 106–107; and John B. Rae, *The American Automobile: A Brief History* (Chicago: University of Chicago Press, 1965), 47–48.

25. Epstein, *Automobile Industry*, 109–111, and James Flink, *The Automobile Age* (Cambridge: MIT Press, 1988), 213. For a selection of industry articles that chart the progress toward a completely enclosed car by American manufacturers, see D. R. Hobart, "Present Trend of Body Design at the New York Show," *Automobile Trade Journal*, 18 (Feb. 1914): 104A–106A; George Mercer, "Motor Body Evolution in 25 Years," *Automobile Trade Journal* 29 (April 1925): 48–50; Paul Dumas, "The Trend of Design as Seen in 1928 Cars," *Automobile Trade Journal* 32 (Jan. 1928): 25–27, 55.

26. "Converting Touring Car into Sedan," *Popular Mechanics*, Oct. 1924, 688; "Disappearing Top Converts Coupe into Roadster," *Popular Mechanics*, Sept. 1924, 440; "Preventing Draft in Touring Car," *Popular Mechanics*, Aug. 1924, 334.

27. "Beach Umbrella As Auto Top New Motor Accessory," *Popular Mechanics*, Oct. 1927, 377.

28. Murray Fahnestock, *Those Wonderful Unauthorized Accessories for Model A Ford* (Arcadia, Calif.: Post Publications, 1984). See also Kline, *Consumers in the Country*, 55–86.

29. "Specially-Equipped Car," *Fordowner*, June 1914, 36.

30. Burt Reid, "Disguising the Ford," *Illustrated World*, Jan. 1915, 813–815.

31. For observations of the auto as incomplete, see Arthur B. Maurice, "The Complete Motor Tourist," *Collier's*, 12 Aug. 1911, 18–19; "Making the Automobile Complete," *Scientific American*, 3 Jan. 1920, 10; Harold P. Shertzer, *No Charge: A Brief, Soul-Inspiring Collection of Practical Hints for This and That* (Kansas City, Mo.: privately printed, 1925), 11–12.

32. "From the Motorist's Viewpoint," *Scientific American*, 6 Jan. 1917, 11.

33. Letter to Ford Motor Works from J. C. Tucker, Union Trust Company, Pittsburgh, 3 Nov. 1928, accession 94, box 204, folder: Accessories—Sept.-Dec., The Henry Ford (hereafter THF).

34. Letter from R. H. Halton, Hot Springs, Ark., to Henry Ford, Feb. 1925, accession 94, box 144, folder 238, THF.

35. Letter from V. E. Paul, Shelton, Wash., to Ford Motor Company, 24 June 1926, accession 94, box 168, File: Complaints General 1926, THF.

36. Marguerite S. Shaffer, *See America First: Tourism and National Identity, 1880–1940* (Washington, D.C.: Smithsonian Institution Press, 2002)

37. Letter to Henry Ford, from Einar Lund, Fargo, N. Dak., 13 July 1923, accession 94, box 27, folder 113, THF.

38. Jessup, *Motor Camping Book*, 104.

39. "The Editor's Personal Page," *Motor Life*, Oct. 1914, 12.

40. "Equipment Review," *Fordowner*, March 1915, 50.

41. "Nomads of the Automobile," *Literary Digest*, 30 April 1921, 40–43.

42. Harry Irving Shumway, "The Camper on Tour," *Field and Stream*, June 1922, 200.

43. "They Gypsy Trail," *Outing*, May 1918, 134.

44. James J. Flink, "Three Stages of American Automobile Consciousness," *American Quarterly* 24 (Oct. 1972): 457 and Warren James Belasco, *Americans on*

the Road: From Autocamp to Motel, 1910–1945 (Cambridge: MIT Press, 1979), 7–24.

45. "Seeing America on 50 Cents a Day," *Ford Times*, Nov. 1915, 173–177.

46. Frederick L. Beers, "Dollars and Horse Sense," *Ford Owner and Dealer*, July 1920, 98.

47. "The Gypsy Trail," 134.

48. Walter Farlow, "Tents for Motor Gypsies," *Motor*, May 1922, 26.

49. Emily Post, *By Motor to the Golden Gate* (New York: D. Appleton, 1916), 259–277.

50. Elon Jessup, "The Flight of the Tin Can Tourists," *Outlook* 25 May 1921, 167.

51. Clark, "Six Weeks in a Ford," 164.

52. Thaddeus S. Dayton, "Camping Out with an 'Auto,'" *Harper's Weekly*, 2 Sept. 1911, 12.

53. Post, *By Motor*, 80, 187. See also Edwin Post, *Truly Emily Post* (New York: Funk & Wagnalls, 1961), 169–194.

54. James Montgomery Flagg, *Boulevards All the Way—Maybe* (New York: George H. Dornan, 1925), 12, 137.

55. J. C. Long, "Somewhere Else," 637.

56. J. C. Long and John D. Long, *Motor Camping* (New York: Dodd, Mead, 1923), 25.

57. For articles on motor touring that claimed to solve the problems of physical comfort, see Warren H. Miller, "Camping Out in Comfort," *New Country Life*, Aug. 1918, 53–56; "All the Comforts of Home," *Fordowner*, May 1916, 21; E. Saunderson, "Camping in Comfort," *Outing*, Oct. 1916, 47–48; Frank Brimmer, "Home Away from Home; Vacation Motor Camping in Comfort," *Woman's Home Companion*, May 1923, 47–48; "Going Light With Comfort," *Field and Stream*, June 1922, 211. Manufacturers also addressed the idea of comfort in their advertising; see Gold Medal Camp Furniture Mfg. Co., "Comfort Guide for Sportsmen, Campers, Tourists," (Albany, N.Y.: Albany HDWE & Iron Co., 1920), Trade Catalog Collection, THF; "Comfortable Camping," *Field and Stream*, May 1921, 84.

58. Frank E. Brimmer, "Autocamping—The Fastest-Growing Sport," *Outlook*, 16 July 1924.

59. Jessup, *Motor Camping Book*, 9, 10.

60. On material comfort as an expression of middle-class life style, see Blumin, *Emergence of the Middle Class*, 12–13; Baritz, *Good Life*, 57–58, 76.

61. Katherine Grier, *Culture and Comfort: People, Parlors, and Upholstery, 1850–1930* (Rochester, N.Y.: Strong Museum, 1988), 3. On comfort and the cultural importance of household furnishings, see John Gloag, *Victorian Comfort: A Social History of Design, 1880–1900* (New York: St.. Martin's Press, 1973); Kenneth Ames, *Death in the Dining Room and Other Tales of Victorian Culture* (Philadelphia: Temple University Press, 1992).

62. Baritz, *The Good Life*, 57–58, 76.

63. Jessup, *Motor Camping Book*, 9.

64. Peck, "Practical Hints," 80; Opal Haynes, "For Nomads of the Open Road," *Touring Topics*, June 1929, 42.

65. William Charles Bettis, *A Trip to the Pacific Coast by Automobile Across the Continent—Camping on the Way* (Toledo, Ohio: privately printed, 1922), 5.

66. Shertzer, *No Charge*, 11–12.

67. "Accessories Page," *Automotive Industries* 22 (Jan. 1910), n.p.

68. For a discussion of early automotive assembly processes, see James Flink, *The Automobile Age* (Cambridge: MIT Press, 1988), 40–43.

69. "The Automotive Equipment Association," *Automobile Trade Journal*, 29 (Jan. 1925): 46–47.

70. See "Ford Owners' Supply Book," Western Auto Supply Company, Chicago, 1926, held in trade catalog collection, Chicago Historical Society.

71. W. S. Smith, "Opportunities for Selling Accessories by Garage Men," *Automobile Trade Journal*, 20 (Jan. 1916): 113.

72. "Windows that Sell," *Automobile Trade Journal*, 29 (March 1925): 75–76. See also "Chain Store Methods Will Sell More Merchandise," *Automobile Trade Journal*, 31 (June 1927): 34–35.

73. "Ellis Turns Accessory Stock 9 to 10 Times a Year," *Automobile Trade Journal*, 30 (March 1926): 34.

74. Western Auto Supply, "Ford Owner's Supply Book," 1926, 2; American Auto Supply Company, Catalog 1915, Trade Catalog Collection, Chicago Historical Society.

75. "Get 'Em While They're Dreaming!" *Automobile Trade Journal*, 29 (Jan. 1925): 102.

76. "Tourist Profit," *Automobile Trade Journal*, 31 (April 1927): 41.

77. Ibid.

78. Stephen Hardy, "'Adopted by All the Leading Clubs': Sporting Goods and the Shaping of Leisure, 1800–1900," in Richard Butsch, *For Fun and Profit: The Transformation of Leisure into Consumption* (Philadelphia: Temple University Press, 1990), 71–94.

79. See "The History of Wilson Sporting Goods (1913–1919)," *www.wilson-sports.com/wilson/corporate/history/1913s.html*, January 1997. For Wilson products marketed to autocampers, see "Outing Service Honor Roll," *Outing*, April 1921, 47. For trade catalogs, see "Restgood," Wilson and Co. 1925, TC-0637 Trade Catalog Collection, Harpers Ferry Center Library, National Park Service, Harpers Ferry, Va. (Hereafter cited as HFC Library).

80. For trade catalogs of tent and awning companies that made autocamping equipment, see TC-Doughtery Bros. Tent and Awning Co., Catalogue No. 66, St. Louis, Mo., 1917; TC-George B. Carpenter and Co., Chicago, 1921; TC-Allen-Lawrence Co. Catalogue No. 46, "Efficient Camp Equipment," Guttenberg, N.J., 1920; TC-Dickey MFG. Co., Toledo, Ohio, 1925; all in the collections at Henry Ford.

81. Edward T. Tandy, "Building a National Business Out of a Local Need," *Printers' Ink*, 4 August 1921, 61–62.

82. F. J. Burch Manufacturing Company, Trade Catalog Collection, THF.

83. For a brief corporate history of Coleman, see Coleman Inc. Annual Reports, Historical Corporate Reports, Baker Business Library, Harvard University; and Herb Ebendorf, "Notes on the Gasoline Camp Stove," unpublished history of the Coleman stove (June 1983), Clipping Files, Division of Transportation, NMAH.

84. Hardy, "Adopted by All the Clubs," 82, 89.

85. Frank Brimmer, *Coleman Motor Campers Manual* (Wichita, Kans.: Coleman Company, 1923), inside cover.

86. Brimmer, *Coleman Motor Campers Manual*, 9.

87. For one traveler's assertion that gasoline stoves were dangerous, see Frederic Van de Water, *The Family Flivvers to Frisco* (New York: Appleton, 1927), 31–32.

88. W. C. Coleman, "President's Report to the Stockholders of the Coleman

Lamp and Stove Co." 1928, Coleman, Inc., Annual Reports, Historical Corporate Reports, Baker Business Library, Harvard University.

89. "How to Get the Most from the Shows," *Horseless Age,* 9 Dec. 1914, 843.

90. See Sears, Roebuck Spring and Fall Catalogs, 1909 to 1930, Library Collection, NMAH.

91. Marshall Field & Co., *Motoring Catalog* (Chicago: Marshall Field, n.d.), Trade Catalog Collections, Chicago Historical Society.

92. Marshall Field & Co., *Motoring to and from Marshall Field & Co.* (Chicago: Marshall Field, n.d.), 1, Trade Catalog Collection, Chicago Historical Society.

93. Nina Wilcox Putnam, *West Broadway* (New York: George H. Doran, 1921), 57–58.

94. Dixon, *Westward Hoboes,* 6. See also Hillman, "Selecting Motor Touring Equipment," 20.

95. Post, *By Motor to the Golden Gate,* 37. See William Bettis, *A Trip to the Pacific Coast,* 6; Will Irwin, "Pike's Peak, Lizzie, or Bust," *Saturday Evening Post,* 7 Oct. 1922, 14.

96. William Leavitt Stoddard, ed., *The Motorists' Almanac* (Boston: Houghton Mifflin, 1916), n.p.

97. "Making the Automobile Complete: Some Interesting Motor Car Accessories for the 1920 Market," *Scientific American,* 3 Jan. 1920, 14.

98. For annual reviews of automotive accessories, see *Scientific American* issues for 3 Jan. 1914, 12–15; 2 Jan. 1915, 20; 1 Jan. 1916, 20; 6 Jan. 1917, 21–22;, 5 Jan. 1918, 20–21; 3 Jan. 1920, 21. See also "New Accessories for Car Owners," *Motor Life,* Jan. 1914, 24 "Fitments of All Sorts," *Motor Life,* June 1921, 38; "More or Less Feminine," *Motor,* Dec. 1921, 44.

99. O. O. McIntyre, "How Many Gadgets on Your Car?" *Motor,* Nov. 1924, 54.

100. Jessup, *Motor Camping Book,* 12–13.

101. "Increasing the Pleasure by Camping Out," *Motor Life,* July 1914, 34; "We Announce Ourselves," *Fordowner,* April 1914, 1.

102. H. H. Dunn, "Touring Automobile Rivals Limited Train," *Motor Car,* Nov. 1909, 13.

103. "The Complete Tourist," *Popular Mechanics,* July 1927, 155.

104. See Roger White, *Home on the Road: The Motor Home in America* (Washington, D.C.: Smithsonian Institution Press, 2000).

105. *Outing,* May 1921, 75, and "Home Comforts in Auto Bed with Kitchenette Case," *Popular Mechanics,* Oct. 1925, 609.

106. H. C. Newton, *Six Weeks in a Motor Car: Camping and Sleeping Out* (Syracuse, N.Y.: Franklin Automobile Company, 1911), 4. Newton discussed why and how he sawed his seats in an interview: "A Luxurious Touring and Camping-Out Car," *Carriage Monthly,* April 1911, 96.

107. L. W. Peck, "Practical Hints for the Motor Camper," *Sunset,* June 1919, 81.

108. "Letters," *Field and Stream,* Aug. 1922, 468.

109. Belasco, *Americans on the Road,* 42–53.

110. "Mr. and Mrs. J. W. Lawlor, Motor Nomads, and Their Camping Outfit," *Motor Age,* 1 July 1915, 38.

111. "Double-Deck Auto Bed Billets Whole Family," *Popular Mechanics,* Nov. 1920, 717.

112. For articles on companies which produced automobiles with beds, see "Jackson Builds Standard Touring Car Sleeping Body," *Automobile,* 27 May 1915: 941; "Dodge Brothers Convertible Car" advertisement in *Polk's City Directory,* Dis-

trict of Columbia, 1919; "Spauding 'Thirty' from Iowa," *Horseless Age*, 6 April 1910, 517; "Wants Sleeping Car Body" *Automobile*, 13 Nov. 1913: 926–927; "Spaulding Sleeper," advertisement *Grinnell Herald*, 30 March 1915: 4, 1. The Flapper, a conversion built by a New York company, appeared in 1922 and featured a bed, luggage space, and ice box, according to Beverly Rae Kimes and Henry Austin Clark, Jr., *The Standard Catalog of American Cars, 1805–1942*, 543, Clipping Files, Division of Transportation, NMAH.

113. Dunn, "Touring Automobile Rivals Limited Train," 13;; "Adjustable Bed for Open or Closed Cars," *Popular Mechanics*, Nov. 1925, 743; "Auto Bed Concealed in Top Simplifies Touring," *Popular Mechanics*, Oct. 1928, 617.

114. "Line's Auto Sleeper," *Field and Stream*, May 1921, 105. Similarly, illustrations of the Universal Car Bed showed two tourists comfortably wedged beneath the roof of their car. The text claimed: "Will in three minutes make ANY size, kind or type of touring car a private palace of Pullman Comfort." T. C. *Doublservice*, ABC Mfg. Co., Kansas City, Mo., 1922, Trade Catalog Collection, THF. See also "Newman's Comfort Cot," *Field and Stream*, May 1921, 109. Several Ford beds also claimed they were "as comfortable as the lower berth in a Pullman"; *Modell's Camp Outfitters*, 1927, Trade Catalog Collection, THF.

115. Sigfried Giedion, "Railroad Comfort and Patent Furniture," in *Mechanization Takes Command: A Contribution to Anonymous History* (New York: Oxford University Press, 1948), 394–481.

116. For a social history of metamorphic furniture, see Rodris Roth, "Nineteenth-Century American Patent Furniture," and "Multiple Functions," in David Hanks, ed., *Innovative Furniture in America From 1800 to the Present* (New York: Horizon Press, 1981), 23–46, 169; Jan Seidler, *Artful Toil: Artistic Innovation in an Age of Enterprise* (Boston: Brockton Art Center-Fuller Memorial, 1977), 22–23.

117. Giedion, "Railroad Comfort and Patent Furniture," 395.

118. Robert I. Martin, "Automobile-Body with Traveling and Housekeeping Conveniences," patent 1,392,955, Oct. 11, 1921, and "Camp Outfit Combines Four Articles in One," *Popular Mechanics*, Oct., 1925, 628; "Hotel on Wheels," *Popular Mechanics*, Aug. 1925, 228; "Auto Dash box and Desk," *Popular Mechanics*, Nov. 1925, 864; "Wash Basin on Running Board Serves Auto Tourist," *Popular Mechanics*, Jan. 1929, 66.

119. For cultural histories of Taylorism and the efficiency movement in the United States, see Pursell, *The Machine in America*, 207; Sam Haber, *Efficiency and Uplift: Scientific Management in the Progressive Era, 1890–1920* (Chicago: University of Chicago Press, 1964); Martha Banta, *Taylored Lives: Narrative Productions in the Age of Taylor, Veblen, and Ford* (Chicago: University of Chicago Press, 1993).

120. "The Editor's Personal Page," *Motor Life*, July 1914, 12.

121. Brimmer, "Autocamping—the Fastest-Growing Sport," 438. See also C. O. Nichols, "Field and Stream's Outfit and Mine," *Field and Stream*, August 1923, 490.

122. Winifred Dixon, *Westward Hoboes: Ups and Downs of Frontier Motoring* (New York: C. Scribner's Sons, 1921), 9.

123. George J. Mercer, "Trends in Touring Body Designs," *Automobile* 8 July 1915, 66–68.

124. For a brief history of trunk manufacture, see Jack Trefney, "Have Trunk Will Travel," *Classic Car*, Sept. 1987, 42. For early debates on integrating trunks into the design of the car, see "Solving the Baggage Problem," *Automobile*, 25 Feb. 1915, 366–368, and Victor Page, "The Refinement of Details," *Scientific American*, 3 Jan. 1920, 6.

125. "Solving the Baggage Problem"; "Carrying the Ford's Burdens," *Ford Owners and Dealer,* Aug. 1920: 54–57; "Brief Review of Madison Square Car Exhibition," *Cycle and Automobile Trade Journal,* 15 (Feb. 1910): 174.

126. Ralph S. Roberts, "Odd Nooks and Crannies for the Tourists' Small Baggage," *Motor Life,* June 1921, 34, 62.

127. "Carrying the Ford's Burdens."

128. Petman, "Storing the Tourists' Needs," 490. See also "Interesting New Patents," *Popular Mechanics,* Feb. 1915, 318; "The Gemco Luggage Carrier," *Automobile Journal,* 21 (Jan. 1917): 298A; "Luggage Carriers," *Motor,* May 1922, 46.

129. Ethan Viall, "A Practical Flivver Trunk Rack," *Outing,* July 1925, 30–32;

130. "Suitcase Holder for Running Board of Automobile," *Popular Mechanics,* April 1917, 639; "Tent Poles and Auto Luggage Rack Are Combined for Tourists," *Popular Mechanics,* Aug. 1924, 233.

131. "Carrying the Ford's Burdens," 54–57.

132. Ibid.

133. "Luggage Carriers," *Motor,* May 1922, 46.

134. See Trefney, "Have Trunk Will Travel," 42.

135. M. Goodfriend, "Auto 'Kitchen' for the Tourist," *Popular Mechanics,* April 1928, 682; "Tourists' Kitchen Built on Front of Auto Bumper," *Popular Mechanics,* June 1931, 1025; "Boland Auto Food Cabinet," advertisement, 1922, Autocamping Clipping File, Division of Transportation, NMAH.

136. Donald H. Cole, "Autocamping Deluxe," *Field and Stream,* June 1929, 95–96.

137. General Motors declared that the integrated trunk was one of their historical landmarks; see General Motors news release on styling, c. 1957, held in folder 83–1.7–114, Kettering Archives, GMI. See also Trefney, "Have Trunk Will Travel," 42.

138. For an example of early auto beds, see "Pierce-Arrow Touring Landau," *Horseless Age,* Feb. 16, 1910: 265. On Willys-Overland's attempt to compete in a glutted market of the mid-1920s with their convertible Champion, which included a bed, see Keith Marvin, "The Rise and Fall of the Overland Champion," Clipping Files, Division of Transportation, NMAH. See also, "America's Only Versatile Car: The New Champion" *Saturday Evening Post,* 1923, Clippings Files, Division of Transportation, NMAH; "Another Innovation: The Overland Champion," *Motor World,* 3 Oct. 1923, 66–67.

139. Marvin, "Rise and Fall of the Overland Champion."

140. *Hudson Service Magazine,* March 1939, 83, Clipping Files, Division of Transportation, NMAH.

141. Flink, *The Automobile Age,* 241. See also David Hounshell, *From the American System to Mass Production,* 276 and Nevins and Hill, *Ford: Expansion and Challenge,* 595. For a detailed examination of the evolution of the Model T, see Ray Miller, *The Model T Ford: A Look at the Changes in an Unchanging Car, 1909–1927* (Oceanside, Calif.: Evergreen Press, 1971).

142. Letter to Henry Ford from C. F. Booher, Cleburne, Texas, 14 Sept. 1926, accession 94, box 182, folder, Accessories—July–Dec. 1926, THF.

143. Letter to Ford Motor Company from A. Medicus, Philadelphia, 14 March 1927, accession 94, box 189, folder: Complaints, THF.

144. For a complete description of the Model A's features, see Victor Pagé, *The Ford Model A Car: Construction, Operation, Repair* (1929; reprinted Los Angeles: Floyd Clymer Publications, 1961), 22–28.

Chapter 2. Women's Ingenuity
Note to epigraph: Laura Dent Crane, *The Automobile Girls at Newport* (Philadelphia: Henry Altemus, 1910), 78.

1. For samples of motor girl images in popular culture, see Arthur Weld, *The Motor Girl: A Musical Play in Three Acts* (New York: Arthur Weld, 1902); "The Automobile Girl," Peninsular Engraving Company, Detroit, Mich., 1903–1905, Box 19, Folder 4, Warshaw Collection, Archive Center, National Museum of American History, Smithsonian Institution, Washington, D.C. (hereafter cited as Archives Center, NMAH); C. N. Williamson and A. M. Williamson, *The Motor Maid* (New York: Doubleday, Page, 1910).

2. On middle-class women's changing relationship to public leisure, see James R. McGovern, "The American Woman's Pre-World War I Freedom in Manners and Morals," *Journal of American History* 55 (Sept. 1968): 315–33. For an overview of the historical debates surrounding women's ability to drive and the use of cars by suffragists, see Virginia Scharff, *Taking the Wheel: Women and the Coming of the Motor Age* (New York: Free Press, 1991). On gender difference and the use of the automobile between 1910 and 1920, see Clay McShane, *Down the Asphalt Path: The Automobile and the American City* (New York: Columbia University Press, 1994), 149–171.

3. Scharff, *Taking the Wheel*, 35–50, 59–63, and Michael Brian Shiffer, *Taking Charge: The Electric Automobile in America* (Washington, D.C.: Smithsonian Institution Press, 1994).

4. Constance Penley and Andrew Ross, eds., *Technoculture* (Minneapolis: University of Minnesota Press, 1991), xiii. On technological imagination and the potential for gender equality, see Linnda R. Caporael, E. Gabriella Panichkul, and Dennis R. Harris, "Tinkering with Gender," *Research in Philosophy and Technology* 13 (1993): 73–99. On technological imagination in serial fiction, see Cynthia Golomb Dettelbach, *In the Driver's Seat: The Automobile in American Literature and Popular Culture* (Westport, Conn.: Greenwood Press, 1976), 4–5, 52–57. On methodological approaches for exploring gender and the history of technology, see Lana F. Rankow, "Gendered Technology, Gendered Practice," *Cultural Studies in Mass Communication* 5 (1988): 57–70; and Nina E. Lerman, Arwen Palmer Mohun, and Ruth Oldenziel, "Versatile Tools: Gender Analysis and the History of Technology," *Technology and Culture* 38, no. 1 (Jan. 1997), 1–9. For a reading of women as active participants in the history of technology, see Judith McGaw, "No Passive Victims, No Separate Spheres: A Feminist Perspective on Technology's History," in Stephen H. Cutcliffe and Robert C. Post, eds., *In Context: History and the History of Technology* (Bethlehem, Pa.: Lehigh University Press, 1989), 172–191.

5. For background on the historical debates surrounding first-wave feminism, the New Woman, and how feminism changed after the passage of suffrage, see Nancy Wollach, *Women and the American Experience* (New York: Knopf, 1984), 269–325; Karen Offen, "Defining Feminism: A Comparative Historical Approach" *Signs* (Autumn 1988 –1989): 119–157,195–202; Estelle Freedman, "The New Woman: Changing Views of Women in the 1920s," *Journal of American History* 61 (Sept. 1974): 372–393.

6. On the Stratemeyer syndicate, see Bruce Watson, "Tom Swift, Nancy Drew and Pals All Had the Same Dad," *Smithsonian,* 22 (1991): 50–61; Diedre Johnson, *Edward Stratemeyer and the Stratemeyer Syndicate* (New York: Twayne, 1993), 7, 110–124; Carol Billman, *The Secret of the Stratemeyer Syndicate* (New York: Unger,

1986). For an overview of automobile juvenile fiction, see David K. Vaughan, "The Automobile and American Juvenile Series Fiction, 1900–1940," in Jan Jennings, ed., *Roadside America: The Automobile in Design and Culture* (Ames: Iowa State University Press, 1990), 74–81.

7. McShane, *Down the Asphalt Path*, 168–169, and Johnson, *Edward Stratemeyer*, 9.

8. Sherrie Inness, "On the Road and in the Air: Gender and Technology in Girls' Automobile and Airplane Serials, 1909–1932," *Journal of Popular Culture* 30 (Fall 1996): 37–46.

9. On adolescent fiction as providing role models, see Susan P. Montague, "How Nancy Gets Her Man: An Investigation of Success Models in American Adolescent Pulp Literature," in W. Arens and Susan P. Montague, eds., *The American Dimension: Cultural Myths and Social Realities*, 2nd ed. (Sherman Oaks, Calif.: Alfred, 1981), 77–89. For a dissenting view, see Sean McCann, "A Roughneck Reaching for Higher Things: The Vagaries of Pulp Populism," *Radical History Review* 61 (Winter 1995): 4–34. For a review of automobile fiction as a site for heroism, see "Not Yet Immortalized in Fiction: A Review of Attempts to Introduce Motoring Heroes and Heroines," *Motor*, 22 May 1923, 293.

10. Crane, *Automobile Girls at Newport*, 61; Crane, *Automobile Girls at Palm Beach*, 56–57, 135; Katherine Stokes, *The Motor Maids' School Days* (New York: Hurst, 1911), 69.

11. Clarence Young's Motor Boys series often took the heroes far from home; see *The Motor Boys in Mexico* (New York: Cupples & Leon, 1908); *The Motor Boys over the Rockies* (New York: Cupples & Leon, 1911); *The Motor Boys on the Border* (New York: Cupples & Leon, 1913); and *The Motor Boys in the Army* (New York: Cupples & Leon, 1918).

12. Michael Denning, *Mechanic Accents: Dime Novels and Working-Class Culture in America* (New York: Verso, 1987), 82–83. For a similar argument that recovers the political meanings of popular forms for women, see Janice Radway, *Reading the Romance: Women, Patriarchy, and Popular Literature* (Chapel Hill: University of North Carolina Press, 1984). On using popular fiction as historical evidence of women's experiences, see Mary Ryan, "The Projection of a New Womanhood: The Movie Moderns in the 1920s," in Jean E. Friedman and William G. Shade, eds., *Our American Sisters: Women in American Life and Thought*, 3rd ed. (Lexington, Mass.: D.C. Heath, 1982), 500–518; Regina Kunzel, "Pulp Fictions and Problem Girls: Reading and Rewriting Single Pregnancy in the Postwar United States," *American Historical Review* 100 (Dec. 1995): 1465–1487.

13. Susan Ware, *Still Missing: Amelia Earhart and the Search for Modern Feminism* (New York: W. W. Norton, 1993), 32.

14. Scharff, *Taking the Wheel*, 78.

15. Frances Willard quoted in Susan Ware, *Modern American Women: A Documentary History* (Chicago: Dorsey Press, 1989), 18. For a feminist history of the bicycle, see Ellen Gruber Garvey, "Reframing the Bicycle: Advertising-Supported Magazines and Scorching Women," *American Quarterly*, 47 (March 1995): 66–101.

16. On women and airplanes, see Joseph Corn, *The Winged Gospel: America's Romance with Aviation, 1900–1950* (New York: Oxford University Press, 1983), 71–90.

17. On leisure and women's public life, see Kathy Peiss, "Commercial Leisure and the 'Woman Question,'" in Richard Butsch, ed., *For Fun and Profit: The Transformation of Leisure into Consumption* (Philadelphia: Temple University Press, 1990); and Scharff, *Taking the Wheel*, 138–139.

18. Nancy Cott, *The Grounding of Modern Feminism* (New Haven: Yale University Press, 1987), 16.

19. On ham radio operators as heroes, see Susan J. Douglas, *Inventing American Broadcasting, 1899–1922* (Baltimore: Johns Hopkins University Press, 1987), 187–215. On a culture of invention that defined inventors as predominantly male, see Lisa A. Marovich, "'Let Her Have Brains Too': Commercial Networks, Public Relations, and the Business of Invention," *Business and Economic History*, 27, no. 1 (Fall 1998): 141–161. On gender and technical communication and the historical exclusion of women, see Katherine T. Durack, "Gender, Technology, and the History of Technical Communication," *Technical Communication Quarterly*, 6, no. 3 (Summer 1997): 249–260.

20. Pursell, "The Long Summer of Boy Engineering," 37.

21. For example, see Fay Leone Faurote, *A Boy's Text Book on Gas Engines* (Lansing, Mich.: privately printed, 1908).

22. On debates over the woman's fitness for driving, especially physical strength, see "Do Women Make Good Drivers?" *Motor*, May 1914, 61–62; Margaret R. Burlingame, "Insurance for the Woman Driver," *Motor*, June 1914, 56; and "Woman and the Motor," *Motor Digest*, 1 Nov. 1915, 28. For arguments on women's inability to drive or master mechanics, see Michael L. Berger, "Women Drivers! The Emergence of Folklore and Stereotypic Opinions Concerning Feminine Automotive Behavior," *Women Studies International Forum* 9 (1986): 257–263.

23. Hamblen Rossiter, "The Woman and the Motor Car," *Harper's Weekly*, 8 Jan. 1910, 24.

24. On the electric starter developed by Charles Kettering and the dangers of hand cranking the car, see James J. Flink, *The Automobile Age* (Cambridge: MIT Press, 1988),162; Scharff, *Taking the Wheel*, 59–63. On the invention of the starter, see T. A. Boyd, "The Self-Starter," *Technology and Culture* 9 (Oct. 1968): 585–591. On the electric starter, see Philip Drew, "We Have Women Drivers," *American Weekly* 12 Feb. 1950, 7, and Christy Borth, "He 'Liberated the Women,'" in Folder 12–36, both in Kettering papers, Kettering Archives, GMI Alumni Foundation Collection of Industrial History, Flint, Mich. (hereafter cited as Kettering Collection, GMI).

25. Penrose, *Motor Girls in the Mountains*, 84.

26. Crane, *Automobile Girls at Newport*, 60. For another example of caution and skill, see Crane, *The Automobile Girls at Palm Beach* (Philadelphia: Henry Altemus, 1913), 116–117.

27. Laura Dent Crane, *The Automobile Girls at Chicago* (Philadelphia: Henry Altemus, 1912), 146–147, 228–229.

28. Crane, *Automobile Girls at Newport*, 57–58.

29. Margaret Penrose, *The Motor Girls in the Mountains* (New York: Cupples and Leon, 1917), 87; Penrose, *The Motor Girls on a Tour* (New York: Cupples and Leon, 1910), 191.

30. Margaret Penrose, *The Motor Girls on Waters Blue* (New York: Cupples and Leon, 1915), 118.

31. "Women Make Good Motor Car Drivers," *New York Times*, 31 July 1910, p. 8, sec. C; "Driving a Car," *Woman's Home Companion*, May 1919, 52 "Safety, Thy Name Is Woman!" *Literary Digest*, 3 April 1926, 22; "Men Versus Women at the Wheel," *Literary Digest*, 26 Dec. 1931, 34.

32. "Women Make Good Motor Car Drivers."

33. "Motoring as a Woman's Profession," *Motor*, 1 May 1923, 523.

34. Mary Mullet, "Women and the Automobile," *Outing*, July 1906, 500–501.

35. Mrs. Andrew Cuneo quoted in Robert Sloss, "What a Woman Can Do with an Auto," *Outing*, April 1910, 68.

36. Sloss, "What a Woman Can Do with an Auto," 67–68.

37. On the poor quality of roads and the difficulties of driving between 1900 and 1920, see Bruce Seely, *Building the American Highway System* (Philadelphia: Temple University Press, 1987); John B. Rae, *The American Automobile: A Brief History* (Chicago: University of Chicago Press, 1965); Flink, *Automobile Age*, 29–33, 169–180.

38. Crane, *Automobile Girls at Newport*, 55.

39. Margaret Penrose, *The Motor Girls on Crystal Bay* (New York: Cupples and Leon, 1914), 100, 159, 167. For examples of technological expertise among fictional heroines, see also Penrose, *The Motor Girls on a Tour* (New York: Cupples and Leon, 1910), 2; Penrose, *The Motor Girls Through New England* (New York: Cupples and Leon, 1911), 34, 94–94; Katherine Stokes, *Motor Maids Across the Continent* (New York: Hurst, 1911), 82–85.

40. On the importance of mechanical knowledge for women drivers, see Mrs. Aria, *Woman and the Motor-Car: Being an Autobiography of an Automobilist* (London: Sidney Appleton, 1906), 109–132; Dorothy Levitt, *The Woman and the Motor Car* (London: John Lane, The Bodley Head, 1909), 31, 51; Luellen Cass Teters, "Fair Woman as a Motorist," *Motor*, Jan. 1904, 19; Blanche McManus, "The Woman Who Drives Her Own Car," *Harper's Bazaar*, July 1912, 354; Anna Phillips See, "Flivverous Miss Mary," *Ford Owner and Dealer*, Dec. 1924, 63. For prominent examples of women's mechanical know-how, see Alice Huyler Ramsey, *Veil, Duster, and Tire Iron* (Covina, Calif.: privately printed, 1961), 11, 12, 46; Mrs. Andrew Cuneo, "Why There Are so Few Women Automobilists," *Country Life in America*, March 1908, 515–516.

41. "Little Things About a Car," *Ladies' Home Journal*, March 1917, 32.

42. Sloss, "What a Woman Can Do with an Auto," 67.

43. For another comparison between domestic knowledge and automotive know-how, see Ramsey, *Veil, Duster, and Tire Iron*, 35–36. In her memoirs, Ramsey recalled that changing inner-tubes reminded her of "extracting the entrails of a turkey preparatory to stuffing it for Thanksgiving dinner."

44. "Women Make Good Motor Car Drivers."

45. On experience as informal technical training, see Charles B. Hayward, "The Price of Experience," *Harper's Weekly*, 7 June 1913, 16–17.

46. Blanche McManus, "The Woman Who Drives Her Own Car," *Harper's Bazaar*, July 1912, 354.

47. Winifred Hawkridge Dixon, *Westward Hoboes* (New York: Charles Scribner's Sons, 1921), 2. For reviews that present Dixon and her companion as role models of gender equality, see "Westward Hoboes," *Outlook*, 23 Nov. 1921, 129; "Westward Hoboes," *New York Times Book Review*, 1 Jan. 1922, 8.

48. For articles that reported the numbers of women motor travelers to be small but significant because women did the driving or traveled without male escort, see "Practical Uses of the Ford," *Fordowner*, Aug. 1916, 21; "Lucky Ladies Who Motor Alone," *Literary Digest*, 11 Aug. 1923, 50–53; T. H. Peterson, "Just Girls, They Motor Across Half the Continent and Over the Rockies," *Ladies' Home Journal*, April 1925, 205–208; Harriet B. Skidmore, "A Man-less Motor Trip: Two Women Prove the Delights of the Open Road in France," *Woman's Journal*, April 1928, 14–15, 37. For book-length narratives see, Caroline Rittenberg, *Motor West* (New York: Harold Vinal, 1926); Melita L. O'Hara, *Coast to Coast in a Puddle Jumper and Other Stories* (Tessier, Saskatchewan: privately printed, 1930).

49. "The Lone Woman Traveler," *Scribner's*, June 1937, 12–13.

50. For descriptions of the lone woman traveler, see W. G. Blaikie, "Lady Travellers," *Blackwoods*, July 1896, 49–66; Eleanor Gates, "The Girl Who Travels Alone," *Cosmopolitan*, Nov.–Dec. 1908, 1–3, 163–172; "The Lone Female Traveler," *Scribner's Magazine*, June 1937, 12–13. For advice on protection, consumption, and packing, see "Practical Hints by Women Who Have Travelled," *Ladies' Home Journal*, June 1904, 26; Laura Smith, "When a Girl Travels Alone," *Ladies' Home Journal*, May 1911, 43. Etiquette books also addressed the problem of the lone woman traveler; see John Young, *Our Deportment, or the Manners, Conduct and Dress of the Most Refined Society* (Detroit: F. B. Dickerson, 1883), 167–183; Florence Howe Hall, *Social Customs* (Boston: Estes and Lauriant, 1887), 175–181; and Margaret E. Sangster, *Good Manners for All Occasions* (New York: Cupples & Leon, 1910), 42. For a scholarly look at women travelers, see Bonnie Frederick and Susan H. McLeod, eds., *Women and the Journey: The Female Travel Experience* (Pullman: Washington State University Press, 1993).

51. Gates, "Girl Who Travels Alone," 163.

52. Ibid., 166.

53. Ramsey, *Veil, Duster, and Tire Iron*, 35–36, 46. On a similar trip by a lone woman automobilist, see "Woman Transcontinentalist Makes Progress," *Automobile Topics*, 28 May 1910, 469.

54. Ramsey, *Veil, Duster, and Tire Iron*, 42.

55. Vera Marie Teape, "The Road to Denver" (1907), reprinted in *Palimpsest*, 61 (1980): 4, 2–11.

56. Carolyn Wells, *Patty's Motor Car* (New York: Dodd, Mead, 1911), 177–189.

57. Sinclair Lewis, *Free Air* (New York: Grosset & Dunlap, 1919), 21–26.

58. Penrose, *Motor Girls on Crystal Bay*, 32.

59. See "Planning a Motor Ship," in Clarence Young, *The Motor Boys in the Clouds* (New York: Cupples and Leon, 1910), 81–95; Clarence Young, *The Motor Boys Over the Ocean* (New York: Cupples and Leon, 1911), 1–7, 91.

60. Mary Mullett, "Women and the Automobile," *Outing*, July 1906, 502; Ann Murdock, "The Girl Who Drives a Car," *Ladies' Home Journal*, July 1915, 11; Katherine Parrott Gorringe, "A Terrible Tour with Henrietta," *Sunset*, Sept. 1919, 25, Pauline Bell, "An Overland Ford Trip," *Fordowner*, July 1920, 51; Miss D. Chilton, "Motoring as Woman's Profession," *Motor*, 1 May 1923, 523.

61. Chilton, "Motoring," 523.

62. Bell, "Overland Ford Trip," 50.

63. Ibid., 51.

64. Dixon, *Westward Hoboes*, 349–352.

65. Bell, "Overland Ford Trip," 51.

66. Ibid., 50; Dixon, *Westward Hoboes*, 351; Teape, "Road to Denver," 7.

67. F. G. Moorhead, "Women Drive to Fortune," *Illustrated World*, Feb. 1915, 336.

68. Kathryn Hulme, *How's the Road* (San Francisco: privately printed, 1928), 32.

69. Teape, "Road to Denver," 3.

70. Christine Frederick, "The Commuter's Wife and the Motor Car," *Suburban Life*, July 1912, 13–14.

71. Crane, *Automobile Girls at Newport*, 49.

72. Penrose, *Motor Girls on a Tour*, 7.

73. Katherine Stokes, *Motor Maids' School Days* (New York: Hurst and Company, 1911) 90; Margaret Penrose, *The Motor Girls Through New England* (Cleve-

land: Goldsmith, 1911), 63, 94–95; Margaret Penrose, *The Motor Girls in the Mountains* (New York: Goldsmith, 1917), 81–82; Penrose, *Motor Girls on Crystal Bay,* 100–101.

74. Crane, *Automobile Girls at Newport,* 32.

75. Penrose, *Motor Girls in the Mountains,* 136–137, 139, 140.

76. Corn, *Winged Gospel,* 71–90.

77. Margery Rice, "Ready to Take the Wheel!" *American Motorist,* Sept. 1933, 3.

78. On the companionate marriage, see Lesse Lynch Williams, "The New Marriage," *Good Housekeeping,* Feb. 1914, 182; Washington Gladden, "Who Should Marry? Part II—Marriage as Friendship," *Good Housekeeping,* April 1912, 488; Judge Benjamin Lindsay and Wainwright Evans, *The Companionate Marriage,* ed. David Rothman and Sheila Rothman, Family in America series (1928; reprint New York: Arno Press, 1972). For the companionate marriage in the context of women's history, see Christine Simmons, "The Companionate Marriage and the Lesbian Threat," *Frontiers,* 4 (1979): 54–59.

79. For visions of the companionate vacation as reuniting families, see Charles I. O'Neil, "Motor Touring as a Family Affair," *Sunset,* Oct. 1916, 76–77; Frank Brimmer, *Motor Campcraft* (New York: Macmillan, 1923), 2–5; Elon Jessup, *Roughing It Smoothly: How to Avoid Vacation Pitfalls* (New York: G. P. Putnam's Sons, 1923), 203–207; Katherine Lafitte, "Burning Gas on the Gypsy Trail," *Outing,* April 1922, 298–301; "Friend of the Children—The Family Car," *Literary Digest,* 8 Jan. 1927, 65. For historians who have argued that the automobile reunited the family and made men and women equal partners on the road, see Warren Belasco, *Americans on the Road: From Autocamp to Motel, 1910–1945* (Cambridge: MIT Press, 1979)., 69 and Flink, *Automobile Age,* 158–160, 162–163.

80. Simmons, "Companionate Marriage," 55.

81. Lewis, *Free Air,* 240, 369–370. For a review, see "Free Air," *New York Times Book Review,* 19 Oct. 1919, 580.

82. Lewis, *Free Air,* 158–159, 160–161.

83. Ibid., 273, 367.

84. For a selection of articles that emphasized companionship and family togetherness as the best form of motor travel, see J. Constantine Hillman, "Cross-Country Fording," *Fordowner,* May 1916, 13–17; Emerson Hough, "Maw's Vacation," *Saturday Evening Post,* 16 Oct. 1920, 14–15,109; R. M. King, "Family Takes a Vacation," *Sunset,* Aug. 1925, 32–33; "Friend Wife on the Trail," *Outing,* April 1925, 34–35; "The Motor Trip for You," *Ladies' Home Journal,* May 1929, 16. For book-length narratives, see Effie Price Gladding, *Across the Continent by the Lincoln Highway* (New York: Brentano's, 1915); Beatrice Larned Massey, *It Might Have Been Worse* (San Francisco: Harr Wagner Publishing, 1920); William Charles Bettis, *A Trip to the Pacific Coast by Automobile Across the Continent* (Toledo, Ohio: By the Author, 1922), 4; Mary Crehore Bedell, *Modern Gypsies* (New York: Brentano's, 1924); James Montgomery Flagg, *Boulevards All the Way—Maybe* (New York: George H. Doran, 1925); Gula Sabin, *California by Motor* (Milwaukee: privately printed, 1926); Frederic Van de Water, *The Family Flivvers to Frisco* (New York: Appleton, 1927).

85. Jessup, *Roughing It Smoothly,* 203–204.

86. Mary Carolyn Davies, "Motor Honeymoon" *Sunset,* May 1925, 32; Vivian Gurney, "An Auto-Burro Honeymoon," *Sunset,* June 1921, 40–42.

87. Gurney, "Auto-Burro Honeymoon," 42.

88. Brimmer, *Motor Campcraft,* 5.

89. "Friend Wife on the Trail," *Outing*, April 1925, 34–35. For representations of wives as partners, see J. Constantine Hillman, "Selecting Motor Touring Equipment," *Fordowner*, July 1916, 19–24; Frank Farrington, "You Can't Awe a Woman: Touring Adventures in Which Friend Wife Stars," *Motor Life*, June 1921, 28, 64–65; "Something for the Ladies," *Field and Stream*, June 1922, 205–206; Jessie Rockefeller, "When Friend Wife Goes Camping," *Motor Camper and Tourist*, Sept. 1925, 257; R. E. Smith, "Madam Goes Along," *Field and Stream*, July 1927, 51–52.

90. Hillman, "Cross-Country Fording," 17.

91. Belasco, *Americans on the Road*, 65.

92. Margaret Marsh, "Suburban Men and Masculine Domesticity, 1870–1915," *American Quarterly* 40 (June 1988):166–167.

93. Brimmer, *Motor Campcraft*, 39,137. For more articles by Brimmer illustrating him and his wife sharing equally in domestic tasks, see "Home Away from Home," *Woman's Home Companion*, May 1923, 47–48; "Following the Open Road in Your Car," *Woman's Home Companion*, June 1925, 42; "Motor Camping Made Comfortable," *Woman's Home Companion*, July 1927, 34.

94. Marsh, "Suburban Men and Masculine Domesticity," 167, 177. For an image of male auto campers caring for children, see E. S. Shipp, "Tourists at Lolo Hot Springs, Lolo, Montana," United States Forest Service, North Dakota, the Division of Transportation, NMAH, Smithsonian Institution, Washington, D.C. (hereafter cited as Division of Transportation, NMAH).

95. Herbert Ladd Towle, "The Woman at the Wheel," *Scribner's*, Feb. 1915, 219.

96. "Efficiency Around the Camp," *Field and Stream*, Aug. 1922, 465.

97. Gorringe, "A Terrible Tour with Henrietta," 25–28; Harriet Wilkin Johnson, "Housekeeping on Wheels," *Motor*, May 1922, 26; "A Woman's Advice on Motor Camping," *Literary Digest*, 4 April 1925, 82–86; Sabin, *California by Motor*, 3; Lois E. Buriff Brown, "Modern Gypsies," *Nation*, 4 May 1927, 500–501.

98. Sabin, *California by Motor*, 4–8, quotation on 5.

99. Scharff, *Taking the Wheel*, 137–138.

100. Estella M. Copeland, *Overland by Auto in 1913: Diary of a Family Tour from California to Indiana* (Indianapolis: Indiana Historical Society, 1981), 43–44, 50, 56. See also Dorherty Family Diary, *Gilkey Trailer Travels, 1929–1938*; Rushton Coutelyou travel diary, 1919; and Stimson Auto Journal, Nov. 20, 1929–Nov. 6, 1930, Jonathan Cass Stimson Collection, Acc. 1997.0245, all held in the Division of Transportation, NMAH.

101. Bedell, *Modern Gypsies*, 104.

102. Letter, Anne Kerr Crawford to Rushton Cortelyou, Ottawa, Dec. 11, 1988, Division of Transportation, NMAH.

103. Rushton Cortelyou travel diary, 1919, p.159, Division of Transportation, NMAH.

104. Gilkey Trailer Travels diary, July 4, 1932, Aug. 1, 1932, Aug. 5, 1932, July 12, 1935, July 8, 1935.

105. Bedell, *Modern Gypsies*, 215.

106. "Mammoth Public Auto Camp," 1923, LC-USZ62–66079, Library of Congress, Prints and Photographs Division, Washington, D.C.

107. Simmons, "Companionate Marriage," 55.

108. Ruth Schwartz Cowan, "Two Washes in the Morning and a Bridge Party at Night: The American Housewife Between the Wars," in *Our American Sisters*, 519–520.

109. Van de Water, *Family Flivvers to Frisco*, 70.

110. Winfield A. Kimball and Maurice H. Decker, *Touring with Tent and Trailer* (New York: McGraw-Hill, 1937), 249.

111. Ibid., 248–249.

112. Van de Water, *Family Flivvers to Frisco*, 146–147, 148.

113. Priscilla Hovey Wright, *The Car Belongs to Mother* (Boston: Houghton Mifflin, 1939), 78, 79, 80.

114. "Who's Who in Outing," *Outing*, April 1919, 2.

115. Adelaide Ovington, "Camping and the Motor Car," *Outlook*, 12 June 1918, 274. For background on Horace Kephart and his career as a camping authority, see Horace Kephart, *Camping and Woodcraft*, introduction by Jim Casada (1917; reprint, Memphis: University of Tennessee Press, 1988), vii–xxxiii.

116. Ovington, "Camping and the Motor Car," 274.

117. See "Who's Who in Outing" and "Contents," *Outing*, April–Sept. 1919.

118. For a brief biography of Frank Brimmer with list of publications and editorial affiliations, see Frank Brimmer, *Coleman Motor Campers Manual* (Wichita, Kans.: Coleman Lamp Company, 1926), 3.

119. For a list of Jessup's publications, see Jessup, *Roughing It Smoothly*, v.

120. For advice on how to make cooking easy, Bannister Merwin, "A Good Way to Cook a Trout," *Outing*, April–Sept. 1910; "What to Bring in the Grub Bag," *Outing*, June 1918, 205–206; Lawrence Clark, "Six Weeks in a Ford," *Outing*, July 1922, 163; "For Cooking Delicious Meals," *Field and Stream*, July 1925, 60; Maurice H. Decker, "Motor Camping Made Easy," *Woman's Home Companion*, April 1931, 55–56.

121. Orin Crooker, "Motor Camping—the New Sport," *American Motorist*, March 1922, 19–20.

122. Stewart Edward White, *The Outdoor Omnibus* (New York: Grosset & Dunlap, 1904), 182.

123. E. L. Chicanot, "A Bachelor's Breadmaking," *Outing*, July 1921.

124. Stewart Edward White, *Camp and Trail* (New York: Doubleday, Page, 1915), 135.

125. "A Woman's Advice on Motor Camping," *Literary Digest*, 4 April 1925, 82.

126. Betty M. Orr, "Tips for Trailer Housekeepers," *Trailer Travel*, March–April 1936, 33.

127. On the assertion that trailer travel was easier on women than auto-camping, see W. W. Bauer, M.D., "Prairie Schooner, 1935–36," *Trailer Travel*, May–June 1936, 24–25. For advice on how to make trailer housekeeping simpler and more efficient, see Trailer Wife, "Tasty Trailer Meals from the Shelf," *Trailer Travel*, March–April, 1936, 32; "Discoveries in the Field of Accessories to Comfort Trailer Wives," *Trailer Travel*, Sept. 1936, 48; Kathryn Moross, "Dean of Trailer House Wives Tell How She Keeps the Inner Man Satisfied," *Trailer Caravan*, Sept. 1936, 9.

128. Ruth Schwartz Cowan, *More Work for Mother: The Ironies of Household Technology from the Open Hearth to the Microwave* (New York: Basic Books, 1983); Susan Strasser, *Never Done: A History of American Housework* (New York: Pantheon Books, 1982).

129. Elizabeth Allyse, "The Cook and the Can Opener," *Trailer Caravan*, March–April 1937, 13, 31; Edrey Bullis Miles, "More Time for the Cook," *Trailer Caravan*, Aug. 1937, 15, 33.

130. "Edwin Fisher Forbes, "A Trailer Made Marriage," *Trailer Caravan*, Aug.

1937, 11; Bruce V. Crandall, "Just Rolling Along," *Trailer Caravan*, May–June 1937; Edwin Teale, "Five Weeks in a Trailer," *Popular Science Monthly*, April 1937, 46–48,121. For trailer fiction that featured families and companionate romances, see Harriet F. Bunn, *Trailer Tracks* (New York: Macmillan, 1937), and Marion Short, *The Trailer Man* (New York: Samuel French, 1938).

131. Hallie Whitaker, "'Patent Applied For: Two Girls Turn Trailer Minded and as Usual Romance Enters," *Trailer Caravan*, Nov. 1936, 43.

132. On women as supposedly mechanically unskilled, see Berger, "Women Drivers!" 56–60; Margaret R. Burlingame, "Needs Must, When—Woman Asks," *Motor*, May 1913, 50; Margaret R. Burlingame, "Insurance for the Woman Driver," *Motor*, June 1914, 56; "Do Women Make Good Drivers?" *Motor*, May 1914, 16–62; Herbert Towle, "The Woman at the Wheel" *Scribner's*, February 1915, 214; "Feminine Foibles Through Masculine Eyes," *Motor*, 5 June 1923, 733; Patricia Cox, "Woman—Her Ignorance: The Garage Owner and His Attitude to Women Customers," *The Motor*, 15 May 1923, 611; "You Can't Tell What a Woman'll Do Next," *Ford Owner and Dealer*, Sept. 1923, 4; "Can A Woman Drive A Car?" *Literary Digest*, 4 July 1925, 36–37; Frederick Russell, "Lifting the Hood," *American Motorist*, Oct. 1933, 8; "Women Drivers," *Scientific American*, April 1937, 35.

133. "Do Women Make Good Drivers?" 61.

134. Towle, "Woman at the Wheel," 214 and "Feminine Foibles," 733.

135. Van de Water, *Family Flivvers to Frisco*, 187.

136. For descriptions of male tinkerers and their motor equipment as ingenious, see "Camping on the Running Board," *Outing*, April 1919, 41; "Take Your Hotel with You in Your Ford," *New York World*, 16 July 1916; "Six Weeks in a Ford," *Outing*, July 1922, 163; J. C. Long, *Motor Camping* (New York: Dodd, Mead, 1923), 23.

137. Harry Irving Shumway, "What Do You Get Out of Auto-Camping, Anyway?" *Field and Stream*, May 1922, 58. See also Bertha Streeter, "Vacations by Motor Car," *Parents*, July 1929, 24–25.

138. Massey, *It Might Have Been Worse*, 48; Post, *By Motor to the Golden Gate*, 241–250.

139. Nancy Barr Mavity, "Woman at the Wheel," *Sunset*, April 1927, 30.

140. A. D. Hard, "Incidents of an Automobile Trip," *Motor Life*, Aug. 1914, 39; Murray Fahnestock, "Spark and Throttle: A Discourse on the Problem of Teaching Woman to Drive!" *Ford Owner and Dealer*, Oct. 1924, 71–73; Mavity, "Woman at the Wheel," 30; Barbara Lane, "How My Husband Taught Me to Drive," *American Motorist*, Feb. 1935, 8.

141. "When Friend Wife Rocked the New 'Boat,'" *Literary Digest*, March 13, 1920, 96.

142. Fahnestock, "Spark and Throttle," 71.

143. Conversation with Dr. Patrick Malone and Louis Azza, Providence, R.I., 6 May 1999.

144. On the dangers of driving with the planetary transmission, see E. B. White, "Farewell, My Lovely!" in White, *The Second Tree from the Corner* (New York: Harper & Row, 1978). For a similar description, see Ralph Stein, *The Treasury of the Automobile* (New York: Golden Press, 1961), 167.

145. *Instruction Book for Ford Model T Cars* (Detroit: Ford Motor Company, 1913), 11; International Correspondence Schools, *The Automobile Handbook* (Scranton: International Textbook Company, 1913), 123.

146. Fahnestock, "Spark and Throttle," 71–72.

147. Lane, "How My Husband Taught Me," 8; Cox, "Good and Bad Driving," 705; Geraldine Sartain, "You and Your Car," *Independent Woman* 18 (May 1939): 135.
148. Mavity, "Woman at the Wheel," 31.
149. Gurney, "An Auto-Burro Honeymoon," 40.
150. Van de Water, *Family Flivvers to Frisco*, 187.
151. Kimball and Decker, *Touring with Tent and Trailer*, 258, 259–260.
152. "Feminine Foibles," 733.
153. Wright, *Car Belongs to Mother*, xi, xii, xiii.
154. Sartain, "You and Your Car," 135, 136.

Chapter 3. Consumers Become Inventors

1. Milton Wright, "Commercial Property News," *Scientific American*, April 1926, 284.
2. David Nobel, *America by Design: Science, Technology, and the Rise of Corporate Capitalism* (New York: Knopf, 1977), and Thomas Hughes, *American Genesis: A Century of Invention and Technological Enthusiasm, 1870–1970* (New York: Viking, 1989).
3. Hughes, *American Genesis*, 9.
4. See Alfred P. Sloan, Jr., *My Years with General Motors* (Garden City, N.Y.: Doubleday, 1964); Daniel M. G. Raff, "Making Cars and Making Money in the Interwar Automobile Industry: Economies of Scale and Scope and the Manufacturing behind the Marketing," *Business History Review* 65 (Winter 1991): 721–753.
5. Peter Whalley, "The Social Practice of Independent Inventing," *Science, Technology, and Human Values*, 16 (Spring 1991): 208–209,213.
6. Carolyn Cooper, "Invention, Authorship, 'Intellectual Property,' and the Origin of Patents: Notes Toward a Conceptual History"; Cooper, "Crossover Inventors and Technological Linkages: American Shoemaking and the Broader Economy, 1848–1901," in Carolyn Cooper, ed., *Technology and Culture* 32 (Oct. 1991): 846–884.
7. Orson Munn, ed., *Patents: A Book of Facts Every Inventor Should Know* (New York: Munn & Company, 1927), 9.
8. Library of Congress has an extensive collection of advice manuals written by patent attorneys. For a representative selection, see L. D. Snook, *Snook's Inventors' Helper* (Dundee, N.Y.: Observer Print, 1879); A. J. O'Brian, *Patent Pointers* (Denver, Colo.: Scientific Agency of Denver, 1891); Joseph Allen Minturn, *The Inventor's Friend; or, Success With Patents* (Indianapolis, Ind.: Meridian, 1893); Charles Labofish, *How to Win Fortune by Inventing: Couched in a Readable Story* (Washington, D.C.: privately printed, 1911); Richard B. Owen, *Stepping Stones: A Reliable Treatise on Invention* (Washington, D.C.: privately printed, 1911); George M. Hopkins, *Inventor's Manual: How to Work a Patent to Make it Pay* (New York: Norman W. Henley, 1924); A. F. Gillett, *Valuable Hints to Inventors* (Washington, D.C.: Inventors' Publishing, 1933); George R. Roesch, *Your Invention: What to Do with It* (Syracuse, N.Y.: Roesch & Associates, 1934); Raymond Francis Yates, *Inventors' Selling Guide* (New York: Donley, 1934).
9. Simon Deutsch, "Invention by Effort and Study," in Owen, *Stepping Stones*, 10.
10. Labofish, *How To Win a Fortune*, 111, 115, 119.

11. Edwin C. Axe, *Inventors' Pocketbook: The ABC of Patents* (London: S. & M. Bayles, 1933). On hairpins, paper clips, and pencil erasers, see Labofish, *How to Win a Fortune*, 21; Owen, *Stepping Stones*, 11; Hopkins, *Inventor's Manual*, 4; Gillet, *Valuable Hints*, 5; Leo Parker, "Don't Throw Away Your Ideas," *Popular Mechanics*, Oct. 1925, 745.

12. "An Outside Inventor," *Scientific American*, Jan. 1929, 94.

13. John M. Staudenmaier, *Technology's Storytellers: Reweaving the Human Fabric* (Cambridge: MIT Press, 1985), 143.

14. R. S. Woodworth, "The Mechanism of Progress: A Theory of Inventiveness," *Scientific American Supplement*, 30 April 1910, 279.

15. Adam Fisher, *Plain Talk, or Dollars and Sense in Inventions* (St. Louis: privately printed, 1929), 1.

16. Larry Owens, "Patent, the 'Frontiers' of American Invention, and the Monopoly Committee of 1939: Anatomy of a Discourse," *Technology and Culture* 32 (Oct. 1991): 1093.

17. Simon Broder, "The Psychology of Invention: An Inquiry into the Nature and Causes of Invention," *Journal of the Patent Office Society* 9 (April 1927): 357

18. Lowell Julliard Carr, "The Patenting Performance of 1,000 Inventors During Ten Years," *American Journal of Sociology* 37 (Jan. 1932): 569–580; Carr, "A Study of 137 Typical Inventors," in *Papers and Proceedings of the 23rd Annual Meeting of the American Sociological Society* (Chicago: University of Chicago Press, 1928), 204–206.

19. Joseph Rossman, "The Negro Inventor," *Journal of the Patent Office Society* 12 (April 1928): 552; and Rossman, "Women Inventors," *Journal of the Patent Office Society* 10 (Sept. 1927): 18–30.

20. On audiences for technical magazines as largely white, middle-class, and male, see Tom Pendergast, *Creating the Modern Man: American Magazines and Consumer Culture, 1900–1950* (Columbia: University of Missouri Press, 2000). See also Carroll Pursell, "The Long Summer of Boy Engineering," in John L. Wright, ed., *Possible Dreams: Enthusiasm for Technology in America* (Dearborn, Mich.: Henry Ford Museum & Greenfield Village, 1992), 34–43.

21. Henry Robinson, *Inventors and Inventions* (New York: privately printed, 1911), 14, 1.

22. For a more complete and sophisticated discussion of women inventors and inventive culture in the United States, see Lisa Marovich, "Fueling the Fires of Genius: Women's Inventive Activities in American War Eras," Ph.D. diss., UCLA, 1998.

23. Minturn, *Inventor's Friend*, 21

24. Labofish, *How to Win a Fortune.*

25. Minturn, *Inventor's Friend*, 2–3.

26. Labofish, *How to Win a Fortune*, 22.

27. Owen, *Stepping Stones*, 11.

28. Labofish, *How to Win a Fortune*, 21.

29. Hopkins, *Patent Knowledge for Inventors*," 71.

30. Fisher, *Plain Talk*, 3.

31. For popular histories of invention, see S. E. Forman, *Stories of Useful Inventions* (New York: Century, 1919); B. A. Fiske, *Invention, the Master-Key to Progress* (New York: Dutton, 1921); Edward Cressy, *Discoveries and Inventions of the Twentieth Century*, 2nd ed. (New York: Dutton, 1923); Wademar Kaempffert, *A Popular History of American Invention* (New York: Charles Scribner's Sons, 1924).

32. James M. Chalfant, "Fortunes from Little Ideas," *Popular Mechanics*, Sept. 1932, 429.

33. Milton Wright, "Inventors Who Have Achieved Commercial Success," *Scientific American* 136 (Feb. 1927): 105.

34. Minturn, *Inventor's Friend*, back cover.

35. Carolyn Cooper, "Social Construction of Invention Through Patent Management: Thomas Blanchard's Woodworking Machinery," *Technology and Culture* 32 (Oct. 1991), 962–963.

36. "What Is a Patent Attorney," *Scientific American* (April 1928): 380;

37. Minturn, *Inventor's Friend*, 61.

38. Labofish, *How to Win a Fortune*, 150.

39. Steven Lubar, "New, Useful, and Non-Obvious," *American Heritage of Invention and Technology* 6 (Spring–Summer 1990): 18–25.

40. Minturn, *Inventor's Friend*, 1.

41. Gillet, *Valuable Hints*, 76.

42. George Kimmel, *Patent Knowledge for Inventors* (Washington, D.C.: privately printed, 1916), 6.

43. Hopkins, *Inventor's Manual*, 68.

44. For a sample, see "More Than $128,400 Offered for Your Ideas," *Popular Mechanics*, Aug. 1924, 177–183; "Your Idea May Be Worth a Fortune," *Popular Mechanics*, Dec. 1931.

45. Leo Parker, "Don't Throw Away Your Ideas," *Popular Mechanics*, Oct. 1925, 745, 746.

46. Gillet, *Valuable Hints*, 13–14.

47. For examples of tinkering in selected travel narratives, see Mary Crehore Bedell, *Modern Gypsies* (New York: Brentano's, 1924), 83; Maria L. Stocket, *America First, Fast, and Furious* (Baltimore: Norman-Remington, 1930), 2; William Bettis, *A Trip to the Pacific Coast by Automobile Across the Continent—Camping on the Way* (Toledo: Booth Type Setting Company, 1922), 7; Andrew Wilson, *The Gay Gazel: An Adventure in Auto Biography* (Cooperstown, N.Y.: privately printed, 1926), 82.

48. The research for this study was derived from a survey of the *Patent Index* for all automobile tourist accessories that duplicated domestic functions (beds, kitchenettes, food boxes, stoves, etc.) between 1910 and 1939. There were no patents for tourist items before 1915 and very few (3 or 4) after 1930. I traced patents related to beds, bedding, and shelter (tents) both alone and in combinations such as bed and tent, bed and table. I compiled a list of 100 tourist accessories from the subcategories of "automobile-bed," "bed-automobile," "tent-automobile," and "trunks." I included inventors from the patent index in popular journals and advertisements.

The following data was recorded from the patent specifications letters: names and locations of the inventors, whether the patent was assigned at the time of application, and the justifications for the usefulness of the idea. Each patentee was checked against two additional sets of documents—city directories (held in the Library of Congress) and assignment records (held in National Archives II). Thirty-nine inventors were successfully located in city directories. City directories provided the inventors' occupations. The majority of patentees were middle-class managers and professionals who did not work in an automotive-related field.

Finally, I checked assignment records for all patents in the sample (through the seventeen-year duration of the patent) in order to see if the patentee sold the patent to a manufacturer or a retail outlet. The overwhelming majority of patentees studied never assigned and did not hold other patents.

Patents for all automobile accessories ended between 1930 and 1933. In order to chart the effect of the national depression and the rise of professional design on amateur invention, I examined the *Patent Index* for 1945–1955. Even in this era of material prosperity, patent records for automobile accessories did not approach the pre-1930s numbers.

I used collections of the *Index of Patents* held by the National Museum of American History, Smithsonian Institution, and the Providence Public Library, Providence, R.I. The rise in patents corresponds with the rise in automobile registrations after between 1920 and 1933. For statistics on registration, see National Automobile Chamber of Commerce, *Facts and Figures of the Automobile Industry, 1926 Edition* (New York: NACC, 1926), 72–73, and *National Automobile Chamber of Commerce, Facts and Figures of the Automobile Industry, 1934 Edition* (New York: NACC, 1934), 12–13.

49. See "Alphabetical List of Inventions," *Patent Indexes* (Washington, D.C.: Government Printing Office, 1910–1937).

50. General Motors initiated the first formal consumer survey in 1933. See "The Proving Ground of Public Opinion" (Detroit: General Motors, 1934), Kettering Archives, GMI Alumni Foundation Collection of Industrial History, Flint, Mich.

51. Most of the historical work done on a patents and invention has focused on a limited number of famous inventors and on the nineteenth century. On patents as historical evidence, see Nathan Reingold, "U.S. Patent Office Records as Sources for the History of Invention and Technological Property," *Technology and Culture* 1 (Spring 1960): 156–167. For general essays on the patent system and invention, see Thomas P. Hughes, "Inventors: The Problems They Choose, the Ideas They Have, and the Inventions they Make," in Patrick Kelly and Melvin Kranzburg, eds., *Technological Innovation: A Critical Review of Current Knowledge* (San Francisco: San Francisco Press, 1978), 166–182; Lubar, "New, Useful, and Non-Obvious"; Ruth Schwartz Cowan, "Inventors, Entrepreneurs, and Engineers," in *A Social History of American Technology* (New York: Oxford University Press, 1997), 118–147; Kenneth L. Sokoloff and B. Zorina Kahn, "The Democratization of Invention During Early Industrialization: Evidence from the United States, 1790–1846," *Journal of Economic History* 50 (1990): 363–378.

52. Brooke Hindle, *Emulation and Invention* (New York: Norton, 1981).; Merritt Roe Smith, *Harper's Ferry Armory and the New Technology: The Challenge of Change* (Ithaca, N.Y.: Cornell University Press, 1977); Carolyn Cooper, *Shaping Invention: Thomas Blanchard's Machinery and Patent Management in Nineteenth-Century America* (New York: Columbia University Press, 1991); Ruth Schwartz Cohen, "Inventors, Entrepreneurs, and Engineers," in Cowan, *A Social History of American Technology* (New York: Oxford University Press, 1997), 119–147; Zorina Kahn, "The Patent System and Inventive Activity in Britain and America, 1790–1865," paper given at the Lemelson Center, Smithsonian Institution, July 1997.

53. See patents and city directory records for Joseph Smith, 30 June 1925; James Young, 6 Nov. 1923; John Turner, 28 Dec. 1920; Claude Eaton, 30 May 1922. For numbers of doctors and other professionals who owned cars during this period, see NACC, *Facts and Figures of, by and for the Automobile Industry* (New York: NACC, 1919), 15; See also *Facts and Figures* 1921, 22; and *Facts and Figures* 1922, 53.

54. Michael B. Fox, patent 1,322,100, 18 Nov. 1919; see also Lester E. Ike, patent 1,744,701, 21 Jan. 1930. See also "When the Car Becomes Your Bedroom," *Outing*, April 1921, 25.

. See personal memoir of George Reid Clapp, "A Pierce-Arrow Camper," *The Arrow,* no date, vertical files, Division of Transportation, NMAH. Clapp recalled his father taking their Pierce Arrow to a mechanic to have the seats hinged and the interior converted for sleeping. See also "Studebaker Sedan Equipped with Berths for Touring," *Motor Age,* 16 Sept. 1915, 25; "A 7-Passenger Landau-Type Sedan Arranged by Judkins as an Emergency Sleeping Car," *Autobody,* Dec. 1924, 218; and how-to literature such as C. G. Cook, "Amplified Method of Reconstructing the Front-Seat Back of a Closed Car so It Can Be Lowered to Form a Bed," *Motor Vehicle Monthly,* July 1924, 44–45.

56. "A 7-Passenger Landau-Type," 218.

57. For representative examples, see "Converting the Car Into a Sleeping Compartment," *Scientific American,* 24 April 1915, 383, which discussed E. L. Thompson's patent as the first convertible auto bed. I located 100 patents for automobile beds or convertible automobiles between 1915 and 1930. See also patents for the following: Judson E. Wright, "Foldable Seat for Converting Two-Seated Automobile-Bodies into Lounges," patent 1,149,931, 25 May 1915; Burton E. Haney, "Auto-Bed," patent 1,304,966, 27 May 1919; Clifford K. Aldrich, "Automobile-Bed," patent 1,291,704, 21 Jan. 1919; Michael B. Fox, "Bed Structure for Automobiles," patent 1,322,100, 8 Nov. 1919; Liven Grubb Taylor, "Combination Seat and Bed for Automobiles," patent 1,390,177, 6 Sept. 1921; Charles E. Putnam, "Automobile-Bed," patent 1,318,589, 14 Oct. 1919; John Lawrence, "Auto-Body," patent 1,316,488, 16 Sept. 1919; James J. Rehanek, "Automobile-Sleeper," patent 1,378,615, 17 May 1921; Frank Mitchell, "Convertible Automobile Body," patent 1,401,177, 21 Dec. 1921; Marjoree Steel, "Camping Bed for Automobiles," patent 1,465,925; 21 Aug. 1923; Elvira R. Fischer, "Automobile-Bed," patent 1,259,220, 12 March 1918; James W. Kippen and Elma Kippen, "Convertible Automobile Body," patent 1,410,192, 21 March 1922; Etta H. Goodrich, "Convertible Automobile Body," patent 1,437,751, 5 Dec. 1922; Lester E. Ike, "Automobile Bed," patent 1,744,701, 21 Jan. 1930.

58. John F. Kerrigan, Automobile-Bed, patent 1,306,258, 10 June 1919.

59. "Sleeping in a Ford Sedan," *Popular Mechanics,* May 1924, 796.

60. Joseph B. Smith, Automobile Bed, patent 1,554,277, 30 June 1925, p. 1, and John S. Turner, Automobile-Bed, patent 1,363,627, p. 1.

61. William H. Groverman, Automobile-Bed, patent 1,255,307, 5 Feb. 1918, 1. These were extremely popular designs, perhaps because they took little mechanical knowledge and did not involve restructuring the interior of the car.

62. Herrick S. Cole, Folding Automobile-Bed, patent 1,233,645, 17 July 1917; Otis W. Cook, Tent Attachment for Automobiles, patent 1,267,979, 28 May 1918.

63. Delbert M. Westcott and Harry M. Vincent, Folding Bed for Automobiles, patent 1,226,426, 15 May 1917; Wilbur E. Cummings, Auto Spring-Bed, patent 1,349,268, 10 Aug. 1920.

64. James W. and Elma Kippen, "Convertible Automobile Body," patent 1,410,192, 21 March 1922.

65. Samuel F. Donnell, "Convertible Bed and Table Attachment for Automobiles," patent 1,282,391, 22 Oct. 1918, 1. See also Clarence C. Starr, "Folding Automobile Bed," patent 1,415,727, 9 May 1922. Starr's bed could also be used as a table.

66. Elvira Fischer, "Automobile-Bed," patent 1,259,220, 12 March 1918.

67. Charles Putnam, "Automobile-Bed," patent 1,318,589, 14 Oct. 1919.

68. Marjorie Steel, "Camping Bed for Automobiles," patent 1,465,925, 21 Aug. 1923.

69. *Popular Mechanics Automobile Tourist's Handbook No. 1* (Chicago: Popular Mechanics Press, 1924). See also Opal Haynes, "For Nomads of the Open Road," *Touring Topics,* June 1929, 43, 54.; Peter Schaefer, Horace D. Hulse, and George M. Livingstone, auto-porch bed, patent 1,347,412, 20 July 1920, 1.

70. Milton Wright, "Successful Inventors—XIII," *Scientific American,* Jan.. 1928, 28. See also "A Quick Sale," *Scientific American,* Oct. 1925, 258; "How to Sell an Invention," *Popular Mechanics,* Nov. 1931, 810–814.

71. For a concise overview of the various ways of profiting from a patent in the interwar years, see Gillet, *Valuable Hints,* 50.

72. Fisher, *Plain Talk,* 21.

73. See Charles Davis, assignor, to Handy Auto Bed Company of Bend, Oregon, patent 1,502,498, 22 July 1924; John Rietshel assignor to Tentobed Company of Chicago, Illinois, patent 1,404,145; Isaac Pursell assignor to the Tentobed Company, patent 1,434,962, Peter Schaefer, Horace Hulse, and George M. Livingstone, assignors to Peter C. Schaefer, Denver, Colorado, patent 1,347,412. The remaining were assigned to manufacturers after application, to friends and relatives, or to named individuals but not to companies. See assignments for Claude Eaton; Ralph Hosner, George Blake, Theodore Schmeiser; John McBrady; Henry Moffett; Burton Crain; John Line; Louis Clergy; Lonza Windsor; Henry Moffett; Fred Horton; Lester Ike.

74. "Spotlight Turned on Refined Motor Camping," ABC Manufacturing Company Trade Catalog, 1922, accession T. C. Dublservis, ABC Mfg. Co., Trade Catalog Collection, THF.

75. Patentees lived and worked in areas that supported high rates of automobile ownership and motor tourism. More than half (53) of patentees came from the western states of California, Washington, Oregon, and Colorado. The Midwest (Kansas, Michigan, Missouri) was second largest region, claiming 30 percent of the patentees. Eastern and the southern states contributed less than a quarter of the patents. These figures reflected national averages of automobile ownership and registration, as well as patterns of tourism. Western states had the highest ratio of automobiles to people in the 1920s. See *Facts and Figures,* 1922, 53; and James Flink, *The Automobile Age,* (Cambridge: MIT Press, 1988), 24.

76. *Field and Stream,* May 1921, 109.

77. On the difficulties of patent management in the nineteenth century, see Cooper, "Construction of Invention Through Patent Management," 960; For texts on patent management in the twentieth century, including those that advised patentees to advertise, see Roger Sherman Hoar, *Patents: What a Business Executive Should Know About Patents* (New York: Ronald Press, 1926); Milton Wright, *Inventions and Patents: Their Development and Promotion* (New York: McGraw-Hill, 1927), 123; Alf K. Berle and L. Sprague de Camp, *Inventions and Their Management* (Scranton, Pa.: International Textbook Company, 1937).

78. Harry Irving Shumway, "The Camper on Tour," *Field and Stream,* June 1922, 200. Shumway's "Camper on Tour" series ran in *Field and Stream* from May to Nov. 1922,

79. "Outing Service Honor Roll," *Outing,* April 1921, 47.

80. Kimmel, *Patent Knowledge for Inventors,* 34.

81. Fisher, *Plain Talk,* 22–23.

82. Ibid.

83. Yates, *Inventors' Selling Guide,* 13.

84. Ibid., 23.

85. On the dominance of Ford and GM over automotive design, see David

Hochfelder and Susan Helper, "Suppliers and Product Development in the Early American Automobile Industry," *Business and Economic History* 25 (Winter 1996): 39 –51.

86. Charles Kettering and Allen Orth, *The New Necessity: The Culmination of a Century of Progress* (Baltimore: Williams and Wilkins, 1932), 47–48. For a selection of letters to Ford addressing modification, design, and pricing, see Maxwell H. Emmer, Detroit, to Henry Ford, Dearborn, 24 Sept. 1933; John Radovich, Los Angeles, to Edsel Ford, Dearborn, 17 Oct. 1935; E. L. Davis, Hollywood, California, to Edsel Ford, Dearborn, 21 Nov. 1935, Personal Correspondence, THF.

87. Stuart W. Leslie, *Boss Kettering* (New York: Columbia University Press, 1983), 187; Alfred Sloan, President of General Motors, Detroit, to General Managers of Divisions, General Operating Officers, Relations Committees, 3 Aug. 1925, memo in folder 18–17, New Devices Committee, GMI. On Kettering's influence, see Harry Dumville, Director of New Devices Section, Interview by T. A. Boyd, 23 Jan. 1961, 1–7; George H. Willits, Patent Staff, Interview by T. A. Boyd, 19 Dec. 1960, 1–7, accession 1673, Kettering Collection, GMI.

88. Sloan to General Managers of Divisions, 3 Aug. 1925, 1, New Devices Committee, folder 18/17, Kettering Collection, GMI.

89. "Do Inventors Get a Fair Shake?" and "How General Motors Handles New Ideas," *Automotive Industries* 55 (23 Dec. 1926): 1035. See also Leslie, *Boss Kettering*, 187.

90. Although I was able to access some of Charles Kettering's personal papers, company records at General Motors were closed and I could not search for documents or letters from the New Devices Committee.

91. On letters to Henry Ford, see Reynold M. Wik, *Henry Ford and Grass-roots America: A Fascinating Account of the Model-T Era* (Ann Arbor: University of Michigan Press, 1973), 59.

92. Wik, *Henry Ford*, 34–58; and Robert Lacey, *Ford: The Men and the Machine* (Boston: Little, Brown, 1986), 87–181.

93. On Ford as a popular hero, see Warren Susman, "Cultural Heroes: Ford, Barton, Ruth," in *Culture as History: The Transformation of American Society in the Twentieth Century* (New York: Pantheon, 1984): 122–49.

94. Lacey, *Ford*, 214.

95. Letter to Henry Ford from B. H. Snape, Toronto, Ontario, Canada, 19 Nov. 1928, accession 94, box 204, Accessories Sept.–Dec.; see also letter to Ford Motor Company from W. L. Haverty, Valley Center, Kan., 7 March 1928, accession 94, box 204-Accessories—Jan.–April, THF.

96. Letter to Ford Motor Company from Dr. Charles A. Boyd, Long Beach, Calif., 2 Aug. 1926, accession 94, box 182, Accessories—July–Dec. 1926, THF.

97. Letter to Henry Ford from Frank M. Beach, c/o Kingsway Products Company, Tampa, Fla., 31 March 1928, accession 94, box 204, Accessories—Jan.–April, THF. Punctuation as in original.

98. See "Automobile Construction," transcript of speech given by L. S. Sheldrick, Ford Motor Company Engineering Department, 21 July 1932, with organizational chart, accession 674, THF. On Ford's relationship to the company and his staff, see Ford R. Bryan, *Henry's Lieutenants* (Detroit: Wayne State University Press, 1993).

99. For examples of letters from lawyers, see letter to Ford Motor Company from John A. Nordin, Minneapolis, 29 July 1926, accession 94, box 182, folder: Accessories—July–Dec. 1926; letter to Ford Motor Company from M. L. Okun, Toledo, Ohio, 5 March 1928, accession 94, box 204, folder: Accessories—Jan.–

April; and letter to Ford Motor Company from Howard L. Fisher, St. Paul, Minn., 18 Jan. 1926, accession 94, box 182, folder: Accessories—Jan.–June 1926. For an example of letters from small accessory manufacturers, see letter to Ford Motor Car Co from Fred Whipple, Likely Luggage, Fitchburg, Mass., offering a patented trunk for sale, 28 Nov. 1928, accession 94, box 204, folder: Accessories Sept.–Dec., THF.

100. For this project, I surveyed approximately five hundred letters in accession 94, records of the engineering department, which has not been inventoried or sorted. I chose a sample of two hundred letters related specifically to automotive accessories and written by individuals held in the files of W. T. Fishleigh and C. H. Foster. Almost all letters had replies from the engineering department attached, allowing me to see the response from Ford Motor Company. The summary statements here about amateur inventors are drawn from this sample of two hundred writers.

101. For example, see letter to Ford Motor Co. from Ralph J. Simmons, Pittsburgh, 20 July 1928, accession 94, box 204, folder: Accessories—May–Aug., THF.

102. Letter to Ford Motor Company, Dearborn, MI from M. A. Zielinski, Trenton, N.J., 27 Oct. 1926, accession 94, box 182, folder: Accessories—July–Dec. 1926, THF.

103. Letter to M. A. Zielinski, Trenton, N.J., from W. T. Fishleigh, Ford Motor Company, 2 Nov. 1926, accession 94, box 182, folder: Accessories—July–Dec. 1926, THF.

104. Letter to Ford Motor Company from D. J. Carrall, Bay City, MI 4 Aug. 1928, accession 94, box 204, folder: Accessories—May–Aug., THF.

105. Rolland Marchand, *Advertising the American Dream: Making Way for Modernity, 1920–1940* (Berkeley: University of California Press, 1985), 353–363. See also Michael Shudson, *Advertising the Uneasy Persuasion: Its Dubious Impact on American Society* (New York: Basic Books, 1984).

106. Letter to Ford Motor Co. from Ralph J. Simmons, Pittsburgh, 20 July 1928, accession 94, box 204, folder: Accessories—May–Aug., THF.

107. Letter to Henry Ford Motor Company from J. H. Herzer, Los Angeles, 6 Dec. 1928, accession 94, box 204, Accessories—Sept.–Dec., THF.

108. See letters to Ford Motor Co. from John E. Zeiher, Seattle, 23 Dec. 1927; from H. P. Take, Smackover, Ark., 21 April 1928, accession 94, box 204, folder: Accessories Jan.–April, THF.

109. Letter to Chief Engineer, Ford Motor Co. from J. C. Long, Charleston, S.C., 24 July 1924, accession 94, box 91, folder J-K 316, THF.

110. Letter to Ford Motor Company from F. L. Costenbader, Richmond, Va. 30 May 1928, accession 94, box 204, folder: Accessories—May–Aug., THF.

111. Letter to Ford Motor Company from Vera Wells, Pukwana, S. Dak., 12 Sept. 1924, accession 94, box 113, folder T-2, THF. For examples of people who asked Henry Ford for a new car in exchange to their ideas, see letters from C. Walter Lawrence, Lynn Brothers Hospital, Pocatello, Idaho, 27 April, 1920, accession 94, box 27, folder 112, and from Ed C. Thomson, Contractor and Builder, Lebanon, Ky., 3 June 1923, accession 94, box 42, folder 173, THF.

112. Letter to Ford Motor Company from Ralph Simmons, Pittsburgh, 20 July 1928, accession 94, box 204, folder Accessories—May–Aug., THF.

113. Letter to Ford Motor Company from Riea Krug, Gardner, Ill., 29 Aug. 1928, accession 94, box 204, Accessories—May–Aug., THF.

114. Letter to Ford Motor Company from Paul J. Tatum, Hallsville, Texas, 17 Feb. 1926, accession 94, box 182, Accessories—Jan.–June 1926.

115. Undated letter to Henry Ford, Dearborn, Mich., from Edward O'Donnell, Brooklyn, N.Y., accession 94, box 97, folder 393, THF.

116. Letter to Henry Ford from W. H. Nunamacher, Newark, N.J., 28 March 1924, accession 94, box 97, folder 389.

117. Anderson, "Women's Contributions." No supporting documentation remains for this report. Anne L. Macdonald also uses the report in her *Feminine Ingenuity: Women and Invention in America* (New York: Ballantine Books, 1992). She confirms the nonexistence of supporting documents, namely the correspondence upon which the report was based. There are discussions of the report in other published sources. See "Fifth Annual Report of the Director of the Women's Bureau for the Fiscal Year Ended June 30, 1923," (Washington, D.C.: Government Printing Office, 1923), 14–15; Joseph Rossman, "Women Inventors," *Journal of the Patent Office Society* 10 (Sept. 1927): 16–30; and Rossman, "Women Contribute Heavily to Automotive Patents," *Automotive Industries* (17 May 1923): 1083.

118. Anderson, "Women's Contributions," 15, 26–27, 6.

119. On sociotechnical networks and power, see Steven Lubar, "Representation and Power," *Technology and Culture* 36 (Supplement to April 1995): 554–558; and Michael Callon and John Law, "On the Construction of Sociotechnical Networks," *Knowledge and Society* 9 (1989): 57–83.

120. Letter to Henry Ford from Addie C. Pickard, Guthrie, Okla., 22 Nov. 1923, accession 94, box 32, folder 141, THF.

121. Letter to Henry Ford from Mrs. Bertha A. P'Diamond, Port Jervis, N.Y., 5 May 1923, accession 94, box 32, folder 141, THF.

122. Anderson, "Women's Contributions," 7. For later studies of amateur invention that drew similar conclusions, see "Technological Trends and National Policy: Including the Social Implications of New Inventions," Report to the Subcommittee on Technology to the National Resources Committee (Washington, D.C.: Government Printing Office, 1937). For a history of patent reform in the 1930s, see Larry Owens, "Patents, and the 'Frontiers' of American Invention, and the Monopoly Committee of 1939: Anatomy of a Discourse," *Technology and Culture* 32 (Oct. 1991): 1076–1093.

123. Letter to Ford Motor Company from Joseph A. Conroy, Detroit, 8 Aug. 1923, accession 94, box 8, folder H-I 35, THF.

124. Letter to Henry Ford from Louis P Cook, Mt. Healthy, Ohio, 13 Nov. 1923, accession 94, box 8, folder H-I 35. THF

125. Letter to President, Ford Motor Co., from D. O'Brian, Punta Alegre Sugar Co., San Juan, Cuba, 26 Aug. 1924, accession 94, box 97, folder 93, THF.

126. Letter to Edsel B. Ford from William Bassett, Richmond, Va., 8 April 1926, accession 94, box 182, Accessories—Jan.–June 1926, THF.

127. Letter to Rudolph Weirup, Maquoketa, Iowa from Ford Motor Company, 25 Aug. 1924, accession 94, box 113, folder N-S, THF.

128. Letter to Henry Ford from A. L. Huber, Indianapolis, 29 Dec. 1924, and reply from R. H. Cromwell, Ford News, 7 Jan. 1925, accession 94, box 144, folder 241.

129. For example, see letter to D. G. Leigh, Coleman, Fla., from Ford Motor Company, 22 Oct., 1923, accession 94, box 27, folder 113, THF.

130. See reply to C. F. Boohr, Cleburne, Texas, from W. T. Fishleigh, Ford Motor Company, 20 Sept. 1926, accession 94, box 182, folder Accessories—July–Dec. 1926, THF.

131. Letter from C. H. Foster, Engineering Department, Ford Motor Com-

pany, to Mrs. H. A. Stalker, Emmett, Idaho, 1 Aug. 1928, accession 94, box 204, folder Accessories May–Aug., THF.

132. Letter to Einar Lund, Fargo, N. Dak., from W. T. Fishleigh, Experimental Engineering, Ford Motor Company, 27 July 1923, accession 94, box 27, folder 113, THF.

133. Letter from W. T. Fishleigh, Engineering Department, Ford Motor Company, to W. W. Davis, Old Orchard Beach, Me., 21 Dec. 1928, accession 94, box 204, folder: Accessories Sept.–Dec., THF.

134. Letter to W. T. Fishleigh, Ford Motor Company, from Norman J. Wood, Miami, 18 July 1928, accession 94, box 204, folder: Accessories—May–Aug., THF.

135. Labofish, *How to Win a Fortune,* 171.

136. See Don Glassman, "This Inventing World," *Popular Mechanics,* Aug. 1930, 202–206.

137. "Bringing Inventors and Manufacturers Together" *Scientific American,* Jan. 1928, 91.

138. Yates, *Inventors' Selling Guide,* 25.

139. General Motors Convention Committee, "White Sulphur Entertainment," White Sulphur Springs, N.Y., 19 Oct. 1934, 6–8, script in William Powers Collection, NAHC.

140. Kettering and Orth, *New Necessity,* 48, 56.

141. On patent reform in the 1930s and the changing landscape of invention, see Nobel, *America by Design,* 84–110.

142. Kaempffert, "Invention as a Social Manifestation," 64.

Chapter 4. A Tinkerer's Story

1. My work here draws on the following to distinguish individual and grass-roots inventors: Thomas Hughes, *American Genesis: A Century of Invention and Technological Enthusiasm, 1870–1970* (New York: Viking, 1989), 14–15; Peter Whalley, "The Social Practice of Independent Inventing," *Science, Technology, and Human Values,* 16, no. 2 (Spring 1991): 209–210.

2. For a list of all of Tupper's inventions prior to the plastic containers that made him famous, see his own data sheet compiled in the mid-1930s, c. 1930, Earl S. Tupper Papers, accession 470, box 3, folder: "Notes on Invention," Archives Center, National Museum of American History, Smithsonian Institution (hereafter cited as NMAH). For a full discussion of these earlier inventions as part of a utopian vision, see Alison J. Clarke, *Tupperware: The Promise of Plastic in 1950s America* (Washington, D.C.: Smithsonian Institution Press, 1999), 1–35.

3. Brooke Hindle, *Emulation and Invention* (New York: Norton, 1983), 5, 13. On spatial thinking, creativity, and fingertip knowledge, see Douglas Harper, *Working Knowledge* (Chicago: University of Chicago Press, 1987); Eugene Ferguson, "The Mind's Eye: Nonverbal Thought in Technology," *Science* 197 (26 Aug. 1977): 827–836.

4. On the myth of the Yankee inventor-hero, see Carolyn Cooper, "Myth, Rumor, and History: The Yankee Whittling Boy as Hero and Villain," *Technology and Culture,* 44, no. 1 (2003): 82–96.

5. "Biographical/Historical Note" on the Earl S. Tupper Papers, accession 470, NMAH.

6. On the rise of modern corporations, see Alan Trachtenberg, *The Incorporation of America: Culture and Society in the Gilded Age* (New York: Hill and Wang,

1982); David F. Noble, *America by Design: Science, Technology and the Rise of Corporate Capitalism* (New York: Oxford University Press, 1977); Carroll Pursell, *The Machine in America: A Social History of Technology* (Baltimore: Johns Hopkins University Press, 1995), 203–271.

7. Tupper notes, "Facts and Dates Concerning the Conception of the Tupper Folding Rumble Seat Top," c. 1934, Earl S. Tupper Papers, accession 470, series 2, box 3, folder 4: "Notes on Inventions, 1930s," NMAH. Memo can be dated as a response to a January 1934 letter from Warren Ogden to Earl Tupper requesting a written statement that Tupper conceived of his rumble top accessory prior to 1932 in order to defeat an earlier claim by another patentee. See letter to Warren Ogden, Boston, to Earl Tupper, Fitchburg, Mass., 25 Jan. 1934, in Earl S. Tupper Papers, accession 470, box 3, folder 9, NMAH.

8. Steven M. Gelber, *Hobbies: Leisure and the Culture of Work in America* (New York: Columbia University Press, 1999), 11, 20.

9. Tom Pendergast, *Creating the Modern Man: American Magazines and Consumer Culture, 1900–1950* (Columbia: University of Missouri Press, 2000), 111. See also Lisa Jacobson, "Manly Boys and Enterprising Dreamers: Business Ideology and the Construction of the Boy Consumer, 1910–1930," *Enterprise and Society* 2 (June 2001): 225–258, and Carroll Pursell, "The Long Summer of Boy Engineering," in John Wright, ed., *Possible Dreams: Enthusiasm for Technology in America* (Dearborn, Mich.: Henry Ford Museum and Greenfield Village, 1992), 34–42.

10. Pendergast, *Creating the Modern Man*, 39.

11. C. Francis Jenkins, "Hobbies that Led to Inventions," *Popular Mechanics*, Sept. 1927, 379.

12. Tupper diary, 23 Sept. 1934, Earl S. Tupper Papers, accession 470, series 2, box 4, NMAH. All citations from Tupper's diary are at this location.

13. John L. Wright, "Introduction: An American Tradition," in Wright, ed., *Possible Dreams*, 14. On the establishment of inventors as leaders of national progress, see Hindle, *Emulation and Invention*, 127.

14. "The American Leonardo Da Vinci," Earl S. Tupper papers, accession 470, series 2, box 1, NMAH.

15. Janice Radway, *A Feeling for Books: The Book-of-the-Month Club, Literary Taste, and Middle-Class Desire* (Chapel Hill: University of North Carolina Press, 1997), 161.

16. Tupper diary, 2 Jan. 1933.

17. For a discussion of the physical fitness craze as promoted by magazines, see Pendergast, *Creating the Modern Man*, 111–142.

18. Tupper diary, 12 Jan. 1933.

19. Tupper diary, 20 Jan. 1933.

20. Radway, *A Feeling for Books*, 296.

21. Ibid., 15, 167.

22. Tupper diary, 7 Jan. 1936 and 2 Jan. 1937. Tupper stated that he went to the library to read *Popular Mechanics* and patent law.

23. "Thoughts," Earl S. Tupper Papers, accession 470, series 2, box 1, folder 8, NMAH.

24. Tupper Invention Diary and Sketch Book, c. 1935–1937, "How to Invent."

25. Tupper Invention Diary and Sketch Book, c. 1935–1937, "How to Realize an Invention."

26. Radway, *A Feeling for Books*, 13, 182, 262.

27. Ibid., 284.

28. Tupper diary, 25 June 1933.

29. "Answers to Examination Questions: Advertising as a Business Force," Earl S. Tupper Papers, accession 470, box 3, folder 9, NMAH.

30. Ibid.

31. Tupper Invention Diary and Sketch Book, c. 1935–1937, "My Purpose in Life."

32. On the social superiority of inventors, see Joseph Allen Minturn, *The Inventor's Friend; or, Success With Patents* (Indianapolis: Meridian Company, 1893), 1.

33. Don Glassman, "This Inventing World," *Popular Mechanics*, Aug. 1930, 202.

34. Tupper diary, 18 June 1933.

35. Tupper diary, 7 Jan. 1933.

36. Robert S. McElvaine, *The Great Depression: America, 1929–1941* (New York: Times Books, 1993), 134, 73; Robert S. McElvaine, ed., *Down and Out in the Great Depression: Letters from the Forgotten Man* (Chapel Hill: University of North Carolina Press, 1983), 35–48.

37. Tupper diary, 26 July 1933.

38. McElvaine, *Great Depression*, 90.

39. Tupper diary, 10 Feb. 1933.

40. Tupper diary, 27 Jan. 1933.

41. McElvaine, *Great Depression*, 131. On the left and American popular culture in the 1930s, see Michael Denning, *The Cultural Front* (New York: Verso, 1997); Alan Brinkley, *Voices of Protest: Huey Long, Father Coughlin, and the Great Depression* (New York: Vintage, 1983).

42. Tupper diary, 12 Aug. 1937.

43. Tupper diary, 25 Dec. 1933.

44. Tupper diary, 4 March 1933.

45. Tupper diary, 10 Sept. 1933.

46. Tupper diary, 7 Jan. 1933.

47. On the reorganization of public space in the interwar period and the growing reliance on automobility, see Joseph Interrante, "You Can't Go to Town in a Bathtub: Automobile Movement and the Reorganization of Rural American Space, 1900–1930," *Radical History Review* 21 (Fall 1979): 151–168. On suburbanization and the automobile, see Kenneth Jackson, *Crabgrass Frontier: The Suburbanization of America* (New York: Oxford University Press, 1985), 172–189. and Martin Wachs and Margaret Crawford, eds., *The Car and the City: The Automobile, the Built Environment, and Daily Urban Life* (Ann Arbor: University of Michigan Press, 1992), 7–25.

48. Tupper diary, 9 Dec. 1933.

49. Tupper diary, 17 and 24 Feb. 1933.

50. Tupper diary, 18 June 1933.

51. Ibid.

52. See diary entries for details on buying cars, Tupper diary, 3 April and 18 Aug. 1934.

53. See Index of Invention Sketch Book, Earl S. Tupper Papers, accession 470, series 2, box 3, folder, "Notes on Invention," NMAH.

54. On the Model A, see Victor Pagé, *The Ford Model A Car: Construction, Operation, Repair* (1929; reprint, Los Angeles: Floyd Clymer Publications, 1961). After 1925 the Ford Model T included accessories such as windshields, as standard equipment. See Ray Miller and Bruce McCalley, *The Model T. Ford . . . A Look at the Changes in an Unchanging Car, 1909–1927* (privately printed 1971), 211–212, 217.

55. For a detailed list of cars with rumble seats, see *Automobiles of America*, 5th ed., rev. (Sidney, Ohio: American Automobile Manufacturers Association, 1996), 32, 39.

56. See Robin Ad-Finem-Ville, Jr., "The Origin of the Mother-in-Law Seat," *Automobilist*, 8, no. 5 (Aug. 1958): 29–30, held in the collections of the National Automotive Collection, Detroit Public Library.

57. For a sample, see William C. Linton, *The Inventor's Advisor* (Washington, D.C.: privately printed, 1921); Adam Fisher, *Plain Talk: Or Dollars and Sense in Inventions* (St. Louis, Mo.: privately printed, 1929); and Hopkins, *Inventor's Manual.*

58. Tupper notes, "Have Courage for Your Convictions," Earl S. Tupper Papers, accession 470, series 2, box 1 folder 11, NMAH.

59. On the early automobile industry in New England and its shift to Detroit, see James Flink, *The Automobile Age* (Cambridge: MIT Press, 1988), 15–26.

60. "A Few Facts About Fitchburg, Mass.," *Fitchburg City Directory* (Fitchburg, Mass.: S&C Shepley, 1933).

61. National Automobile Chamber of Commerce, *Facts and Figures of the Automobile Industry 1933.* (New York: NACC, 1933), 64.

62. Tupper notes, "Raker Rumble Top," Earl S. Tupper Papers, accession 470, series 2, box 3, folder 9, NMAH.

63. See description with drawing of "Rumble Seat Umbrella Slicker Top," Earl S. Tupper Papers, accession 470, series 2, box 3, folder 9, NMAH.

64. Patent 2,002,514, 28 May 1935.

65. On empirical approaches of independent inventors, see Hughes, *American Genesis*, 52; Hindle, *Emulation and Invention*, 127–142; and Ferguson, "Mind's Eye."

66. Tupper notes, "Facts and Dates," Earl S. Tupper Papers, accession 470, series 2, box 3, folder 4, NMAH.

67. Ibid.

68. For a discussion of the patent office criteria for invention, see Steven Lubar, "New, Useful, and Non-Obvious," *American Heritage of Invention and Technology* 6 (Spring–Summer 1990): 18–25.

69. Although I could not find any letters from Earl Tupper in the Henry Ford Collection, many other consumers and tinkerers wrote with their suggestions on rumble seat tops, several of whom offered patented rumble seat covers for sale. For examples, see letters to Henry Ford from Herbert Davis, Malden-on-Hudson, N.Y., 22 Oct. 1928; and to Ford Motor Company from Norman Browning, Guernsey, Ohio, 21 June 1928; from Chas Thurmond, Edgewater, Fla., 16 July 1928; from Edna Mantell, Columbus, Ohio, 12 June 1928; and from H. Mirsky, Toledo, Ohio, 12 Nov. 1928, held in Engineering Files, accession 94, box 204, folder: Accessories Sept.–Dec., THF.

70. Letter to Ford, from H. Mirsky, Toledo, Ohio, 12 Nov. 1928, Engineering Files, accession 94, box 204–Accessories Sept.–Dec., The Henry Ford.

71. Letter from C. H. Foster, Engineering Department, Ford Motor Company, to Herbert Davis, Malden-on-Hudson, N.Y., 25 Oct. 1928. Engineering Files, accession 94, box 204–Accessories Sept.–Dec., THF.

72. Letter from W. T. Fishleigh, Engineering Department, Ford Motor Company, to H. Mirsky, Toledo, Ohio, 12 Nov. 1928, Engineering Files, accession 94, box 204–Accessories Sept–Dec., THF.

73. "Slicker for the Rumble Seat Keeps Passengers Dry," *Popular Mechanics*, July 1930, 46, and "Rumble Seat Top on Rollers Supported by Lazy Tongs," *Popular Mechanics*, June 1933, 873.

74. Tupper diary, 5 May 1933.

75. Tupper diary, 14 June 1933.

76. For example, see "Your Idea May Be Worth a Fortune," *Popular Mechanics*, Dec. 1931, 920–925, and James M. Chalfant, "Fortunes from Little Ideas," *Popular Mechanics*, Sept. 1932, 424–429.

77. R. George Roesch, *Your Invention: What to Do with It* (Syracuse, N.Y.: Roesch & Associates, 1934), 35–36.

78. On advertising appeals that spoke to social class mobility, see Marchand, *Advertising the American Dream*, 194–200. On the rise of branding, see Susan Strasser, *Satisfaction Guaranteed: The Making of the American Mass Market* (New York: Pantheon Books, 1989).

79. Tupper notes, "Raker Rumble Top," in Earl S. Tupper Papers, accession 470, series 2, box 3, folder 9, NMAH.

80. Tupper notes, "Some of the Important Features," in Earl S. Tupper Papers, accession 470, series 2, box 3, folder 9, NMAH.

81. Ibid.

82. "Holder of Patent Cannot Fix Retail Price," *Popular Mechanics*, Aug. 1913, 256.

83. Tupper notes, "On Selling Tops," Earl. S. Tupper Papers, accession 470, series 2, box 3, folder 4, NMAH.

84. Flink, *Automobile Age*, 205.

85. Milton Wright, "Bringing Inventors and Manufacturers Together," *Scientific American*, Jan. 1928, 91.

86. Carolyn C. Cooper, "Social Construction of Invention Through Patent Management: Thomas Blanchard's Woodworking Machinery," *Technology and Culture* 32, no. 4 (Oct. 1991): 972.

87. Roesch, *Your Invention*, 2.

88. Tupper notes, "Facts and Dates," Earl S. Tupper Papers, accession 470, series 2, box 3, folder 4, NMAH.

89. Orson Munn, ed., *Patents: A Book of Facts Every Inventor Should Know* (New York: Munn & Company, 1927), 9.

90. Tupper notes, "Facts and Dates," Earl S. Tupper Papers, accession 470, series 2, box 3, folder 4, NMAH.

91. Fisher, *Plain Talk*, 22.

92. For Tupper diary entries on relationship with Sheedy, see 1 July, 24 Aug., and 31 Dec. 1933.

93. Letter to Earl S. Tupper, Shirley, Mass., from Warren G. Ogden, Boston, 14 July 1932. On Tupper's fear that someone would steal his ideas see, Tupper notes, "Facts and Dates." See also letter to Earl S. Tupper, Shirley, Mass., from Warren G. Ogden, Boston, 4 Aug. 1932, Earl S. Tupper papers, accession 470, series 2, box 3, NMAH.

94. Letter to Earl S. Tupper, Fitchburg, Mass., from Warren G. Ogden, Boston, 25 Jan. 1934, Earl S. Tupper Papers, accession 470, series 2, box 3, NMAH.

95. Tupper diary, 7 Feb. 1934.

96. Tupper notes, "Facts and Dates Concerning the Conception of the Tupper Folding Rumble Seat Top," c. 1934, Earl S. Tupper Papers, accession 470, series 2, box 3, folder 4, NMAH.

97. Letter from A. W. Hawkins, Montgomery Ward & Company, Baltimore, to Earl S. Tupper, Shirley, Mass., 4 Aug. 1932. Earl S. Tupper Papers, accession 470, series 2, box 3, folder 9, NMAH.

98. Letter from M. T. Shipley, Statistical Department, Chrysler Corporation, Detroit, to Earl S. Tupper, West Groton, Mass., 6 July 1933, Earl S. Tupper Papers, accession 470, series 2, box 3, folder 9, NMAH.

99. Letter from Stephen D. Bryce, Jr. Information Department, National Automobile Chamber of Commerce, New York, N.Y., to Earl S. Tupper, West Groton, Mass., 27 June 1933, Earl S. Tupper Papers, accession 470, series 2, box 3, folder 9, NMAH.

100. *Facts and Figures of the Automobile Industry, 1933*, 17.

101. Letter from N. P. Madsen, LaSalle Extension University, Chicago, to Earl S. Tupper, Fitchburg, Mass., 24 Feb. 1934, Earl S. Tupper Papers, accession 470, series 2, box 3, folder 9, NMAH.

102. Tupper notes, "Please note" undated, Earl S. Tupper Papers, accession 470, series 2, box 3 folder 9, NMAH, and Tupper diary, 17 Feb. 1934.

103. Tupper diary, 23 July 1933.

104. Tupper diary, 10 and 12 Aug. 1933.

105. Tupper diary, 10 Aug. 1933.

106. Tupper diary, 1 Nov. 1933.

107. Tupper diary, 22 and 8 March 1934.

108. Tupper diary, 20 March 1934.

109. Letter from Earl S. Tupper, Lunenburg, Mass., to Mr. A. Shapiro, Back Bay Auto Co., Boston, 17 April 1934, Earl S. Tupper Papers, accession 470, series 2, box 3, folder 9, NMAH.

110. Tupper diary, 30 and 18 April 1934.

111. Tupper diary, 7 Sept. 1934.

112. Tupper diary, 1 March 1934.

113. Tupper diary, 14 Jan. and 2 March 1936.

114. Letter from National Service Bureau, St. Louis, Mo., to Mr. Tupper, 31 July 1935, and reply from Earl Tupper, Lunenburg, Mass., to National Service Bureau, St. Louis, Mo., 3 Aug. 1935, Earl S. Tupper Papers, accession 470, box 3, folder 9, NMAH.

115. Tupper diary, 5 April 1937.

116. Roesch, *Your Invention*, 50.

117. Tupper diary, 22 Jan. 1937.

118. Tupper diary, 16 June and 30 July 1937.

119. Tupper diary, 30 July 1937. For a detailed account of Tupper's work as a fledgling designer in the late 1930s, see Clarke, *Tupperware*, 26–35.

120. Clarke, *Tupperware*, 28.

121. Tupper diary, 5 Aug. 1937.

122. Tupper diary, 10 Dec. 1937. See also Clarke, *Tupperware*, 34.

123. See Tupper letterhead, Earl S. Tupper Papers, accession 470, series 2, box 3, folder 2, NMAH.

124. Ibid.

125. For an analysis of Tupper's career in plastics, with attention to his continued struggles to market his novelties, see Clarke, *Tupperware*.

126. Larry Owens, "Patents, the 'Frontiers' of American Invention, and the Monopoly Committee of 1939: Anatomy of a Discourse," *Technology and Culture* 32, no. 4 (Oct. 1991): 1076–1093.

127. Ibid., 1080.

128. "Inventors Keep After Auto Improvements," *Scientific American*, July 1939, 42. For two studies of the patent office records that argue the percentage of individual patents had fallen after World War I, Lowell J. Carr, "A Study of 137 Typical Inventors," *American Sociological Society*, 23 (Chicago: University of Chicago Press, 1928); Lowell J. Carr, "The Patenting Performance of 1,000 Inventors During Ten Years," *American Journal of Sociology*, 37 (Jan. 1932): 562–580.

129. Carr, "Patenting Performance," 569.

130. On patent legislation and its relationship to corporate control of invention, see Nobel, *America by Design*, 84–89.

131. On the transition from autocamping to staying in motels, see Belasco, *Americans on the Road*. For the history of the trailer industry, White, *Home on the Road*; Carleton Edwards, *Homes for Travel and Living: The History and Development of the Recreational Vehicle and Mobile Home Industries* (East Lansing: privately printed, 1977); and Allan D. Wallis, *Wheel Estate: The Rise and Decline of Mobile Homes* (New York: Oxford University Press, 1991), 31–81. For a brief history of motels, see Chester Liebs, *Main Street to Miracle Mile: American Roadside Architecture* (Boston: New York Graphic Society/Little, Brown, 1985).

132. See John Dashiell Myers, "The Plight of Industrial Designs," *Automotive Manufacturer*, May 1926, 21; Ray Lyman Wilbur, "Slide Rule of Civilization: The Engineering Mind as an Aid to Progress," *Technological Review*, Dec. 1931, 13; Joseph Rossman, "Do Engineers Invent? And Why Do They Abhor the Label 'Inventor'?" *Technological Review*, Dec. 1931, 117–119.

Chapter 5. The Automotive Industry Takes the Stage

1. Untitled press release on V-8, Box 172, Fairlane Papers, Ford Motor Company (FMC) advertising, The Henry Ford (hereafter THF).

2. Stuart Hall, "Notes on Deconstructing the Popular," in Ralph Samuel, ed., *People's History and Socialist Theory* (London: Routledge, 1981), 227.

3. Robert Rydell, *World of Fairs: The Century of Progress Expositions* (Chicago: University of Chicago Press, 1993), 99.

4. On the professionalization of research and innovation in the 1920s, see Noble, *America By Design*, 33–49, and Pursell, *The Machine in America*, 203–270.

5. Jesse Frederic Steiner, *Americans at Play: Recent Trends in Recreation and Leisure Time Activities* (New York: McGraw-Hill, 1933), 34, 60, 183.

6. Rydell, *World of Fairs*, 82–91.

7. Ibid., 118.

8. On utopianism at the fairs, see Folke T. Kihlstedt, "Utopia Realized: The World's Fairs of the 1930s," in Joseph J. Corn, ed., *Imagining Tomorrow: History, Technology and the American Future* (Cambridge: MIT Press, 1986), 97–117.

9. Rydell, *World of Fairs*, 119.

10. Howard Florence, "Will Automobiles Lead the Way?" *Review of Reviews and World's Work*, January 1933, 38–41.

11. James Flink, *The Automobile Age* (Cambridge: MIT Press, 1988), 231, and Robert Lacey, *Ford: The Men and the Machine* (Boston: Little, Brown, 1986), 306.

12. For statistics of passenger car sales increases in 1934, the second year of the fair, see "The National Survey of Spending Power," *Sales Management* 34 (20 April 1934): 357–361. For one of the earliest references to Ford, GM, and Chrysler as the "big three," see J. C. Clifford, "Big Three in Motordom Contend for Sales Leadership," *Magazine of Wall Street*, 23 June 1934, 242–244.

13. Flink, *Automobile Age*, 218.

14. On the effects of the Depression on auto manufacturers, see John B. Rae, *The American Automobile: A Brief History* (Chicago: University of Chicago Press, 1965), 105–121, and Daniel Raff, "Making Cars and Making Money in the Interwar Automobile Industry: Economies of Scale and Scope and the Manufacturing Behind the Marketing," *Business History Review* 65 (Winter 1991): 721–753.

15. Quoted in Lacey, *Ford*, 344.

16. Ibid., 337.

17. "Finding Out What the Customer Thinks About the New Cars," *Automotive Industries* 73 (21 Dec. 1935): 820.

18. On the organizational differences between the Association of Licensed Automobile Manufacturers (ALAM, the group headed by Selden) and the American Motor Car Manufacturers' Association (AMCMA which included independents Ford, REO, and Maxwell-Briscoe), see Flink, *The Automobile Age*, 52–55. The trade association duties were assumed by the Automobile Board of Trade in 1914, which would later become the National Automobile Chamber of Commerce and then the Automobile Manufacturers Association in 1932.

19. "Great Show Ready in Madison Square Garden," *Automobile Topics*, 7 Jan. 1911, 883; "Garden Show a Marvelous One," *Automobile Topics*, 14 Jan. 1911, 935–956.

20. "National Show Impression," *Automobile Trade Journal* 21 (1 Feb. 1917): 170.

21. Morris A. Hall, "America's Best Motor Show Opens," *Motor Life*, Feb. 1914, 7.

22. "A Car for Every Man," *Automobile Trade Journal* 18 (1 Jan. 1914): 64–65; "National Show Impression," 167; C. L. Edholm, "Prosperity Seen in New York Show," *Automobile Trade Journal* 21 (1 Feb. 1917): 168.

23. "Twenty-five Years of Automobile Shows," *Automobile Trade Journal* 29 (Jan. 1925): 27–32; "The Silver Jubilee Show," *Automobile Trade Journal* 29 (Jan. 1925): 24–26; A. V. Comings, "The New York Silver Jubilee Show: Marking Twenty-five Years of Automotive Progress," *Automobile Trade Journal* 29 (1 Feb. 1925): 19–21.

24. Ibid. For more discussion of Sam Miles, see "National Shows Usher in Prosperity," *Automobile Trade Journal* 32 (Jan. 1928): 23–24; Don Blanchard, "Attend the Show," *Automobile Trade Journal and Motor Age*, 34 (Jan. 1929): 28–29; "A People Motor Mad Sees New York Show," *Automobile Trade Journal* 32 (Feb. 1928): 28.

25. "Stage All Set for National Shows," *Automobile Trade Journal* 28 (Jan. 1924): 29–30; "New York's Greatest Automobile Show," *Automobile Trade Journal* 28 (Feb. 1924): 26–27.

26. *The Book of Grand Central Palace: Home of All the Large Industrial Expositions Held in New York* (New York: Merchants and Manufacturers Exchange, 1923), 5. See also "Do Exhibits in Local Automobile Shows Pay?" *Horseless Age*, 1 Jan. 1918, 49.

27. "The Significance of the Shows," *Motor*, Feb. 1922, 21.

28. Roland Marchand, "The Corporation Nobody Knew: Bruce Barton, Alfred Sloan, and the Founding of the General Motors 'Family,'" *Business History Review* 65 (Winter 1991): 825–875.

29. "Winners Announced in Children's Essay Contest," *New York Times*, 8 Jan. 1934, 13. For other descriptions of "pantomime and pretty girls," see "Motorists in Buying Mood," *Sales Management* 33 (15 Jan. 1934): 67; L.G. Peed, "Primitive Man's Floating Log a Discovery in Streamlining," *New York Times*, 7 Jan. 1934, p. 18 sec. A; "Progress of Transportation Depicted in Marionette Show Presented by De Soto," *New York Times*, 7 Jan. 1934, p. 10.

30. "International Day," *New York Times*, 8 Jan. 1934, p. 13; "Women Appraise New Auto Models," *New York Times*, 13 Jan. 1933, p.11. On Women's Day, see also "Observed at the Show," *New York Times*, 15 Jan. 1933, p. 8; "Women Are Guests at the Auto Show," *New York Times*, 2 Nov. 1937, p. 27.

31. Arthur H. Little, "Automobiles at an Auto Show Are Out of Place," *Printers' Ink Monthly* 28 (Feb. 1934): 23.

32. Flink, *Automobile Age*, 215.

33. Rae, *American Automobile*, 113.

34. "An Eye to the Future and An Ear to the Ground," GM Hall of Progress, Century of Progress Exposition, 1934, pamphlet held in General Motors Clipping File, National Automotive History Collection, Detroit Public Library, Detroit, MI. (Here after known as NAHC.) See also General Motors, "Milestones of Progress," in *We Drivers* (Detroit: General Motors Corporation, 1935), pamphlet, General Motors Clipping File, NAHC. On knees, see General Motors, "The Story of Knee Action" (Detroit: General Motors Corporation, 1935), booklet, General Motors Clipping File, NAHC.

35. Rae, *American Automobile*, 113–114.

36. Jeffrey L. Meikle, *Twentieth Century Limited: Industrial Design in America, 1925–1939* (Philadelphia: Temple University Press, 1979), 14.

37. Morris Hall, "America's Best Motor Show Opens," *Motor Life*, Feb. 1914, 8.

38. "Chrysler Offers This Streamlined Sedan," *New York Times*, 7 Jan. 1934, p. 2, sec. A; "Primitive Man's Floating Log: A Discovery in Streamlining," *New York Times*, 7 Jan. 1934, p. 18, sec. A; "Varied Improvements Mark New Bodies Built by Fisher," *New York Times*, 7 Jan. 1934, p. 19, sec. A; "New Type of Auto on Exhibit Today," *New York Times*, 6 Jan. 1934, 17; "Stout Announces a New Scarab," *Automotive Industries* 73 (2 Nov. 1935): 601.

39. On the debates concerning the engineering and economic value of streamlining that accompanied the introduction of the Airflow, see "The Transportation of Tomorrow," in Joseph Corn and Brian Horrigan, *Yesterday's Tomorrow's: Past Visions of the American Future* (New York: Summit Books, 1984), 90–94; John Heskett, *Industrial Design* (London: Thames and Hudson, 1980), 120–126; Meikle, *Twentieth Century Limited*, 140–151.

40. "Motorists in Buying Mood; Airflow Dominates Auto Show," *Sales Management* 33 (15 Jan. 1934): 67.

41. "Cars for All Are on Display," *New York Times*, 5 Jan. 1930, p. 1, sec. A.

42. Meikle, *Twentieth Century Limited*, 148.

43. Ibid., 45–46.

44. Walter Dorwin Teague, "Basic Principles of Body Design Arise from Universal Rules," *SAE Journal* 35 (Sept. 1934): 18–19 and "Body Design Session," *SAE Journal* 35 (Aug. 1934): 27. See also Walter Dorwin Teague, *Design This Day: The Technique of Order in the Machine Age* (London: Trefoil, 1947).

45. On user modification as improving the fit between machines and consumers, see Donald Norman, *The Design of Everyday Things* (New York: Doubleday: 1988), 187–188.

46. For a brief history of steel bodies, see Flink, *Automobile Age*, 213. See also Roger B. White, "Body by Fisher: The Closed Car Revolution," *Automobile Quarterly* 29 (Aug. 1991): 46–63. On self-tapping screws and the difficulties faced by home tinkerers in the 1930s, Joseph Corn, conversation with author, October 15, 1998.

47. Porter Varney, *Motor Camping* (New York: Leisure League of America, 1935), 47.

48. See General Motors press release on styling, c. 1957, folder 83–1.7–114, GMI.

49. General Motors, *Styling the Look of Things* (Detroit: General Motors Public

Relations, 1958), 36. For references to the innovation of the integrated trunk as a product of advanced corporate design and engineering, see "Dodges More Powerful for 1934," *Automotive Industries* 69 (30 Dec. 1933): 795; "Variable Luggage Space," *Automobile Engineer* (Jan. 1936), 40; Huppmobile Catalog, 1933, Warshaw Collection of Business Ephemera, Archives Center, NMAH.

50. W. J. McAneeny, "Automobile Show a Symbol of Young Year's Prosperity," *New York Times*, 5 Jan. 1930, p. 26, sec. A; Alvan Macauley, "People Enriched by Automobiles," *New York Times*, 5 Jan. 1930, p. 1, sec. A.; "Behind the Motor Car: Dreams of Ages," *New York Times*, 7 Jan. 1934, p. 16; "Advances Made in New Cars Show Confidence in Future," *New York Times*, 7 Jan. 1934, p. 18, sec. A; "Array of Evidence Justifies Optimism," *New York Times*, 7 Jan. 1934, p. 11, sec. 1; Don Blanchard, "Huge New York Show Crowds Spur Industry's Hopes for a Good Year," *Automotive Industries* 70 (13 Jan. 1934): 33.

51. McCarthy, "Advances Made in New Cars."

52. Macauley, "People Enriched by Automobiles."

53. Alan Trachtenberg, *The Incorporation of America: Culture and Society in the Gilded Age* (New York: Hill and Wang, 1982), 41. See also Neil Harris, "Great American Fairs and American Cities: The Role of Chicago's Colombian Exposition," in Harris, *Cultural Excursions: Marketing Appetites and Cultural Tastes in Modern America* (Chicago: University of Chicago Press, 1990), 128–129. On fairs and cultural hegemony, see Anders Ekstrom, "International Exhibitions and the Struggle for Cultural Hegemony," *Uppsala Newsletter* 12 (Fall 1989); 6–7.

54. Robert Morris Lovett, "Progress—Chicago Style," *Current History* 39 (Oct. 1933–March 1934): 434, 435; Carroll Pursell, *The Machine in America: A Social History of Technology* (Baltimore: Johns Hopkins University Press, 1995), 251; John E. Findling, *Chicago's Great World's Fairs* (Manchester: Manchester University Press, 1994), 99.

55. For a history of pageants as a cultural form, see David Glassberg, *American Historical Pageantry: The Uses of Tradition in the Early Twentieth Century* (Chapel Hill: University of North Carolina Press, 1990).

56. Bruce Sinclair, "Technology on Its Toes: Late Victorian Ballets, Pageants, and Industrial Exhibitions," in Stephen H. Cutcliff and Robert C. Post, eds., *In Context: History and the History of Technology* (Bethlehem, Pa.: Lehigh University Press, 1989), 81.

57. *Official Guide Book of the Fair* (Chicago: Century of Progress, 1933), 11.

58. Ibid. See also Henry Justin Smith, *Chicago's Great Century of Progress, 1833–1933* (Chicago: Consolidated Publishers, 1933), 185. On the composition of the Fair board of trustees and the role of the National Research Council, see Rydell, *World of Fairs*, 93 and Findling, *Chicago's Great World's Fairs*, 92–94. See also "Chicago's Second World's Fair," *Review of Reviews*, March 1933, 38.

59. Rydell, *World of Fairs*, 93–99.

60. Rae, *American Automobile*, 105–120.

61. Bernard Ostrolenk, untitled speech at GM Previews of Progress dinner, Century of Progress Exposition, 25 May 1934, transcript, Previews of Progress Folder 6/12, Kettering Collection, GMI.

62. On Ford's belief that mass production would foster mass consumption, see David Harvey, *The Condition of Postmodernity: An Enquiry into the Origins of Cultural Change* (Oxford: Basil Blackwell, 1990), 125–126. On Henry Ford's reluctance to advertise, see Alfred Chandler, ed., *Giant Enterprise: Ford, General Motors, and the Automobile Industry* (New York: Harcourt, Brace & World, 1964), 148–157.

63. "Wave of Advertising Rushes Ford Back to Top in Motor Car Sales," *Sales*

Management 34 (1 Sept. 1934): 188; Lawrence M. Hughes, "Custom-Built Local Advertising Helps Ford Double Sales," *Sales Management* 34 (1 Oct. 1934): 298–299, 317. See also "Advertising Talk Given at Branch Managers Meeting," 1935, and memo, "Introductory Advertising Program," 29 Dec. 1934, accession 454, box 1, THF.

64. "Advertising Talk Given at Branch Managers Meeting," 1935, accession 454, box 1, THF. For an in-depth exploration of radio sponsorship and the beginnings of corporate advertising, see Susan Smulyan, *Selling Radio: The Commercialization of American Broadcasting, 1920–1934* (Washington, D.C.: Smithsonian Institution Press, 1994), 98–116.

65. Clifford, "Big Three in Motordom Contend for Sales Leadership,"242. See also Hughes, "Custom–Built Local Advertising," 298.

66. Marchand, "The Company Nobody Knew," 827–828.

67. Interviews by T. A. Boyd with the following: John C. Green, 28 March 1961; Fred Huddle, 10 Nov. 1964; Kenneth A. Meade, 9 Jan. 1961; Allen Orth, 26 Aug. 1960; John W. Reedy, 24 Aug. 1960; Gifford G. Scott, 14 Dec. 1964; George Willits, 19 Dec. 1960; R. K. Evans, 21 Dec. 1960; all transcripts, Kettering Collection, GMI.

68. *Time*, 9 Jan. 1933, 55–60.

69. On Kettering's rural childhood, see Stuart W. Leslie, *Boss Kettering* (New York: Columbia University Press, 1983), 1–4. For a contemporary popular portrayal, see Frazier Hunt, "'Boss Ket': The Country Boy Who Kept His Mind Free," *Popular Mechanics*, Oct. 1932, 587. Kettering published his advice on the economy, education, and the value of research in different venues. For a selection of Kettering's articles, see "Applying New Yardsticks to Automobiles," *Scientific American*, Jan. 1927, 22–23; "Research, Horse-sense and Profits," *Factory and Industrial Management* 75 (April 1928), 735; "Hurdles to Jump for Inventors," *Popular Mechanics*, Dec. 1929, 954–959; "Research Makes Jobs," *Review of Reviews*, May 1937, 38–40; "Coming Out, Yes; But Where To?" *Printers' Ink* (30 March 1933), 10–11;, "The Importance of English to the Engineer in Industry," *Journal of Engineering Education* 27 (Jan. 1937): 442–443.

70. Thomas A. Boyd, *Professional Amateur: The Biography of Charles Franklin Kettering* (New York: E. P. Dutton, 1957). For background on the merger of Dayton with General Motors in 1918–1919, see Leslie, *Boss Kettering*, 90–91. On the electric starter, see Philip Drew, "We Have Women Drivers," *American Weekly* 12 Feb. 1950, 7, and Christy Borth, "He 'Liberated the Women,'" held in Folder 12–36, Kettering Collection, GMI.

71. Leslie, *Boss Kettering*, 120–121.

72. R. K. Evans, interview by T. A. Boyd, 21 Dec. 1960, 7, Kettering Collection, GMI. See also interviews with Felix Brunner, GM public relations, and Allen Orth, 26 Aug. 1960, 1, transcripts, accession 1673, Kettering Collection, GMI.

73. Kenneth A. Meade, interview by T. A. Boyd, 9 Jan. 1961, 7, transcript, accession 1673, Kettering Collection, GMI.

74. Allen Orth, interview by T. A. Boyd, 26 Aug. 1960, 1, transcript, accession 1673, Kettering Collection, GMI. See also Charles F. Kettering and Allen Orth, *The New Necessity: The Culmination of a Century of Progress in Transportation* (Baltimore: Williams & Wilkins, 1932).

75. On the automotive exhibits at the Chicago Fair, see "Our Industries Contribution to a Century of Progress," *Automotive Industries* 68 (20 May 1933): 606–607; "Glimpsing Automotive Achievements at the Century of Progress Exposition," *SAE Journal* 33 (Sept. 1933): 40–47; "Automotive Exhibits Will

Again Dominate Century of Progress," *Automotive Industries* 70 (2 June 1934): 684–687.

76. See speeches given at the GM Previews of Progress Dinner, Century of Progress Exposition, General Motors Building, 25 May 1934, transcripts in Previews of Progress Folder 6/12, Kettering Collection, GMI. On the vague meanings of progress, see "The Progress of Progress," *Nation*, 31 May 1933, 35–43, and "Another Century of Progress: General Motors' Invitation, American Industry Reveals New Products and More Distant Goals," *Business Week*, 26 May 1934, 13.

77. Albert Shaw, "Mr. Sloan Looks Ahead," *Review of Reviews*, July 1934, 47.

78. L. W. Chubb, untitled speech given at the GM Previews of Progress Dinner, 25 May 1934, Previews of Progress Folder 6/12, Kettering Collection, GMI.

79. Charles Kettering, untitled speech given at Advertising Federation of America, 17 June 1931, New York, Folder 5/68, Kettering Papers, GMI. On the same topic, see William Richards, "Kettering Says Boom Awaits New Products," *Detroit Free Press*, 26 Jan. 1932, Kettering Clipping File, GMI.

80. On Roosevelt's support and close connection to the Century of Progress Fair, see Rydell, *World of Fairs*, 147. On New Deal legislation that represented the consumer, see T. J. Jackson Lears, *Fables of Abundance: A Cultural History of Advertising in America* (New York: Basic Books, 1994), 245, 242–243. On the relationship between the automotive industry and the Roosevelt Administration's National Industrial Recovery Act, see Russell Cooper and John Haltiwanger, "Automobiles and the National Industrial Recovery Act: Evidence on Industry Complementarities," *Quarterly Journal of Economics* 108 (Nov. 1993): 1943–1971.

81. On the need to direct public opinion and counteract New Deal sentiment, see speeches by Richard Harte, Randolph Eide, and Niran Bates Pope, managing editor, *Automobile Topics*, given at the GM Previews of Progress Dinner, 25 May 1934, transcripts in Previews of Progress Folder 6/12, Kettering Collection, GMI.

82. Rydell, *World of Fairs*, 115–137.

83. Walter Dorwin Teague, "World's Fair 1893–1933," *Advertising and Selling* 20 (Jan. 1933): 12–14; For discussions of the modern designs at the fair, see "Branding the Buildings at the Chicago Fair," *Literary Digest*, 12 Aug.1933, 15; "Chicago's Second World's Fair," *Review of Reviews*, March 1933, 38; "Chicago Invites the World," *Review of Reviews*, May 1933, 18; "Architecture 1933: Looking Forward at Chicago," *Nation*, 24 Jan. 1934, 109. See also *Chicago and Her Two World's Fairs: Depicting A Century of Progress, 1893–1933* (Chicago: Geographical Publishing, 1933). For color pictures of 1933 Chicago Fair architecture and a discussion of the meaning of the buildings, see James Weber Linn, *Official Pictures of a Century of Progress Exposition* (Chicago: Reuben Donnelley, 1933); *Official Pictures of the 1934 World's Fair* (Chicago: Century of Progress, 1934); *Souvenir Views of Chicago World's Fair* (Chicago: Curt Teich, 1934).

84. Alfred Sloan, President of General Motors, Detroit, to C. F. Kettering, Vice President of Research, Detroit, 8 Sept. 1927, Box 97, Kettering Office Files, Kettering Collection, GMI.

85. Linn, *Official Pictures*, 6–7.

86. "Glimpsing Automotive Achievements at the Century of Progress Exposition," *SAE Journal* 33 (Sept. 1933): 40.

87. Ibid.

88. Ibid., 41. See also "Our Industry's Contribution to a Century of Progress," *Automotive Industries* 68 (20 May 1933): 607.

89. On scientific and industrial processes demonstrated at the fair, see Findling, *Chicago's Great World's Fairs*, 99.

90. Allan D. Albert, "Chicago Invites the World," *Review of Reviews*, May 1933, 17.

91. Linn, *Official Pictures*, 7.

92. Findling, *Chicago's Great World's Fairs*, 103.

93. "Automotive Exhibits," *Automotive Industries* 68 (2 June 1934): 684.

94. Ibid., 687.

95. *Official Guide Book of the Fair* (Chicago: Cuneo Press, 1933), 12.

96. "The Fords Come In," *Commerce* 31 (April 1934): 9; see also radio talk given by Joseph A. Small at the Century of Progress Exposition, 30 April 1934, accession 545, box 3, THF. For a history of Ford's participation in automobile shows and world's fairs, see Lorin Sorenson, *Ford Fairs* (Osceola, Wisc.: Motorbooks International, 1976).

97. On the St. Louis exhibition, see press release from Edsel Ford, President, to the *San Francisco Chronicle*, c. 1939, box 8, accession 554, THF. For a brief history of Greenfield Village, see Michael Wallace, "Visiting the Past: History Museums in the United States," in Susan Porter Benson, et al., *Presenting the Past: Essays on History and the Public* (Philadelphia: Temple University Press, 1986), 137–161, and Lacey, *Ford*, 259–260.

98. Edsel Ford, press release on world's fair participation, c. 1934, accession, box 8, THF.

99. B. E. Hutchinson, "Opportunities for Young Men in the Automobile Industry," *New York Times*, 7 Jan. 1934, p. 19, sec. A.

100. For descriptions of the Ford building and the educational value of Ford's vision, see radio talk by Joseph Small, April 30, 1934; "Ford Flash," July 1934, accession 545, miscellaneous publicity, and "Ford at the Fair," unpaged, accession World's Fairs, THF; "Ford Exhibition at Chicago," *Literary Digest*, 18 Aug. 1934, 6; Thomas Burke, *The History of the Ford Rotunda: 1934–1962* (Hicksville, N.Y.: Exposition Press, 1977); Walter Dorwin Teague, "Designing Ford's Exhibit at A Century of Progress," *Product Engineering* (Aug. 1934): 282–284; "Schoolmaster of Dearborn," *New Outlook*, Sept. 1934, 56; "Welding in the Ford Building at the 1934 Century of Progress," *Architectural Record* 75 (June 1934): 467.

101. Teague, "Designing Ford's Exhibit," 285.

102. *Automotive Industries* 70 (2 June 1934): 687; and *Chicago and Her Two World's Fairs*.

103. "Ford at the Fair."

104. "Ford at the Fair," and "Ford: A Great Chicago Industry," Ford Feature Supplement, *Chicago American*, 16 June 1934, accession 545, box 13, THF.

105. Burke, *History of the Ford Rotunda*, 19.

106. Radio talk, Joseph Small, 30 April 1934, accession: World Fairs, THF.

107. "An Eye to the Future and an Ear to the Ground," GM Hall of Progress, Century of Progress Exposition, 1934, General Motors Clipping File, NAHC.

108. "Research at A Century of Progress," Folder 79–10, GMI. See also John W. Reedy, interview by T. A. Boyd, 24 Aug. 1960, 2, transcript, accession 1673, Kettering Collection, GMI.

109. Boyd, *Professional Amateur*, 218–219.

110. Ford Motor Company hired Walter Dorwin Teague to create an exhibit building in Miami in 1937 to house educational exhibits and display new models. For descriptions of the buildings and their advertising function, see press

releases from N. W. Ayer & Son to national newspapers on 11 Jan. and 19 Feb. 1937, accession 545, box 3, THF.

111. Reedy, interview by Boyd, 24 Aug. 1960.

112. Alfred Sloan, "Bringing Industry Closer to the People," in "Previews of Progress" souvenir program, Kettering Collection, GMI.

113. In the mid-1920s Kettering convinced GM to experiment with and eventually to manufacture buses. GM's Yellow Coach Division became a leader in bus design in the 1930s. See Leslie, *Boss Kettering*, 203–204. On the busses used to carry the Parade of Progress, see "Previews of Progress," Souvenir Program, Kettering Collection, GMI, and "World's Fair on Wheels," *Architectural Record* 79 (April 1936): 333.

114. Reedy, interview by Boyd, 24 August 1960.

115. General Motors, "Second Operating Report of the General Motors 'Previews of Progress' July 20th to December 31st 1937," Folder 87–11.2, Box 95, Kettering Collection, GMI. For statistics on campus appearances, see Reedy, interview by Boyd, 24 Aug. 1960. For later statistics, see General Motors, "A Digest of Facts About General Motors Parade of Progress, "1953, program, Folder 13–38, GMI.

116. Evans, interview by Boyd, 21 Dec. 1960, 8, and Orth, interview by Boyd, 26 Aug. 1960.

117. List of plant cities targeted by the show in "Previews of Progress" promotional package sent by Paul Garrett to plant managers, 23 May 1938, Box 95, Kettering Files, GMI.

118. G. L. Cashdollar, Resident Manager, Grand Rapids, Mich., to Don Hogate, Public Relations, Detroit, 10 May 1938, Box 95, Kettering Collection, GMI.

119. Ibid.

120. "What the Consumer Thinks of Advertising," *Sales Management* (10 April 1934): 323. See also Bruce Bliven, "A Century of Treadmill," *New Republic*, 15 Nov. 1933, 11–13.

121. Orth, interview Boyd, 26 Aug. 1960.

122. For references to the program and technical knowledge explained as highly simplified, see Boyd interviews with Orth, 4, 6, and Evans, 8.

123. On the money spent on Ford and GM exhibits, see Rydell, *American Automobile*, 116, and "Sharply Increased Attendance Marks Reopening of Big Fair," *Sales Management* 34 (15 June 1934): 576.

124. For a selection of letters sent to Henry Ford by visitors to the company's building at the Century of Progress World's Fair, see the following: Maude Munger Hodgman, Princeton, Illinois, 6 July 1934; George Fielding, marketing specialist, Chicago, 10 July 1934; C. W. Becker, Chicago, 9 July 1934; Miss E. Bertram, Affton, Mo., , 24 Sept. 1934; Shirley La Gee, Chicago, 21 Sept. 1934; Etta C. Wilson, Newark, Del., 21 Sept. 1934; all letters in accession 450, THF.

125. "Sharply Increased Attendance Marks Reopening of Big Fair," 576. See attendance records for world's fairs and automobile shows kept by the Ford Motor Company, including: Atlantic City Show, 1935, box 1, accession 450, Chicago Exposition, 1934, box 2, accession 450, "Weekly Comparison, Gross Total Attendance," for the Panama Pacific Exposition, San Francisco 1915, Golden Gate Exposition, 1939, boxes 2 and 3, accession 450, THF.

126. "Record Throngs Indicate Bright Outlook for 1930," *New York Times*, 7 Jan. 1930, p. 14; "Auto Show Crowds Hearten Industry," *New York Times*, 7 Jan. 1930, p. 14; "Attendance Sets Auto Show Record," *New York Times*, 8 Jan. 1934,

p. 13; "Auto Men Forecast Revival of Buying," *New York Times*, 11 Jan. 1934, p. 15; "Largest Attendance for Any Corresponding Day in Several Years," *New York Times*, 7 Nov. 1935, p. 25.

127. "Ford Exposition Attendance" listing Chicago, San Diego, Atlantic City, Cleveland, and Miami, Accession, 545, Box 8, THF.

128. W. N. Moquin, Detroit, to C. W. Olmsted, New York, 10 July 1940, transcript, box 8, accession 545: Ford Fair Buildings, THF.

129. On the history of consumer research in the 1930s, see Lears, *Fables of Abundance*, 244–245; Marchand, *Advertising the American Dream*, 52–87; Meikle, *Twentieth Century Limited*, 71–72. On GM's consumer research program, see Arthur Pound, *The Turning Wheel: The Story of General Motors Through Twenty-Five Years, 1908–1933* (Garden City, N.Y.: Doubleday, 1934), 427–431.

130. Meikle, *Twentieth Century Limited*, 70.

131. On the economic recession after World War I and the general responses of automotive manufacturers, see Flink, *Automobile Age*, 81–87; Rae, *American Automobile*, 118; Pound, *Turning Wheel*, 185.

132. Clyde Jennings, "The Right Method of Selling Cars on a Buyers' Market," *Automotive Industries* 40 (30 Dec. 1920): 1301–1305. See also "Problem for Industries of Today to Keep in Touch with Customers," *New York Times*, 7 Jan. 1934, p. 8, sec. A; "What the Public Wants," *Facts and Figures of the Automobile Industry*, (New York: NACC, 1922), 13; Alfred Smith, "Fortunes Created by Public's Automobile Preferences," *Automobile Manufacturer* 68 (Nov. 1926): 4–7.

133. Leon F. Banigan, "AEA Goes Marketing for a Market," *Automotive Industries* 55 (9 Dec. 1926): 965–966.

134. Chapin Hoskins, "How Field Facts Help Sales and Design," *Machine Design* 1 (November 1929): 22. See also "Ideas of Engineers Face Popular Test," *New York Times*, 7 Jan. 1934, p. 6, sec. A.

135. "Sales Research Cannot Be Neglected," *Machine Design* 3 (June 1931): 52; "Lo, the Consumer!" *Business Week* 33 (19 Aug. 1933): 32; William B. Stout, "What the Traveling Public Wants in the Future," *SAE Journal* 33 (Sept. 1933): 293–297; Norman G. Shidle, "What Does the Public Want," *Automotive Industries* 68 (3 June 1933): 666–669; Norman G. Shidle, "Building Sales by Knowing Customers' Tastes," *Forbes*, 1 June 1934, 6–8; "Public's Wants Should Be Regarded As Most Important Survey Now," *Machine Design* 5 (June 1933): 41; "Finding Out What the Customer Thinks About New Cars," *Automotive Industries* 73 (21 Dec. 1935): 818–821.

136. "Public Taste Is Tested," *New York Times*, 11 Jan. 1933, p. 10. On the initiation of consumer research at General Motors, see "Consumer Research," *Annual Report of General Motors Corporation*, 1933, 24; "What the Public Wants: General Motors Goes Direct to a Million Motorists," *Business Week*, 9 Aug 1933, 14; "Attuning Design to Public's Desire," *Machine Design* 6 (August 1934): 29; "G-M Advertises Consumer Survey," *Printers' Ink* 166 (4 Jan. 1934): 72; "Meeting the Customer," *Machine Design* 5 (Sept. 1933): 34; "Reveals What the Public Really Wants," *New York Times*, 7 Jan. 1934, p. 4, sec. AA. On the automotive industry as a leader in consumer surveys, see "Consider the User," *Machine Design* 3 (Feb. 1931): 56.

137. Henry G. Weaver, "Consumer Questionnaire Technique," *American Marketing Journal* 1 (July 1934): 115–118.

138. "G-M Advertises Consumer Survey," 72; "Finding Out What the Customer Thinks About the New Cars," 818. Alfred Sloan and Arthur Pound also stated that consumer research would repair the gap between the corporation

and consumers; see Sloan, "Customer Research," *Annual Report of General Motors Corporation*, 1933; and Pound, *Turning Wheel*, 427. For a more in-depth exploration of the subject by Weaver, see also Henry G. Weaver, "Consumer Research and Consumer Education," *Annals of the American Academy of Political and Social Science* (Nov. 1935): 1–7, General Motors File, NAHC. On Ford's early consumer research, see "What They Said About Ford at the Cleveland Auto Show," 13–20 Nov. 1937, box 3, accession 545, Auto Show Publicity; Report on Public Attitudes Toward Low-Priced Cars, 11 July 1938, box 1, accession 454; and Curtis Publishing Company, "What the Public Thinks of Big Business" (Cleveland: Curtis Publishing Company, May 1937), accession 454, box 10, Folder: Sales and Advertising, THF.
    139. "Customer Research at the Century of Progress World's Fair," Folder 13–35, Photos 1934, GMI.
    140. See General Motors, *The Automobile Buyer's Guide* (Detroit: General Motors Customer Research Staff, 1934); General Motors, *The Automobile Buyer's Guide* (Detroit: General Motors Customer Research Staff, 1936); General Motors, *The Automobile Buyer's Guide* (Detroit: General Motors Customer Research Staff, 1937), New York Public Library. See also General Motors, *The Story of Knee Action.*.
    141. Weaver, "Consumer Questionnaire Technique," 116.
    142. Shindle, "What Does the Public Want," 667. See also "Picture Book: Auburn Translates Story of Mechanical Features into Simple Terms Layman Can Understand," *Printers' Ink* (5 July 1934): 78–79; "Standard Inquiry Forms Aid Customers in Expressing Wants," *Machine Design*, 5 (June 1933): 34.
    143. General Motors, *Automobile Buyer's Guide* (1935), 18–19.
    144. Ibid.
    145. General Motors, *Automobile Buyer's Guide* (1934), 10–11; General Motors, *The Motorist's Handbook and Buyers Guide*, (Detroit: General Motors, n.d.), 8–9.
    146. Shindle, "What Does the Public Want," 667.
    147. General Motors, "Customer Research" (Detroit: General Motors, 1935), NAHC. On consumers as "cooperative researchers," see Charles Kettering, "The Effect of the Emergency on Scientific and Industrial Progress," speech at the Waldorf-Astoria Hotel, New York, 17 Oct. 1939, Folder 7–29, GMI.
    148. General Motors, *The Motorist's Handbook and Buyer's Guide: A Sequel to the Proving Ground of Public Opinion* (Detroit: General Motors Customer Research Staff, c. 1934), 6.
    149. P. H. Erbes, Jr., "Some Advertising Slants at a Century of Progress," *Printer's Ink* 165 (15 June 1933): 46–49; "Profits of 'A Century,'" *Business Week*, 22 July 1933, 14; "101 Years of Progress," *Business Week*, 5 May 1934, 18–20; R. B. Donnelley, "Fraud, Foliage and Free Samples: Reporter Finds Tastes of Masses Unjaded at Chicago Exposition," *Sales Management* 33 (1 Sept. 1933): 222, 238; (15 Sept. 1933): 278, 284; "Sharply Increased Attendance Marks Reopening of Big Fair,"): 576; Lester B. Colby, "'Free, Gratis' Is Not Enough World's Fair Teaches Makers," *Sales Management* 35 (1 Oct. 1934): 294–295.
    150. "Consumers Create Own Desires," *Printers' Ink Monthly* 166 (June 1934): 53–54; Edmund B. Neil, "Buyers Remember the 'Bugs' Long After Engineers Have Forgotten Them," *Automotive Industries* 68 (27 May 1933): 636–638; "What the Consumer Thinks of Advertising—A Low Down," *Sales Management* 34 (10 April 1934): 322–323; Colby, 294; Donnelly, "Fraud, Foliage and Free Samples," 283–284.
    151. Neil, "Buyers Remember," 636.

152. Ibid., 636.

153. William B. Stout, "What the Traveling Public Wants in the Future," *SAE Journal* 33 (Sept. 1933): 295. See also William B. Stout, "Design for the Eye!" *Machine Design* 5 (Sept. 1933): 41.

154. Stout, "What the Traveling Public Wants," 295.

155. Shindle, "What Does the Public Want," 666.

156. Marchand, Advertising the American Dream, 67–71.

157. Donnelley, "Fraud, Foliage and Free Samples," 237.

158. J. Parker Van Zandt and L. Rohe Walter, "King Customer," *Review of Reviews*, September 1934, 24.

159. Joseph Geschelin, "Which Way Will the Winds of Favor Blow?" *Automotive Industries* 70 (20 Jan. 1934): 63.

160. C. B. Veal, "Motors of Tomorrow in Laboratories Now," *New York Times*, 5 Jan. 1930, p. 26, sec. A.

161. H. J. Klingler, "Conservative Public Resists Sudden Improvement in Cars," *New York Times*, 7 Jan. 1934, p. 8, sec. AA.

162. John D. Rauch, "How Design Affects Sales," *Machine Design* 2 (September 1930): 45.

163. *Printers' Ink Monthly* (Feb. 1934): 52.

164. Charles Kettering and Allan Orth, "Fault Finders," in *The New Necessity,*), 60.

165. "Three Jeers at Some Recent Trends," *Automotive Industries* 68 (8 April 1933): 437.

166. Ibid., 436.

167. Don Blanchard, "They Look Good But—Does the Public Think 1933 Bodies Skimp Comfort and Driving Vision for Style?" *Automotive Industries* 68 (1 April 1933): 391.

168. Cleveland Press, "What They Said About Ford at the Cleveland Show,"13–20 Nov. 1937, 6–8, box 3, accession 545, Auto Show Publicity, THF.

169. Ibid., 9.

170. Maxwell H. Emmer, Detroit, to Henry Ford, Dearborn, 24 Sept. 1933, box 6, accession 23, Miscellaneous, THF.

171. Don Blanchard, "Miss Perkins Would Bar Yearly Models to Even Out Automotive Ups and Downs," *Automotive Industries* 70 (19 May 1934): 626–627.

172. On efforts to change the dates of the auto show from January to November, see "Exhibition of New Motors Challenges the Pessimist," *New York Times*, 5 Jan. 1930, p. 18, sec. A; "Opposition to National Auto Chamber of Commerce Plans to Replace NY and Chicago Shows," *New York Times*, 17 June 1934, p. 8, sec. 16; "Financial and Industry Leaders Endorse Change in Exhibition Period," *New York Times*, 10 Nov. 1935, p. 10; "Period of Annual Exhibits to be Shifted from January to October," *New York Times*, 10 Feb. 1935, p. 8; "Employment Gain Through Fall Shows," *New York Times*, 30 Dec. 1936, p. 19.

173. Myron M. Stearns, "Notes on Changes in Motoring," *Harper's*, Sept. 1936, 443–444.

174. Ibid., 444.

Epilogue

1. Martin Wachs and Margaret Crawford, eds., *The Car and the City: The Automobile, The Built Environment, and Daily Urban Life* (Ann Arbor: University of Michigan Press, 1992.)

2. Warren James Belasco, *Americans on the Road: From Autocamp to Motel, 1910–1945* (Cambridge: MIT Press, 1979).

3. Roger White, *Home on the Road: The Motor Home in America* (Washington, D.C.: Smithsonian Institution Press, 2000), 171–176.

4. On hot rods, see Robert C. Post, *High Performance, The Culture and Technology of Drag Racing, 1950–2000* (Baltimore: Johns Hopkins University Press, 2001).

5. On the outsider esthetics of low riders and hip hop culture, see Brenda Jo Bright, "Nightmares in the New Metropolis: The Cinematic Poetics of Low Riders," in Joe Austin and Michael Nevin Willard, eds., *Generations of Youth: Youth Cultures and History in Twentieth Century America* (New York: New York University Press, 1998). See also Brenda Jo Bright, "Mexican American Low Riders: An Anthropological Approach to Popular Culture," Ph.D. diss., Rice University, 1995.

6. For the Chip Foose bio, see http://tlc.discovery.com/fansites/overhaulin/bio/foose.html.

7. Tom and Ray Magliozzi, "The History of Car Talk," <http://cartalk.cars .com/About/history.html>, April 27, 1999, 2. For background on the show, see also Anna Copeland, "Car Talk: The Brothers Magliozzi go Trisyllabic," *Omni*, December 1993, 10.

8. Magliozzi, "The History of Car Talk," 2.

9. "CarTalk Columns," October 1995, <http://cartalk.cars.com/Columns/CC/CC6601TXT.html>, April 20, 1999, 1–2.

10. For a sample of the numerous references to tinkering, see Tracy Sutton-Masters, "Support Group for Wives Whose Husbands Drive '77 Cars," <http://cartalk.cars.com/Mail/Letters/04-25-97/9.html>, April 25, 1999, 1; "1976 Triumph TR6 Survey Comments," <http://cartalk.cars.com/Survey/Results/Demographics/Comments/Triumph/TR6–1976.html>, May 1999; "1980 Toyota Corolla Survey Comments," <http://cartalk.cars.com/Survey/Results/Demographics/Comments/Toyota/Corolla-1980.html>, May 1999; "1992 Dodge Shadow Survey Comments," <http://cartalk.cars.com/Survey/Results/Demographics/Comments/Dodge/Shadow-1992.html>, May 1999; "1994 Volkswagen Golf Survey Comments,"<http://cartalk.cars.com/Survey/Results/Demographics/Comments/Volkswagen/Golf-1994.html>, May 1999.

11. Tom and Ray Magliozzi, "Women are From Ford, Men are From Mars," <http://cartalk.cars.com/About/CD/html>, April 20, 1999; "Car Talk: Men Are From GM, Women Are From Ford," *Billboard*, 20 December 1997, 68; "Audio Reviews—The Best of Car Talk Written and Read by Tom Magliozzi and Ray Magliozzi," *Publisher's Weekly*, 1 January 1996, 40.

12. On men making uninformed technical statements about their cars, see "CarTalk Columns," June 1996, <http://cartalk.cars.com/Columns/CC/CC6997TXT.html>, April 20, 1999, 1–2. See also David B. Cameron, "From Murky Research: Are Women Loyal to Their Cars—and Men Not?" <http://cartalk.cars.com/Mail/Letters/1999/01.29/1.html>, April 7, 1999, 1–3; "Cartalk Columns," April 1996, , April 25, 1999, 1–2; Jim Whaley, "1986 BMW 325es," <http://cartalk.cars.com/Info/Cyberchumps/Questions/q225.html>, April 25, 1999, 1–2.

13. For examples of women admitting they know little about the car in relation to male partners and mechanics, see "CarTalk Columns" January 1994, <http://cartalk.cars.com/Columns/CC/CC4731TXT.html>, April 20,1999; "CarTalk Columns," December 1997, <http://cartalk.cars.com/Columns/CC/CC769TXT.html>, April 20, 1999; "CarTalk Columns, May 1997, <http://cartalk.cars.com/Columns/CC/CC7167TXT.html>, April 20, 1999.

14. "CarTalk Columns," June 1995, <http://cartalk.cars.com/Columns/CC/CC6282TXT.html>, April 20, 1999, 1.

15. Ibid., 1.

16. For critiques of design by drivers, see Robert C. Barker, MD, "The 1953 Lincoln from Hell: A Reminiscence,"<http://cartalk.cars.com/Mail/Letters/1999/03.20/1.html>, April 7, 1999; Eric Blackwell, "Cosmic Harmony . . . and Interior Auto Design," <http://cartalk.cars.com/Mail/Letters/1999/02.12/9.html>, April 7, 1999, 1–2; Mike Roth, "There Is a Sinister Conspiracy Afoot: Automotive Design Engineers," <http://cartalk.cars.com/Mail/Letters/1999/04.03/2.html>, April 7, 1999, 1–2; Tom, "Is the Car of Tomorrow . . . a 'UV'?" <http://cartalk.cars.com/Mail/Letters/1999/02.19/8.html>, April 7, 1999, 1–2; "Car Talk Moment: Trust Your Dash or Your Mechanic," <http://cartalk.cars.com/Radio/Replay/Transcripts/199804/index.html>, April 25, 1999, 2–4; "Car Talk Moment: Do-It-Yourself Convertible," <http://cartalk.cars.com/Radio/Replay/Transcripts/199802/index.html>, April 25, 1999, 1–4.

17. "Car Talk Moment: Trust Your Dash or Your Mechanic," <http://cartalk.cars.com/Radio/Replay/Transcripts/199804/index.html>, April 25, 1999, 2.

18. Ibid., 3.

19. Mike Roth, "There is a Sinister Conspiracy Afoot," 1–2.

20. Stuart Hall, "Notes on Deconstructing the Popular," in Ralph Samuel, ed., *People's History and Socialist Theory* (London: Routledge, 1981), 228 and George Lipsitz, "The Struggle for Hegemony," *Journal of American History* 75 (June 1988), 146–50.

21. Hall, "Notes on Deconstructing the Popular," 239.

Index

Wilson, Woodrow: opinion on automobiles, 6–7
Wilson Sporting Goods, 29
women: advice literature, 66–67, 79–81; as
  consumers, 11; as drivers, 47–48; and
  family travel, 58–66; as inventors, 96–98;
  as mechanics, 50–53, 68–72; as portrayed in motor fiction, 43–51, 53–54,
57–59; relationship to technology and
  public space, 44–47, 52–53, 56–57; and
  tinkering, 54–56; and trailer travel,
  67–68; travel narratives, 54–56
Women's Bureau, Department of Labor,
  10, 79, 97
women's movement, 45

Acknowledgments

Many people contributed to the ideas in this book and helped me complete the work. I cannot thank them all sufficiently. Several institutions provided financial support and the resources to explore automobility on a national level. These included Brown University; the Lemelson Center at the National Museum of American History, Smithsonian Institution; and the National Science Foundation. I'd also like to thank the Society of the History of Technology for the generous support of Brooke Hindle Fellowship that gave me the time to finish the manuscript.

I also appreciate the assistance of experienced and creative archivists and librarians who helped me navigate the vast body of resources on automobiles. These include staff at the National Automobile Collection at the Detroit Public Library; the Kettering Archives, General Motors Alumni Foundation Collection of Industrial History in Flint, Michigan; and the wonderful archival staff at the National Museum of American History, Smithsonian Institution. Personal thanks go to Linda Skolarus and John Bowen, research archivists at the Benson Ford Research Center, The Henry Ford, in Dearborn, Michigan, who made all of my trips there productive and fun. In addition, Steven Lubar, Susan Tolbert, Mike Harrison, and Roger White gave me free run of the collections at the National Museum of American History, which I deeply appreciate.

At Brown University, Howard Chudacoff and Patrick Malone helped me master the scholarly tools necessary to interrogate the historical and cultural meanings of the automobile. Thanks as well to friends in the Department of American Civilization: Crista Deluzio, Briann Greenfield, Jane Gerhard, Mark Herlihy, Joanne Melish, Miriam Reumann, and Mari Yoshihara, who read my work in its earliest form. Research at the National Museum of American History and many conversations with fellow members of the Society of the History of Technology, such as Bruce Sinclair, Gail Cooper, and Joe Corn, sharpened my questions about grass-roots invention and the role of users. At the University of North Carolina, Greensboro, colleagues including Nan Enstad, Rick and Anne Barton, Tom Jackson, Peter Carmichael, and Bill Link have made my years there productive and happy and gave me valuable time to complete the manuscript. Special thanks to Phyllis Hunter who read drafts of the entire manuscript and to Beth Carmichael for help indexing.

There are a few folks who transcended boundaries, lending their humor and fresh perspectives to the project. Caroline Cortina, Jeff Crews, and Glenn Carroll showed me the links between creativity and technology. I also deeply appreciate the help of several editors who gave special attention to this book, Jeff Hardwick at Smithsonian Institution Press and Robert Lockhart and project editor Noreen O'Connor at University of Pennsylvania Press.

Thanks to my family, Barbara and Will Franz, David and Dana Franz, and my husband, Brendan Danaher, who has been kind and extremely supportive of the demands of academic life. Finally, thanks to my mentor and friend, Susan Smulyan, who offered advice, knowledge, and encouragement through every step of the process. I hope this work is a tribute to her mentorship.

Lightning Source UK Ltd.
Milton Keynes UK
UKHW011544181120
373391UK00009B/239